Chinua Achebe: pure and simple
an oral biography

Chinua Achebe: pure and simple
an oral biography

Phanuel Akubueze Egejuru
Department of English
Loyola University
New Orleans, Louisiana, USA

Malthouse Press Limited

Malthouse Press Limited
8, Amore Street, Off Toyin Street, Ikeja
P.O. Box 500, Ikeja, Lagos State, Nigeria.

Lagos, Benin, Ibadan, Jos, Oxford, Port-Harcourt, Zaria

All rights reserved. No part of this publication may be reproduced, transmitted, transcribed, stored in a retrieval system, or translated into any language or computer language, in any form or by any means, electronic, mechanical, magnetic, chemical, photocopying, recording, manual or otherwise, without the prior permission of Malthouse Press Limited, PO Box 500, Ikeja, Lagos, Nigeria.

This book is sold subject to the condition that it shall not, by way of trade or otherwise be lent, resold, hired out, or otherwise circulated without the Publisher's prior consent, in writing, in any form of binding or cover other than that in which it is published and without a similar condition including this condition being imposed on the subsequent purchaser.

© Phanuel Akubueze Egejuru 2001
First published 2001
ISBN 978 023 148 X

Contents

Acknowledgements v
Preface vii

Part I: Life history

Parentage: a solid foundation	1
Birth	8
Education	16
Primary and Secondary Schools	
University College Ibadan	
Employment	36
Biafra: a challenge	46
Picking up the pieces	53
University of Nigeria Nsukka	
University of Massachusetts at Amherst	
Return to Nsukka	
Retirement Years	64
Turning Point	74
The Paddocks Hospital	79
Bard College: The Hermitage	87
A Triumphal Return	91

Part II: Chinua and his measure

A family man first and foremost	98
Chinua, a big *alusi*	118
A complex simplicity	127
Gentle as a lamb, fierce like a lioness	134

A man of truth and justice	140
A great humanist	145
A man of integrity	150
An unwavering loyalty	154
An empowering force for others	164
A generous soul	167
In possession of his soul	172
A beautiful leisureliness	176
A delicate sense of humor	180
Chinua and the Nobel Prize	185
Points of weakness?	187
Praise names for Chinua	192
Man of the century	199
Appendix: Honorary doctorate degrees to Chinua	206
Index	208

Acknowledgements

I am most grateful to Chinua Achebe for giving his permission and cooperation for this project. I thank Loyola University New Orleans for providing the financial support that enabled me to travel to Europe and Nigeria for research on Chinua. It is with the utmost gratitude and humility that I mention, in alphabetical order, the names of interviewees and references whose contributions made the completion of the project possible: Agnes Achebe, Augustine Achebe, Chidi Achebe, Chinelo Achebe, Chinua Achebe, Christie Achebe, Ernest Achebe, Ikechukwu Achebe, Jane Achebe, Dr. John Achebe, Rev. John Achebe (may his soul rest in peace), Lucy Achebe, Mathilda Achebe, Nwando Achebe and Oyibo Achebe. I would also like to acknowledge the contributions of Achebe's extended family members: Nnaemeka Ikpeze, Okechukwu Ikpeze, Ukamaka Ikpeze, Zinobia Ikpeze, Chike Okocha, Emeka Okocha, Grace Okocha, Tochukwu Okocha and Dr. Sam Okoli. My special thanks to Chinua's friends, teachers, colleagues, employers and employees: F.C. Adi, Chinua's personal physician, Okonkwo Agu, N.T.C. Agulefo, Grace Alele, Reuben Alumona, Nwoye Anene, Ifeanyi Aniebo, Ulli Beier, S.O. Biobaku, Leon Botstein, President of Bard College, S.J. Cookey, Christiana Amachre Graham Douglas, George Egejuru, Chiweite Ejike, Frank Ellah, Godfrey Eneli, Sam Hazley, Aigboje Higo, Bola Ige, V.C. Ike, Godfrey Ikegwuonu, C. L. Innes, Christian Momah, Ethel Momah, John Munonye, Sam Nwaneri, Arthur Nwankwo, Victor Nwankwo, T.C. Nwosu, Sam Nwoye, Ikenna Nzimiro, Emmanuel Obiechina, Dickson Odukwe, Esther Ogadi, Ben Ogbogu, Ephraim Ogbonna, Johnson Okudo (may his soul rest in peace), Michael Olumide, Paddocks Hospital nursing staff, Mabel Segun, Adrian Slater, Wole Soyinka, Michael Thelwell, Ada Udechukwu, Obiora Udechukwu, Grace Ugwoke, Ngozi Ugwoke, Ben Uzochukwu, Theo Vincent and Julian Wasserman.

    I would like to recognize individuals who provided other valuable services in addition to granting me interviews. My heart felt thanks to Chinua and Christie for their hospitality during the numerous times I came to their home for interviews. I thank Chinua for his patience and willingness to answer my questions over the phone throughout the years I worked on the project. Special thanks to Dr. Chidi Achebe for his magnanimous gesture of driving miles to find me in Houston and grant me yet another interview as an eyewitness to his father's visit to Nigeria in 1999. I am very grateful to Rev. John Achebe and his wife Lucy Achebe, for providing me with room and board for most of my extended visits to Ogidi; I thank Mrs. Agnes Achebe, Mrs. Zinobia Ikpeze, Chief Ben Ogbogu and his wife Vicky, Mrs. Grace Okocha, Obiora and Ada Udechukwu, all, for their lavish hospitality. To Professors S.J. Cookey, E. Obiechina and Ikenna Nzimiro, I say a big "Thank You" for providing first hand knowledge of Achebe the humanist and his crucial role as Chairman of Biafra's National Guidance Committee.

I thank Ezenwa Ohaeto for his timely book, *Chinua Achebe* which became a reference point for comparing information or checking for correct names of individuals.

Finally, and by no means the least important, are members of my own immediate and extended families. I thank my husband Dr. Obasi Okorie who made a lot of personal sacrifices to support my project. I am grateful to all my relatives who provided room and board and transportation for me and my children while I tracked down interviewees in different parts of Nigeria: Sir George Egejuru and his wife Selina (may her soul rest in peace), Policarp and Kate Mbajunwa and nephew Chidi Okorie, Kingsley and Chiaka Mbajunwa, Eugene and Chinwe Ekewuba, Beatrice Ekewuba whose motherly care nursed me back to health and ensured the success of the interviews in Nigeria, Macaulay and Blossom Onyeneke. I am especially indebted to my nephews, Israel Okere and Victor Dede Mbajunwa who drove me everywhere in their cars, and stayed for days with me while I conducted interviews. Thank You All!

Preface

Chinua Achebe is undeniably a global social force, a fact testified to by his inclusion on the list of *1000 Makers of the Twentieth Century*. This fact is further supported by the United Nations' choice of Achebe in January 1999, to be their Goodwill Ambassador in matters of health. It was however, the worldwide influence of his works that engendered this recognition. For readers in Asia, Europe and the Americas, and indeed for many readers in Africa, Achebe's works are their window to Africa.

Critical studies on Achebe's works are multiplying by the day. Yet, neither these studies nor the works themselves reveal the human within the spirit-eyed artist. Our knowledge of Achebe, the man, remains vague or superficial at best, because Achebe the artist is so clever that he succeeds in keeping the man out of his art.

This present study specifically focuses on the human as opposed to the artistic side of Chinua. Although Chinua frowns on this arbitrary separation of the man from the artist, he recognizes its validity. When I told him, "My interest is in your human side as opposed to your artistic side," he said:

> I don't draw a line between the human story and the literary story, because to me it is one story, though I understand that one who is at a distance can separate them. I don't think in those categories particularly. I am not saying that these categories don't exist or are not valid, but they are. For me it is one story; there is no way you can say, this is it or that is it, because a person can be so many things. To me the best is to be able to hold all these together without the various components fighting against one another. I am saying that whatever is said about me that is true, I am in accordance with it, but I am not in support of anything that is not true.

In order to find the things that are true about Chinua, he himself was personally involved in talking about his life and in describing his world. Equally crucial to obtaining a reasonable composite picture of Chinua were testimonies of people who have been or are associated with him at various stages of his life.

Thus, what we have here is an oral biography compiled from information obtained during face to face interviews with Achebe himself, his blood relatives and other people who have intimate knowledge of him from infancy through adolescence to adulthood. From these interviews we learn of Chinua the son, the brother, the uncle, the son-in-law, the husband and the father. Chinua, the student is revealed by his teachers, his classmates and his friends. And we learn of Chinua the professional from his employers, his colleagues, his students and his own employees such as his secretary, his house-boy and his driver. On the whole, seventy-one people were interviewed. Of these, one person was interviewed over the phone and two people sent in written responses. There were face-to-face and telephone interviews with Chinua. The rest were face to face interviews.

In addition to family, education and career, other forces and events worked together to chart the course of Chinua's life. These are the "spots in time," the high and low points like his literary success, the Biafran war, and the automobile accident that almost took his life in March 1990.

For a fairly balanced character evaluation of Chinua Achebe, one had of necessity, to retrace the writer's steps over the years, from his hometown Ogidi through various parts of Nigeria, to Europe and to the United States. In the end, this study explored as much as possible, all the forces that combined to shape the character of Chinua Achebe.

What one finds in the end is a character so complex that he is called a big *Alus*i. Despite the enigmatic nature of *Alus*i, Chinua succeeds in holding his life together without the various components fighting against one another. And, paradoxically, underneath this complex character, is a very simple Chinua, an extraordinary ordinary man whose true meaning lies in his genuine concern for the well being of the human community.

Like many scholars of African literature, I "met" Chinua Achebe through *Things Fall Apart*. As I read Achebe's subsequent novels and essays, my respect for his wisdom became boundless. I reached a point where I could not start a scholarly paper or lecture without using Achebe's words as my point of departure.

It was in 1974 that I met Chinua in person for the first time. I had traveled from Los Angeles to interview him at Amherst, Massachusetts. For some unexplainable reason (or due to reckless short sightedness), I had not thought that I might need more than one day for the venture. So, I had made no plans for an overnight accommodation. The Achebes graciously provided room and meals for my overnight stay. They did not call a taxi to take me to the airport the next day. Instead, Chinua drove me to the bus depot where I caught an express bus to the airport. And now, my research has revealed that generosity is second nature to Chinua Achebe.

I saw Chinua again in 1980, at the African Literature Association conference in Gainesville, Florida. Another seven years passed after 1980 before I saw him again. On both occasions, he recognized me and called my name. I was impressed and flattered because none of the other writers I had interviewed ever recognized me at a second meeting.

In spite of the unbounded respect and admiration I have for the man, the thought of doing a biography of him never crossed my mind. What triggered the thought was what I witnessed during the symposium, *Eagle-on-Iroko*, celebrating Chinua's 60th birthday in 1990. I was completely overwhelmed by the activities of the international body that gathered to honor this man. Halfway through the celebrations, I rushed back home to fetch my husband and daughter to come and see this Chinua in the flesh and to be part of the audience in the finale dramatization of *Arrow of God*. I made a wise decision because I didn't have to explain to my family later, the importance of Chinua or why I should spend years researching and writing his biography.

What kept going on in my head while the literary world was "roasting" Chinua *a la* Hollywood was "Who is this ordinary-looking man that commands the respect of this august body of scholars and artists from across the globe? How can this fellow bring such an awesome gathering to its knees in adulation?" After witnessing this unbounded "adoration" of this spirit-eyed artist, I found it particularly disturbing, even painful, that no scholar had done a biography of him yet.[1] Finally, at the symposium's book exhibit, I picked up a pamphlet titled, *In the Beginning, Chinua Achebe at Work,* by Ada Ugah. And that was the final straw! I felt that something more substantial should be done on the human within this artist. Therefore, I decided to go in search of the Chinua Achebe who is not revealed to the world in his novels. I wanted to evaluate Chinua's character, not by deducing from his works but by oral information from people who have known him intimately from his birth to manhood.

---

[1] I had no idea however, that Ezenwa Ohaeto had already started his mammoth biography, *Chinua Achebe,* published in 1997.

In 1991, I visited the Achebes at Bard College. First, I went to welcome them back from the Paddocks Hospital in England, where Chinua was treated after his accident. Second, I went to invite Chinua in person to come and give a speech at Loyola University; my attempt to get him there as the Keynote speaker for the ALA conference in March of 1991 had failed. He accepted the invitation and came in March 1992. At the end of my visit at Bard, I summoned the courage to ask Chinua if he had commissioned anybody to do his biography. He laughed and said, "Oh, no" in a tone that seemed to say, "You don't really know me." I asked if he would mind my doing a biography of him, and he said he wouldn't mind.

I started making plans. I applied to some Foundations in the USA for funds but I didn't get any. However, Loyola University, New Orleans gave me a travel grant that covered my ticket from New Orleans through England to Nigeria and back. I was determined to carry out the project.

I visited Chinua again in 1993. Once more, I brought up the topic of my impending plans to do his biography. I wanted to reassure myself that he had not changed his mind or forgotten our previous conversation. I went away reassured. So, Chinua Achebe's biography became the project for my one-year sabbatical leave in 1995.

On August 15, 1995, I went back to Chinua at Bard College with a tape recorder; the first in the series of interviews started in earnest. Chinua, Christie, Chidi and Nwando, all worked together to come up with names and addresses of potential interviewees. Before I left, I timidly asked Chinua for some written document indicating that I had his permission to carry on with the project. He gave me a very short hand-written note of introduction. I made sure to show that document to everyone I interviewed, and it worked like magic in getting the cooperation of all the people I was able to locate. The note read:

> Professor Phanuel Egejuru is a literary scholar and writer and is well known to me. From what I know of her previous work I expect her present project on my biography to be satisfactorily accomplished.

It was when I started to arrange the information I had gathered into a book, that I reread the above note. I had only thought of it as an important and useful document. But this time, I became truly frightened by the last segment-"I expect her present project...to be satisfactorily accomplished!"

I had no idea of the type of responses I was going to receive to my questions. I was totally confused when people in different parts of the world gave answers that seemed to indicate that they had met and rehearsed their answers! I had set out to explore the character of a "normal" human being, with strengths and weaknesses. Alas! What people said about him didn't sound real at all! However, I kept hoping to get some negative feedback to some of my questions. I became depressed and I panicked because nobody would believe the image of a man who seemed programmed to be good. I desperately tried to find some *bona fide* flaws in Chinua's character. In the end, I could only come up with a tiny segment entitled, "Points of Weakness?" It ends with a question mark because, "Weakness is a matter of perception" according to one interviewee. And when I continued asking one of Chinua's friends to think of a fault in Chinua he said: "One regrettable thing about Chinua is that there are no juicy tales to tell about him." Although I was uneasy about the claim, my research later proved it to be right.

I wrestled with the fear that critics, if not every reader, would throw me to the lions for preposterous claims of near perfection for a human being. But I have made no claims; I merely reported the information given by those who know the man. Indeed, my role is like that of a court recorder, not a lawyer interpreting the words of witnesses.

I am not sure whether I accomplished my goal satisfactorily. However, I consider myself lucky and privileged to have learned so much about Chinua, the man whose true self does not show through his works. I am glad to share what I have learned with all readers who are interested in and inspired by the lives of great souls like Chinua Achebe. I am gratified to know that, in our world where villainy has become a virtue, there are people like Chinua Achebe to remind us that there will always be *"A Remnant"* to exemplify all that is good and virtuous in all of us human beings.

Homage to Chinua Achebe
A Great Man of Complex Simplicity

For my Children: Emezuem, Ugorji and Eze

Part I

... life history...

1

Parentage: a solid foundation

Chinua's father, Isaiah Okafo Achebe was born at Nkwele Ogidi in the late 1800s.[1] Okafo was about two years old when his mother died while giving birth to a second child, who also died. Okafo was raised by his maternal uncle, Udo from Ikenga Ogidi. Udo was a very prosperous farmer known for his huge feasts during ceremonies and festivals. Because no guests could ever finish the meals that Udo presented them, Udo earned the praise name, *Osinyi*. Chinua makes reference to his great uncle in *Things Fall Apart*, in the story of "a wealthy man who set before his guests a mound of *foo-foo* so high that those who sat on one side could not see what was happening on the other."[2] Not too long after his mother's death, Okafo's father also died. His father's second wife, who was also from Ikenga Ogidi, took her children and returned to her home village. Thus, both branches of Achebe's family settled in Ikenga till today.

Okafo grew up to become a remarkable young man admired and respected throughout Ogidi. He was specifically admired for his wrestling prowess, an accomplishment that earned him the praise name, *Okaokwulu*, a contraction of Okafo and Okwulu. Literally, Okafo begotten of okwulu or okwulu incarnate. He was as slippery as okwulu or okra, so slippery that his wrestling opponents could never get a good grip of him let alone throw him down. He participated fully in all traditional rituals and ceremonies such as dancing, masquerading and wrestling. In the words of Johnson Okudo,[3] a contemporary of Isaiah Achebe, "Okafo Achebe lived and enjoyed his youth to the fullest."[4]

While Okafo was still a very young man, the Anglican mission that

---

[1] Chinua wasn't sure of his father's date of birth. He gave the dates of his parents' education and the date of their wedding as he got them from his parents.

[2] Chinua Achebe, *Things Fall Apart*, Heinemann, 1958, p.26.

[3] Johnson Nwosu Okudo (Nwawuluaru, his praise-name) died two years after my interview with him at Ogidi in December 1995. He knew Chinua's father very well. Okudo claimed to be 120 years old at the time of the interview. He was Chinua's valued friend and mentor. "If you divide the stories that Chinua tells you into two, half is mine," he claimed.

[4] Johnson Okudo, interview with Egejuru.

landed at Onitsha in 1857 arrived at Ogidi in 1892. It took them thirty-five years to go from Onitsha to Ogidi, a distance of less than three miles! The arrival of the missionaries in Ogidi would change the lives of Okafo and his people forever.

Like many young men of his village, Okafo, out of curiosity went to listen to the missionaries preaching and singing round the villages. Okafo was soon caught off his guard by the melodious hymns and the spell binding words of the bible read aloud to the listening crowd. Chinua's immediate elder brother, Augustine recalled the stories their father told them about his conversion and subsequent evangelizing mission in his hometown and beyond.

> When he saw the missionaries with strange eye colours and some with no toes, he followed them to listen to their words. What fascinated him about the white men was their book, which told them everything they had to tell people. Any time they opened this thing, it told them the same thing. He was convinced there was something in that book, so he followed them without the knowledge of his uncle. However, his uncle's wife, who became a mother to him, always knew when he left to go to the missionaries. After a few visits, the missionaries gave him a singlet which he then had to wear to the mission. To prevent his uncle from noticing, his aunt would wrap the singlet in cocoyam leaves for him to carry out and put on when he left the compound.[5]

But Okafo's secret rendezvous with the missionaries would not last forever. Words soon leaked out to his uncle that he had been going to listen to the missionaries. His uncle called him and questioned him. Okafo did not deny the story but told his uncle that he would continue to follow the missionaries. His uncle urged him to follow them so as to "find out what type of basket they were weaving" and then come back and report to him. Okafo agreed but never came back. The missionaries had already perceived his intelligence and potential for labour in the Lord's vineyard. They started teaching and indoctrinating him and some other converts. Shortly thereafter, he was baptized and called Isaiah. Chinua would eventually use his father as models for Nwoye in *Things Fall Apart* and Isaac Okonkwo in *No Longer at Ease*. Also, Udo's urging of Okafo to follow the missionaries and find out what they were up to was repeated to Oduche by Ezeulu in *Arrow of God*.

In 1904, Isaiah was sent to Awka College for teachers. Upon his graduation, Isaiah's first accomplishment as a church teacher was the founding of St. Paul's Anglican Church at Ikenga Ogidi. About the same

---

[5] Augustine Achebe, interview with Egejuru.

time, David Okoye, another Ogidi church teacher, started a church at Nkwele Ogidi. Later, Isaiah felt the need for one big church for all Ogidi, so he and David Okoye merged their two small churches to form St. Philip's Church which is located at Akpakogwe Ogidi. St. Paul's was left to serve the elderly who could not make the long trip to St. Philip's. Till today, the Achebes who live in Ikenga, attend church at St. Philip's out of sentimental attachment and loyalty to their father. Chinua said:

> There is St. Paul's, more attractive physically; it's the church for most people from Ikenga, my part of town. My father never accepted that Ogidi should be divided, and until his death in 1962, he believed we should be at St. Philips.[6]

It was when Isaiah was at Awka College that he met his future wife during one of his evangelizing "expeditions" to Awka villages. Before her conversion and baptism, the young girl participated in all traditional rituals and ceremonies of her village. Indeed, when she was much younger, the priestess of their local deity loved her very much. And during one of her bouts with malaria, the priestess carried her on her back over a long distance to the shrine of their deity. There, she asked the deity to cure the child of her illness. That young girl would become the model for Ezinma, Okonkwo's beloved daughter in *Things Fall Apart*.

Something in Isaiah told him to go after this young girl, who seemed to be immersed in the culture and tradition of her people. There followed a brief period of getting to know this young girl and her family. Her name was Anenechi and her father was Iloegbunam of Umuike village in Awka Agulu (not to be confused with Agulu town of the famous lake). Following Awka tradition of adding the prefix, *Nwa* to names, Anenechi was simply called Nwanene, and that explains the initial N for her middle name, according to Chinua. The young lady was soon baptized and given the name Janet. She was then formally betrothed to Isaiah.

In 1905, she was sent to St. Monica's school, the first Victorian finishing school founded in 1894 and located at Iyienu Ogidi. At St. Monica's, Janet actually lived with Miss Warner, one of the missionaries whom she served as a housegirl. In 1906, the school was moved to its present site in Ogbunike, at the strategic spot of Ugwu Ogba, the famous Hills of the Cave of *Things Fall Apart*. It was here that Janet completed her training. In 1909 she and Isaiah were "joined in holy matrimony" by Rev. G. T. Basden, who also became the model for Mr. Brown, the reasonable missionary in *Things Fall Apart*. Mrs. Janet Achebe outlived

---

[6] Chinua, interview with Egejuru.

her husband by five years. She died in 1967, shortly before Ogidi was overrun by Nigerian soldiers. She was among the "lucky" few who died in their homes during the Biafran war.

Isaiah and Janet were blessed with six children, four boys and two girls. Chinua is the youngest of the boys and the last but one of the six children. According to Johnson Okudu, "Isaiah had his children at the hands of white people." This implies that Isaiah's children were born in hospitals or maternity clinics run by white missionaries. Furthermore, they were brought up in the ways of white people or in the ways of Christians. This type of upbringing meant limited interaction with non-Christians and total immersion in Christian living. This was quite easy to do because the family for the most part, lived on church premises where the father worked. However, when they visited their home village and when the father finally came home on retirement, it was quite difficult to avoid mixing with non-Christians in the village. All the same, Isaiah did all he could to limit interaction between his family and *ndi nkiti* or people of nothing as Christians spitefully referred to non-Christians. The latter in turn, referred to Christians as *ndi uka* or church people.

Mrs. Agnes Achebe, Isaiah's daughter-in-law and widow of his first son Frank, fondly recalled the love and discipline that Isaiah gave his children:

> Their father loved them a great deal and he never allowed them to mix with other children. He never allowed visitors or intruders into his compound. It is only recently that people started coming and going as they please in this compound.[7]

This compound that Mrs. Agnes Achebe is referring to, is fondly called *Headquarters* (of Achebe clan). Isaiah's original house was quite large. It was built of mud walls and slate roof. It was destroyed during the Biafran war. While he lived, Isaiah resisted any renovations of his house. After the war, another house was built on the site of the old house. This second house now stands behind a two-story building over looking the old Onitsha/Enugu highway. An eye catching stone escarpment flanks the entrance to the compound. And symbolically guarding the entrance by the left, is the grave and monument to Frank who inherited their parents' homestead. It is here that Mrs. Agnes Achebe, the matriarch of Headquarters, lives with Frank's branch of the Achebe clan. Continuing on her reflections on the semi-seclusion of Isaiah's family, she recalled:

---

[7] Agnes Achebe, interview with Egejuru.

Albert didn't go visiting as such, he didn't mix except at school. That's why it surprises me to read of all those things he wrote in his books. How did he know about them? He didn't follow the masquerades as other children did. How did he know about masquerading? The way their father disciplined them was indescribable and inimitable, and the children obeyed.[8]

Isaiah's grandchildren also experienced his strict discipline. One of his grandsons, Oyibo Achebe, the son of Frank and Agnes, reminisced on his grandfather's ways: "Everybody in our family surrendered to the authority of papa *nnekwu*. He made his presence felt. We were fortunate to watch him."[9]

As a true Christian and especially as a church teacher, Isaiah denounced most traditional practices and beliefs. His son Augustine recalled their father's attitude toward traditional beliefs:

> There are certain stories about tradition and juju our father wouldn't allow people to repeat in his presence, such as rain making, or divination, *ogbanje*, witchcraft and others. His white colleagues regarded such things as superstition.[10]

Isaiah often had confrontations with his non-Christian kinsmen on several traditional beliefs. He saw it as his duty to urge people to turn away from ignorance and embrace the white man's education, which he believed to be the most potent medicine for dispelling ignorance and superstition. Chinua's sister Zinobia recalled:

> Our father went round the villages encouraging parents to send their children to school because, education not farming, will be the saviour in the future. He said that even if you wanted to be a farmer, it would be good to go to school first.[11]

Chinua elaborated on their father's near obsession with education:

> My father believed implicitly in what the missionaries told them about the value of education. Some times he referred to the person who told him that time would come when education would be an item of great value and price. There was nothing my parents would not do in order

---

[8] Agnes Achebe, same interview.
[9] Oyibo Achebe, interview with Egejuru.
[10] Augustine Achebe, interview with Egejuru.
[11] Zinobia Ikpeze, interview with Egejuru.

to enable their children have an education.[12]

The result of all this was that with the pittance he was paid as a church teacher, Isaiah Achebe was able to send his first three sons to the prestigious Denise Memorial Grammar School, Onitsha, before it was Chinua's time to go to secondary school. His two daughters equally finished primary school and attended St. Monica's girls' school Ogbunike. "That was my father's sense of education. So, he put in all he had into our education," Chinua concluded.

Surprisingly, later in his retirement years, Isaiah relented in his rejection of some traditional practices. He saw the need for some aspects of tradition and culture. His grandsons would later be initiated into the societies of masquerades and into their appropriate age grade societies. His sons would join their age grade groups. Chinua for instance, belongs to the age grade called *Government*. Their name indicates that they constitute the majority of the decision-making body of Ogidi local politics.

Despite his iron-clad exterior, Isaiah was described as a very humorous and quiet man. Johnson Okudo said that Chinua inherited his quiet disposition from his father, while Chinua's siblings attribute his sense of humour to their father. Isaiah's wife Janet, was the embodiment of patience and good nature. She and her husband lived so peaceably that their "quietness" was legendary. Chinua could only recall one instance when his parents were loud in their argument:

> I remember one day; in fact, the only day I remember, a neighbour passing through the back of the house heard my father and mother exchanging angry words. He came in and said, 'I have never heard this, what is happening? Isn't there a testimony by the whole town that you never exchange angry words?'

Chinua promptly added:

> But that doesn't mean my parents never disagreed; there were plenty of little disagreements. My father was always complaining about the food placed before him. He was a very difficult person to please, but they didn't live a life of conflict. So, I learned that once you realize that you are different from this other person, the question of how you get along is easy. And my mother's favourite statement was *'onye choka onye n'eme kia, sosia ebili'*—if you keep looking for someone exactly like you for a spouse, you will live alone.[13]

---

[12] Chinua, interview with Egejuru
[13] Chinua, same interview.

Chinua took his mother's favourite statements to heart and literally lives by them. Another favourite dictum of Chinua's mother was, "*Onye n'arapu umu ya n'edunye odibo ozi bu odibo ka o n'azu.*" Literally, if you leave your children and keep sending the servant to do all the chores, you are only raising the servant and not your own children. Chinua and his wife would remember to raise their children instead of servants. It will be later revealed how the wise sayings of Chinua's parents found their applications in Chinua's own life especially in his relationships with his siblings, his spouse, his children, his colleagues and his employees.

Discussions with several members of the Achebe clan revealed two paramount values that Isaiah and his wife inculcated in their children. These are: an unrivalled appreciation of family and a deep sense of right and wrong.

Looking at the results of very important choices Chinua made in his life, one is tempted to speculate that he possesses a very powerful inner voice. Consequently, he was asked what he thought of the idea of an inner voice directing his actions. He said:

> I would say there was something like inner voice. You followed what you thought was right or good or just or valuable. So, it's not surprising because the family in which I grew up, there was a sense of right and justice and the belief that if you followed that way it ought to be alright and it was a mistake to try and short circuit this right and justice. By the way, this right and justice generally involved effort. You had to work; the thing didn't just drop. So, we were on our own with justice and these other things as guide and we did the best we could to follow.[14]

---

[14] Chinua, same interview.

2

A child is born

When he was not yet born, a brother of ours, Julius had died. Our father was wondering what went wrong. One day, papa and I were going to the Ezeokolis at Nnobi. Papa told me that God spoke to him. God told him that the one who would replace the dead child would be a great man. Then papa told his vision to Rev. Amobi of Ogidi. He also told Amobi that he was looking for a name for his next son. Then Rev. Amobi suggested the name, Albertus Magnus. Papa said he would remove Magnus and call the child Albert Chukwunualumogu. Later, when the child was born, he was named Albert Chinualumogu -may God fight for me.[1]

Rev. John Achebe prefaced his responses to questions about his youngest brother Chinua, with the above story. As sacrilegious as it might sound, Rev. Achebe's story is likely to remind some Christians of the Annunciation to the Virgin Mary. The story is even more troubling because, in traditional Igbo society, a child is not given a name before it is born. The Igbo considered and still consider pregnancy a condition froth with danger and uncertainty. Because of that, couples would not make concrete plans such as choosing names or making clothes for the baby. Besides, nobody could predict what the sex of the baby would be. Isaiah Achebe's Christian faith might have influenced his decision to go ahead and predict the sex of his unborn baby and to choose a name for him. What is more, he certainly believed that God spoke to him in his dream. Given the circumstances of his birth therefore, Albert Chinualumogu Achebe would be considered a precious child by anybody's standard.

It was on Nov. 16, 1930, that Albert Chinualumogu was born. At that time, his parents lived at St. Simon's Anglican Church, Nnobi. His father was the catechist there. His eldest sister, Mrs. Zinobia Ikpeze, played a very significant role in his up-bringing. She was his wet nurse, and she seemed to have relished every moment of those early years. She excitedly recalled the daily activities of minding the baby while their mother was away at meetings or at the market or just busy around the house:

---

[1] Rev. John Achebe, interview with Egejuru.

I was old enough to take care of him. When mama went to the market or to a meeting, she would make *akamu* for me to give him. When mama would be cooking, I would be minding the baby, rocking him, singing to him. He started growing and I watched him. I saw him crawl. I saw him stand and walk. Later, when he grew up a little, I would tell him stories while mama cooked. Sometimes I would ask him to tell me the stories that I told him the day before, and he would repeat them exactly as I told them to him.[2]

From here, one gets the first indication of Chinua's aptitude for story telling. Mrs. Ikpeze couldn't resist telling some of Chinua's favourite fairy tales. One was the story of a child who went in search of his sister who married a goat. The sister had moved with her goat husband to the land of goats, so the brother went there to look for her. Another was the story of a boy who forgot his flute at the farm and went back alone to look for it against his mother's advice. Both children succeeded in their search and returned loaded with riches from benevolent spirits because they conducted themselves prudently.

Mrs. Ikpeze was then asked, "what type of child was Chinua? Was he stubborn, aggressive or troublesome?" She replied: "Ever since I have known him, *o daa acho okwu*, he does not seek trouble." His brother John confirmed: " He is not a trouble maker, not a fighter. I never saw him in a fight with other children; he was always at play with them. *O daa acho okwu*."[3]

Stories told by his siblings indicate that Chinua had a normal childhood. He played with other children. He had favourite stories and games. He loved a particular game known as *Dota m ka m dota gi* -pull me and I pull you. This game is a mini tug of war between two people. This seemed quite an unusual type of game for a child who would cry at the very mention of the word fight. From one particular story that was repeated by practically all his siblings, one got the impression that Chinua was subconsciously aware of the significance of his name. The story is told that when Chinua was very young, his mother used to tease him in the way she said his name, *Nualumogu* -fight for me. Whenever she went to the market or to a meeting, she would bring home some delicacy like *akala*, biscuits or groundnuts for Chinua. To give him what she had brought, she would call, "Albert! *bia nualumogu-o-*! The child would tearfully reply, " I will not fight, call Augustine to come and fight for you." Then his mother would laugh and say: "Come my child and take

---

[2] Zinobia Ikpeze, interview with Egejuru.
[3] Chinua's sister, Zinobia and his brother Rev. John, repeated that sentence at separate interviews with each of them.

what I brought for you, that's why I am calling you."[4] Chinua would then heave a breath of relief and go for the goodies.

Chinua lived in reasonable harmony with his siblings. His immediate younger sister, Mrs. Grace Okocha claimed: "Even though he is my elder brother, I can't remember when he ever beat me. We did not fight over things." Unlike other children who would cling to their little "possessions", Chinua loved to share with others. His sister illustrated his giving spirit with this story:

> There is a kind of bean we call *okpo odudu*; Chinua hates it and when it is cooked in our house, our father would give him yam to cook for himself. He would collect vegetables to cook his yam and when it was done he would still share it with me even though I had eaten the *okpo odudu*. Till today, Chinua sends me presents. He has not changed.[5]

When it was suggested that he consciously tried to avoid any confrontations, Chinua quickly put the record straight:

> It doesn't mean we didn't fight. We knew it was not the right thing to do. I was fighting with Grace for instance, and my mother used to call me *Ike ka n'uno* -strong only in the home.[6]

Mrs. Lucy Achebe, Chinua's sister-in-law was asked if Chinua was a spoilt child. She told a story to show that he was not spoilt:

> He was not spoilt but he was pampered. He did chores that children of his age did. He went to the stream quite often, and that was how I came to know him before ever I married his brother John. We all used to fetch water from Iyienu which is not a fast flowing spring. One day, I was at the head of the fountain or spout, and I was washing clothes. I noticed Albert sitting by the spout area. I recognized him as the brother of the girls I used to play with. So, I took his pot and fetched water and put it on his head. He didn't talk to me; he just smiled and went away. After some days I came to wash clothes again. Suddenly, the water stopped flowing. I noticed that somebody was intercepting it from the top. I looked up and saw Albert and he smiled. From then on, any time he saw me at the head of the fountain he would walk straight up there, fetch his water, smile and go away. He must have been around ten

---

[4] Sister Zinobia tried to recapture this incident as it occurred on a number of occasions throughout Chinua's childhood.
[5] Grace Okocha, interview with Egejuru.
[6] Chinua, interview with Egejuru.

years old. That's how I came to know him.[7]

Mrs. Achebe was trying to make the point that a spoilt child would not be going to Iyienu spring to fetch water all by himself. It was a big hassle and a long wait before one could fetch water from there. An incident that happened to Chinua and his sister Grace would serve as a good example of how frustrating it was in those days to get enough water for daily use at Ogidi and other neighbouring towns. Grace recalled the incident:

> In those days, many people used to line up to fetch water from three spouts where water gushed out of the stones. That very Saturday, we went to the one that we normally went to, but there were many people there. We went to Iyienu, the same thing. We went to Nkisa the same thing. So, we carried our dirty laundry home and our mother had to wash the clothes with the water we had at home.[8]

Chinua and his siblings were not spoilt; their mother didn't believe in sending servants to do all the chores in the house. She rightly figured that doing so amounted to raising servants instead of one's own children. But more than the rest of the children, "Chinua was much loved and petted in the family" claimed his sister Grace. " I believe he was my mother's favourite child. I could tell, because if anything fell from mama's hands she would exclaim 'Albert *nwam o-o!*' Chinua passionately dislikes favouritism. Therefore, he found it hard to believe that he might have had a special place in their parents' hearts. It was his brother John who made him realize the special place he held in their father's heart. John had conveyed the idea in a letter he wrote to Chinua when he was at Government College Umuahia. Apparently their father had been complaining that Chinua didn't write him as often as he wanted him to. John then wrote to Chinua saying: " You have a special place in his heart, make sure you write him. Do not ignore this special relationship with him." Referring to the impact of that letter Chinua said:

> It was then that I started noticing that perhaps some siblings might feel jealous rather than encourage you. But John actually revealed this to me. And I began to watch and noticed that each time I came home, my father would be radiantly happy. It wasn't because I was doing anything special for him, I don't know what it was.[9]

Certainly, Chinua didn't reckon with the impact of a longer association with his father after the older boys had left the nest. At that time, when the elders of the village came to discuss matters with his father, Albert would

---

[7] Lucy Achebe, interview with Egejuru.
[8] Grace Okocha, interview with Egejuru.
[9] Chinua, interview with Egejuru.

be around to fetch things from the kitchen or the pantry. He would be sent to get kola nuts and drinks for the guests. He would stand near by to watch and mentally record everything going on. On Sunday, he would carry his father's bible bag and they would go together to church. It was in that way that Chinua learned more about the culture than his older siblings. But more importantly, it was then that the bond between him and his father grew very strong without his realizing it.

It wasn't only his parents who loved him most dearly. His brothers and sisters also love him very much. Chinua claims to have equal love for all his siblings. When it was suggested that he and John seemed to have a father/son relationship, he emphatically denied it: "It's not really so. I don't want to elevate it higher than what I have with my other brothers and sisters. They are all different; each person has something special."[10]

Even when he said that his sister Zinobia was like a mother to him when he was growing up, he didn't mean that he loved her more than the others. On the other hand, he said that he didn't actually know his brothers Frank and Augustine quite well when he was young. Frank had started working and Augustine was living with him at his station. It was not until 1937 when they came home on leave that Chinua really got to know them. He remembered the occasion very well because their homecoming was a big thing for him. "That was the first time I really knew them. They had just become names and I had no idea what they looked like. I grew up with my elder sister and my younger sister."[11] Chinua's reluctance to pick or name favourites seems to run in Isaiah Achebe's line. For instance, all of Chinua's nephews and nieces would not name a favourite uncle or aunt. And Chinua explained:

> I think there is something about our relationships which is difficult to put in words, because we are not 'word' people in talking about relationships, we just let things be. It is difficult to talk about how you relate to this brother or that sister. A lot of it is not spoken about, not formulated in words. But I know that each person in my family has had a role and that I am fortunate because they have all helped me. I, coming last among the boys, had a great advantage.[12]

---

[10] Chinua, same interview.
[11] Chinua, same.
[12] Chinua, same.

Childhood years

"Looking at the mouth of an old man, one would never think he suckled at his mother's breast," says an Igbo proverb. This proverb is enacted each time we ponder the near superhuman achievements of great people or the eternal verities that issue from the mouths of great philosophers. We wonder whether these great people ever said or did any of those naughty, silly and stupid things associated with childhood and adolescence.

Looking at the breath and depth of Chinua's wisdom, one wonders if he ever spoke or behaved like a child. Chinua's wisdom places him among men who are said to be born old. It is not only his works that testify to his deep seated wisdom, his friends and classmates also think that Chinua must have been born old. They claim that even as a young man, he carried himself as an elder and spoke in the manner of village elders.

Yet, Chinua was a normal child. He said and did quite a few childish and funny things when he was a child. Like many children the world over, Chinua loved sweets or candy. He loved biscuits and would do whatever was necessary to have them. His sister Zinobia remembered how much he loved biscuits. She told a story to illustrate. When the family was living at Uboni, their mother's friend, Mrs. Okeke, noticed how much Chinua liked biscuits. From then on, every morning when she came for prayers, she brought biscuits for Chinua. One day, some children were playing outside and Chinua's mother told him to go and join the children and play. Chinua said: "Mrs. Okeke hasn't come yet. If I go out and she comes, keep my biscuits on top of the table for me." If he went out early and came back and there were no biscuits, he would ask if Mrs. Okeke hadn't yet come for morning prayers. Thus, for young Chinua, a voluntary gesture has become a routine obligation.

Sometimes, a child would cause some damage by innocently doing what nobody asked him to do. Some other times he would do the opposite of what he was asked to do. Chinua was no exception. His sister, Zinobia recalled one occasion when her little brother did the opposite of what he was asked to do:

> One day, mama was cooking some meat and she wanted to go over to the neighbour's. She asked Albert to watch the fire and to make sure the pot did not boil over. As soon as mama left, Albert put more firewood into the fire and the pot started boiling over. Then he started yelling, "mama *o lue-e, oku n'agba o-o* -Mama it is time! Fire! Fire!" Then mama came running, laughing and asking Albert if he didn't know that he was supposed to remove the flaming wood from under

the pot.[13]

On another occasion, their mother went to a meeting. Chinua and Grace took it upon themselves to make soup like their mother. They put the pot on the tripod and placed the lid on the pot with the deep side facing up. Then they piled ingredients on to the lid and put fire under the pot. After a little while, they went to remove the lid so as to stir the contents. To their surprise they found the ingredients sitting on the lid while the pot was empty. "They laughed and learned a lesson," Zinobia said.

Chinua loved to watch his mother prepare the family meals, especially when she was making his favourite dishes like *egusi* soup or yam with vegetables. On one occasion, his mother was getting boiled yams ready to be mixed with cooked and seasoned leafy vegetables. When she picked up the head portion of the yam, Chinua asked her if he could have it to eat. His mother said it was too hard for him to chew. Chinua chuckled and said, "Mama *nke a, o si na mmatanwu isi ji, agam atakwia ofuma ofuma* - This mama, she says I can't chew yam head, but I can chew it real well."[14]

Remembering that Chinua grew up in a household where education was highly valued, and its importance drilled into everyone's head, one finds it very hard to believe that Chinua would run away and hide to avoid being sent to school. Yet he did so when he was young. He recalled the incident; it happened at St. Luke's Anglican Mission at Uke, the last station their father worked before he retired and returned to Ogidi in 1935:

> My father used to teach children bible stories in the church building. It was called Monday class. There was a time they tried to get me to go but I refused to attend. I ran away, they pursued and caught me in a nearby bush.[15]

The grown up Chinua claims that that incident wouldn't count as being afraid of school because "Monday Class" wasn't a conventional school. Besides, his father was the teacher. But then, he was afraid of going to the real school too! It happened in 1936 when he was six years old. He was rather too young in those days to start school. His sister Zinobia told the story:

> I would take him to the infant section, then I would go over to the primary section. He used to be afraid and would cry whenever I left him. One day he ran out crying after me. The headmaster stopped him and asked whose son he was and why he was crying. He said his sister

---

[13] Zinobia Ikpeze, interview with Egejuru
[14] Chinua's words as recalled by sister Zinobia, interview with Egejuru.
[15] Chinua, interview with Egejuru.

left him and entered that place; he was pointing at the building. The headmaster led him to my classroom. I stood up and called, 'Albert!' Then the headmaster said I should keep him with me because he was afraid, that when he got over his fears he could go to the infant section.[16]

It was going to take a while for Chinua to get over his fears. Thanks to the headmaster and the quick thinking of Chinua's parents, the problem was solved sooner. Chinua remembered how:

> I remember that story of following my sister to her class in the primary section which was like a university to me. I stayed next to her without knowing what they were doing. It was the headmaster Ezekwesili who drove me out from there. But what is interesting is that I started the same day with my younger sister Grace. She was about three years old. My parents' reason was that if I went to school nobody would stay home with her. So they sent both of us. At the end of the year when the results were announced, Grace was said to have passed but she would have to remain where she was. I was older, so I took off.[17]

---

[16] Zinobia Ikpeze, interview with Egejuru.
[17] Chinua, interview with Egejuru.

3

Primary and secondary education

Officially, Chinua started school in January 1936 at St. Philip's Central school Akpakogwe, Ogidi. The family had returned to Ogidi from Uke, the last place of Isaiah's employment. Chinua recalled the journey home:

> I remember our getting into a lorry. It was my first experience riding in a moving vehicle. I was dizzy watching trees running. When we came back, I started school at St. Philip's C. M. S. Central School Ogidi.[1]

Even though the young Chinua had been afraid to stay in the infant section at the initial stage, once he comfortably settled in, he sort of started "making headlines." It wasn't long before another headmaster, Mr. Anyiwo, who used to make unannounced visits to classes, caught Chinua in the act of giving all the correct answers during oral Arithmetic. That happened a few more times in other subjects, and the headmaster perceived the child's outstanding intelligence. He was so impressed with the child that he paid a visit to Chinua's parents to alert them to the child's intellectual gift. He stressed the need for adequate financial preparation for their son's education:

> You better start preparing yourselves for the education of your son. You need to arm yourselves with head-pads with which to carry loads for people and raise extra cash for this child's education. His brain is such that, for you to send him as far as that brain could carry him, you must think seriously of some other means of making extra money on the side.[2]

The words of the headmaster were a veritable prophecy. Chinua's academic brilliance soon became obvious to all. According to his elder siblings, Chinua excelled in his classes. No student ever outperformed him

---

[1] Chinua, interview with Egejuru.
[2] Words of Mr. Anyiwo, the headmaster, recalled by Chinua's siblings, John, Augustine and Zinobia at separate interviews with each of them.

in any class because he was good in all subjects. Chinua was asked if there were any subjects he didn't like and he replied:

> There were many subjects I didn't care for. I didn't care for History, but later I realized it was because of what went by the name of History. It wasn't really History. It dealt with topics like *The Royal Niger Company*, *Amalgamation* and so on. Math or Arithmetic was not my favourite either, though I got through. I think I enjoyed the English language. If I studied hard, I would know my Arithmetic and the other things, but somehow for the English language, I did not need to study. There were things you did because you liked them, and I liked to read, but apart from that, I had no difficulty getting through my school work.[3]

While Chinua was still in the lower classes, the headmaster picked him to be an assistant to an older boy who was in charge of recording the daily school attendance. This involved going to all the classes after roll call to collect from the teachers, the daily attendance in their classes. Then the attendance monitor would add the total and record it on a little wooden board which was displayed in the assembly hall. By working with the older boy, Chinua was apprenticed to take over the job after the senior pupil shall have left the school.

Chinua did everything he was asked to do in school. He didn't get into fights with the other pupils. He didn't carry on like most brilliant pupils known to be sometimes stubborn and disruptive. Because he conducted himself so well, one assumed that Chinua escaped the corporal punishment that every pupil had to live with in those days. He was not spared. In fact, he was flogged quite frequently. He said that nobody escaped flogging because:

> There were teachers who were neurotic. For instance, if you were given mental or oral arithmetic, you would receive one stroke of the cane for every wrong answer. Sometimes a whole class would be flogged because of something one pupil did and refused to own up. We had a headmaster, Mr. Okongwu who would flog the whole school at least twice a term. So, there was no way you could escape.[4]

Chinua was mercilessly whipped by Mr. Anyiwo, the same headmaster who admired his brilliance and predicted his future academic success. It happened on a rainy day. Chinua and the older boy had not added up the day's attendance by the time the school came in from recess. Chinua recalled: " The headmaster rang the bell and the whole school was summoned for this heavy offence. The two of us were flogged." His sister

---

[3] Chinua, interview with Egejuru.
[4] Chinua, same interview.

Grace also remembered the incident very vividly: " I saw the headmaster flogging Albert. My spirit died and I cried very hard." The grown up Grace rationalized the flogging: "The headmaster flogged him because he loved him so much and he expected him to be perfect in everything he did. He did not flog him out of malice." The elder sister Zinobia also commented on the headmaster's genuine love for her brother: "Anyiwo and his wife loved him so much they said he would marry their daughter when he grew up. When they were leaving Ogidi, my mother presented them with a live chicken on behalf of Albert."

Chinua continued attending school at St. Philip's Ogidi and despite his famed brilliance he was not given any double promotion. Chinua said:

> I was a regular student from the beginning to Standard Five. Then John decided to take me to Nekede for Standard Six. I had to prepare and take entrance examinations to secondary schools. That was the first time I left home.[5]

It was in 1943 that John took him to Nekede Central School, one of the most prestigious Central Schools in Owerri province. John was the Agriculture master at Nekede. Asked why he considered it necessary to remove his brother from Ogidi, John replied:

> Why I came to take him was that I knew what God had told my father about the child. I knew that it was necessary to be careful over him. When I came to take him, it wasn't for him to be my servant. I had other servants. I found out somehow that he needed guidance.[6]

Chinua later understood his brother's reason for taking him away from home. He said, "John took over the overseeing of my education because he really had a sense of what was going to be useful to me. And our father did not protest, they must have discussed it."

The journey to Nekede still remains vivid in Chinua's memory.

> That day we (with his late cousin Eleazar and another boy) did not travel with John. We took Rotibi's lorry from Onitsha to Owerri. Upon reaching Owerri and not knowing the distance, we decided to go and see my sister Zino and her family at Egbu, a distance of three miles. So, we walked carrying our luggage. We had a long trek.[7]

---

[5] Chinua, same interview.
[6] Rev. John Achebe, interview with Egejuru.
[7] Chinua, interview with Egejuru.

From Nekede Central School to Government College Umuahia

At Nekede Central School, Chinua again demonstrated his outstanding academic prowess. Pupils and teachers marvelled at his conduct and academic performance. His brother John remembered: "I did not put pressure on him to read. He read a great deal. Reading was very important to him, and he was good in all subjects." Within a short time, fantastic stories, if not outright myths, were woven around this wonder child at Nekede Central School. Some of Chinua's classmates and teachers talked about one particular incident that turned Albert into an instant hero of the school. Below is a summary of the popular incident, as told by a teacher and a classmate of Chinua's:

> One day, a white Education Officer paid an unannounced visit to Nekede Central School. The pupils in standard six had just finished a dictation class at which Chinua spelled every word correctly. The teacher was telling the other pupils that Chinua had not only spelled every word correctly, but his writing in dictation was more beautiful than the writing of the other pupils during regular writing class. While the teacher was speaking, the Education Officer walked into the class. He listened but did not believe that a pupil could write beautifully as well as score a hundred percent in dictation. The Education Officer demanded to see Chinua's exercise book. After scrutinizing it, he decided to test Chinua himself. He chose a passage and dictated it to Chinua. Chinua again spelled every word right and his writing was the same, very beautiful.[8]

Because Chinua seemed to have mastered the spelling of every word in the English language, he earned the nickname, *Dictionary*. He would eventually give the same nickname to Obi Okonkwo, the hero of *No Longer at Ease*.

Ephraim Ogbonna from Avu town, was one of Chinua's classmates at Nekede. He witnessed the incident. He also claimed to have been friends with Chinua. He talked of the marvels of Albert Achebe as if they happened only yesterday:

> Albert was very clever; he was good in working sums. While we are getting five over ten, he is getting eight, nine. We said it's because his brother was teaching him privately. Albert will not allow anybody to

---

[8] Ephriam Ogbonna, Chinua's classmate at Nekede and Sir George Egejuru, a teacher at Nekede at the time of the incident, both recalled and told me about it. Chinua confirmed it.

touch his pen; nobody can dip into his inkbottle. After writing, he will remove his nib and put his pen in his pocket. He used to carry his inkbottle with him out on recess. During the time for writing, he will bring out his ink. Therefore, we wondered if he had a magic pen and ink.[9]

When Chinua was asked about his academic performance at Nekede and his obsession with his ink and pen, he treated the matter in a casual and modest manner:

> Well, I heard that I had a high reputation at Nekede. As you know, these things get exaggerated with time. I think people were more or less scared of my performance at Nekede. For instance, there was this thing about *ogwu* or medicine. Someone at a lower class at Nekede when I was there, later became a teacher. This fellow was a teacher at the school where my kids were attending. He told the story of how my brother asked me one day if I had taken my medicine, and someone who overheard the question thought it was brain pill. Those thoughts were bandied around, but even at that age, I would have known that any talk about medicine or brain pill was rubbish.[10]

In 1943, Chinua took the entrance examination to Dennis Memorial Grammar School, the first and most famous Anglican Grammar School in Eastern Nigeria. He also took entrance to Government College Umuahia. Finally, he sat for the entrance examination to Aggrey Memorial Grammar School Arochukwu. He sat for this entrance just for the sake of it. But their result came out first and he was admitted in class two! He passed the entrance to Denise Memorial Grammar School and to Government College Umuahia. Chinua said, "I wanted to go to D.M.G.S simply because it was the one we knew. We saw their red caps, their blazers, the students." Not only was D.M.G.S the only one they knew, it was the one that all his brothers had attended. To top it off, he had been awarded a scholarship for D.M.G.S. He hadn't received one for Umuahia. Worse still, he didn't know anything about Umuahia nor did he know anybody who had attended secondary school there. In fact, Umuahia was closed because of World War II. It was about to reopen around the time Chinua was taking the entrance exam. Therefore, Chinua assumed naturally that he would be going to D.M.G.S. "But to my surprise," recalled Chinua, John said no. He said that even if I didn't get a scholarship to Umuahia, that was where I would go. That was a real surprise to me. His brother John confirmed, "I said he wouldn't go to D.M.G.S. It hurt my father that I didn't want my brother to study where I

---

[9] Ephraim Ogbonna, interview with Egejuru.
[10] Chinua, interview with Egejuru.

studied, at a mission school. Why should he go to Government College, a place for non-Christians?"[11]

Chinua was destined to go to Umuahia. Indeed, another headmaster who had taught at Ogidi, but had since left Ogidi, envisioned Chinua attending Government College Umuahia. Nobody had told this headmaster where Chinua was or that he was going to take the entrance to Umuahia, yet he had the premonition that Chinua would be there. Christian Momah, Chinua's friend and classmate, told the story of the headmaster's incredible vision:

> In 1943, I was at St. Michael's Aba and we had a headmaster, Okongwu. When we were preparing for entrance to Umuahia Government College, the headmaster said to me and one other boy, that if we were lucky to pass the entrance exam, he was sure we would meet one boy called Albert Achebe, whom he had taught three years earlier. He said that Albert "*ga ara mmili ga ama anyi*, will unleash the rain that will beat us." Unbeknownst to us in the hall at Aba was Albert taking the same entrance exam; he had come from Nekede. At Umuahia, within a day or two, there was Albert.[12]

John Achebe continued the story of Chinua's admission to Umuahia:

> So he went to Umuahia. Before long, I received a letter from the principal summoning me to Umuahia. I was so surprised. I went to Umuahia and Mr. Simpson the principal told me that he looked at my brother's performance at the entrance exam. He said there was a scholarship available but it belonged to Owerri province. He asked me where I was paying tax and I said Owerri. He told me he would give my brother the scholarship.[13]

In this instance, the British sense of justice and fairness prevailed. Thus, a man working in a province other than his home province, but paying taxes there, was entitled to financial benefits reserved for citizens of that province. In that way, Chinua whose home province was Onitsha, was awarded a scholarship meant for pupils of Owerri province because his guardian was working and paying taxes there.

Right from his first year at Umuahia, Chinua demonstrated his superior intelligence. His performance at mid-year exam was so good that he was promoted to class two along with five other students. Chinua spoke about that unprecedented act by the College:

---

[11] Rev. John Achebe, interview with Egejuru.
[12] Christian Momah, interview with Egejuru.
[13] Rev. John Achebe, interview with Egejuru.

It was a surprise because we were not told it was promotional, and to make matters worse, a few students were demoted from class three to two. So, class two became too large and was split into A & B. It meant I gained one year and finished one year ahead of my classmates.[14]

A number of Chinua's classmates at Umuahia talked about his exceptional academic ability. Momah recalled, "From the first two terms at Umuahia, he was ahead of everybody. Even when he moved to the next class where my elder brother was, after two terms, he went on top and remained there." Another classmate, Ben Uzochukwu had this to say about Chinua's performance:

> As time went on, his brilliance shone and before we knew it, there was this promotion of half a dozen of them to a higher class and that shocked some of us into realizing that we had been left behind. From then the academic rivalry in our class intensified. As for Albert, there was no subject he couldn't master. At school, boys always thought some teachers favoured certain students. Whatever Albert did was far excellent, and some of us thought the masters were biased for Albert. Menakaya, our Geography teacher would pass round Albert's work to show us how it was done. And in literature, you could see it coming that he had a wonderful gift for analysing and making points. He was an all round man.[15]

Mr. Momah also testified to Chinua's mastery of all subjects:

> At Umuahia, our English teacher said that Albert was the best English writer in the whole school, and this was at a time when there was a class ahead of us. He was literally flying; he was tops in all subjects. The only rival he had at one time was Inyang, now a medical doctor.[16]

In addition to his academic achievements, Chinua also held the important office of prefect. He became the prefect for Niger House when he was in class four. It is important to note that he became a prefect just at the time the College initiated a new way of choosing prefects by election. The classes would propose candidates and the principal would appoint them. Chinua was thus first appointed a house prefect when he was in class four. In class five he became a College prefect still holding the post of house prefect. For one student to be the College prefect as well as a house prefect shows the trust and confidence his classmates had in him.

---

[14] Chinua, interview with Egejuru.
[15] Ben. Uzochukwu, interview with Egejuru.
[16] Christian Momah, interview with Egejuru.

Mr. Adrian Slater was the English Master at Government College Umuahia during Chinua's time. Mr. Slater was eighty-one years old when he was interviewed in August 1995. For the interview which took place in the office of Professor C. L. Innes at the University of Kent at Canterbury, Mr. Slater came weighed down by his baggage of Achebe memorabilia. Prominent in his collection were Chinua's novels including an autographed copy of *Arrow of God* which read, "To the man who taught me respect for language." There was also a voluminous album of handwritten cards from students in Nile house at Government College Umuahia. Mr. Slater was the master of Nile house. There were pictures of him and the students about whom he was most eager to speak.

Mr. Slater gave a short summary of the history of Government College Umuahia and the quality of students he encountered there. The first principal was Mr. Fisher. When World War II broke out, the students were sent to King's College Lagos. When the College reopened in 1944, Mr. William Simpson became the principal. He recruited a superior African faculty. The in-take of students was less than ninety. Mr. Slater described the student body as "very selective, the peak of the pick." He spoke nostalgically of his teaching there:

> I realize now after teaching at other institutions including England, that the quality of mind that I was privileged to meet, I didn't appreciate until later. Chinua was one of twenty-five or thirty who were so able but I took it for granted. And I am rather shocked even now to think of how I threw everything at them as if they were native English people, speakers who got enormous European background. I am surprised at my nerves, but I did it and they took it. I never let them get away with incorrect English. They learned and wrote as good English as I could teach. If I were responsible for any of Chinua's style of English, I am very proud of it. What I would say is that this class as a whole would be writing this English of the same calibre. I can't say whether Chinua was always on top or if he spoke better, because I could say that ninety percent of the class was accepted by University College Ibadan just like that. I was right in my unconscious assessment that this was an able class. In my eyes they were the same. I can't say, look I knew Chinua, but he was a part of this good school. The staff cared for them. I was concerned with their written English. I would not let them get away with anything being out of place. I would like to think that I made them realize they couldn't get away with bad English. I am sure I demanded more from non-native students than I did from native born English students. Really, it was a good school and was run like an English boys' school of the better kind. They read books considered suitable for English children. It was a happy place. Our principal was very strict, but he loved his charges. He was brought up in the traditional way, so there was standard of behaviour.

We had morning prayers every morning. The students were a captive audience, intelligent and able students.

Mr. Slater would not end the interview without reference to what he considered a crowning moment in his life. It happened in 1982 when Chinua went to receive an honorary degree from the University of Kent at Canterbury. Mr. Slater and his wife Rachael were invited for this first time degree ceremony in Canterbury Cathedral. Slater recalled:

> We met Chinua and Christie over dinner. It was very thrilling. There were six honourees and Chinua was asked to speak. Chinua said, 'I am pleased to see the person who first introduced me to the English language.' All the Nigerians came to shake hands with me. I was ten feet high, and then he came to have tea with us.[17]

One of the first rate African teachers who taught Chinua at Umuahia was Professor Biobaku, former vice Chancellor of the University of Lagos. When Mr. Slater left in 1946, Biobaku was recruited from Cambridge University where he had been studying and sent straight to Umuahia in 1947. He recalled his brief experience with Chinua:

> I was to teach English and History to the senior class, Achebe was in that class. The boys became my friends. From the word go, I noticed Achebe and his writing. A day before their exam we went on a picnic. That's how I came to know Achebe. It was very brief, the last term of 1947, but I noticed and recognized him. From the beginning I was close to the boys and I could tell what each of them was going to become. *Things fall Apart* was the type of thing he would write. Even at College he punctuated his essays with sayings from old people.[18]

After such sustained adulation, one is somehow relieved to know that there were things Chinua wasn't good at when he was in school. He was not good in sports or athletics. He participated in sports because no boy escaped the evening games supervised by the masters. "In soccer, he will kick the ball to wherever he was facing, whether it was against his own team or not. He doesn't have a good voice for singing, so singing wasn't his thing either," recalled Momah. When it came to getting things done, "He was a slacker," said Uzochukwu. Chinua's calculated deliberateness remains with him and is seen by some members of his family as a weak point in his character.

---

[17] Adrian Slater, interview with Egejuru
[18] Professor S.O. Biobaku, interview with Egejuru.

His extra curricular activities included debating, ballroom dancing, reading fiction, and doing some carpentry. The activity that would be of most service to Chinua was the compulsory reading of non-textbooks at weekends. In several of his public lectures, Chinua talked about his joyous encounter with books in the library of Government College Umuahia. It was his first time of seeing so many books in one room. It was at that time that he and his classmates and their contemporaries at other good colleges literally devoured works of fiction by Rider Haggard, Bertha Clay, Joyce Cary, Graham Greene and John Buchan. Most of the staples included, *The Return of She* and *She* by Haggard, *The Sorrows of Satan* and *Beyond Pardon* by Clay, *Mr. Johnson* by Cary, *The Heart of the Matter* by Greene and *Prester John* by Buchan. Feeding on the fantastic stories by Haggard, the highly impressionable boys took "the side of the enemy against the savage Africans," as Chinua would later describe his reaction to the stories. It was much later, at the University that Chinua and most of his classmates became aware of the full implications of the fiction they read at school. Through their reading of European fiction on Africa, they got the picture about themselves wrong. And of course, Chinua's response to this realization would be *Things Fall Apart*. One cannot over emphasize the crucial role played by Government College Umuahia in the making of Chinua Achebe.

Throughout his secondary school years, Chinua was both a model student and a model son, "His life was totally different," said his brother John. "Whatever money you gave him as pocket money, he was contented and he accepted it." His parents' special love for him became obvious at this time as would be noted by his brother John and sister Grace. He spent his holidays in the home of this brother or that sister. Wherever he went, he carried himself with extreme humility not seen in boys who attended secondary schools, especially those who attended Dennis Memorial Grammar School and the almighty Government College Umuahia. When he went home on holidays, Chinua still took part in house chores such as pounding *foo-foo* or fetching water from the stream. Sister-in-law Agnes Achebe said:

> He never fussed about anything and he accepted whatever you gave him. Once, when he was returning from us in Kano, I cooked rice and stew and put in tins for him and he took them. My mind never told me that this boy was going to be different in life.[19]

In his final year at Umuahia, Chinua took the school certificate examination which was then administered by Cambridge University. He scored the highest marks in the Sciences throughout the country. He left

---

[19] Agnes Achebe, interview with Egejuru.

Umuahia in class six after taking the entrance exam to the University College Ibadan. The result of the exam would be published in Nigeria's top newspaper, *Daily Times* while Chinua was on holiday at Ogidi.

University College Ibadan

Nothing could be more logical than Chinua finishing his academic race at his country's highest seat of learning- UCI, University College Ibadan, an affiliate of London University. Perhaps, it was fortuitous that Chinua should be among the pioneer students to open the University in 1948. He had been among the fresh in-take to reopen the Government College at Umudike, Umuahia in 1944. Thus, next to his good parentage and upbringing, these two extraordinary institutions of learning played a very significant role in shaping the future novelist. And as if to emphasize the importance of college education, Chinua's admission to the University College Ibadan, made headlines in the country's leading newspaper. Therefore, the news of his admission reached his hometown in a spectacular manner via the Nigerian *Daily Times*.

Chinua's sister, Zinobia recalled how the news reached the Achebe family:

> A neighbour ran into our compound calling, 'Mama Achebe! Mama Achebe o-o! We hear your son has collected all the tax paid in Nigeria. He is going to Ibadan College to study without paying any fees. Don't you hear the pandemonium in the newspaper?' Within a short time, our compound was filled with people coming to rejoice with us.[20]

Before the end of the day the news "spread like bush fire in the harmattan" and all of Ogidi learned that their son not only gained admission to Ibadan, but had also received a MAJOR scholarship for his studies. This news reminded the Achebe family of the prediction by the headmaster Anyiwo who had told them that the child's academic future was very bright. No one was surprised when it was revealed that Chinua had scored the highest marks in the Sciences in the whole country! Very few people outside the higher echelon of the University administration actually understood the full implication of the adjective qualifying scholarship. Other students received scholarships, but only a couple received MAJOR scholarships. So rare was it that only Chinua and Inyang, his academic rival at Umuahia, received it in their set. In addition to having all academic expenses paid, spending money was given to the

---

[20] Zinobia Ikpeze, interview with Egejuru.

Major Scholar. He was given a private room. In addition, he enjoyed the title, MAJOR SCHOLAR.

Chinua's Major Scholarship was for studies in Medicine. This made a lot of sense because he had consistently scored his highest marks in the Sciences throughout his secondary school years. Therefore, this Major Scholarship was a just reward for Chinua's hard work.

Like his classmates at Umuahia, Chinua's classmates at Ibadan came from the peak of the pick. If the country could have afforded it, this first set of students deserved to be Major Scholars. By all accounts, they all seemed to possess the intellectual versatility associated with Renaissance men. For this set of students, that one was in the Sciences did not mean that one could not be literary. Examples abound of pioneer students of Ibadan who would have felt at home in any discipline. Bola Ige, who was a Major Scholar in Classics, mentioned some of those brilliant minds. For example, James Ezilo, is one of the best known mathematicians in Africa. Ige described Ezilo as "One of the best literary minds that I know; one who has read *The Rise And Fall Of The Roman Empire* and quotes it like any Professor of Roman History." Ige went on to name other graduates like Chijioke, an engineer and a poet; Okoro, a medical doctor who writes short stories; Olumiyiwa, a Professor of Physics who writes in the manner of Achebe; and the late Leslie Harriman, a zoologist who became the finest ambassador that Nigeria ever had. These students were so brilliant that it became almost routine for them upon graduation, to apply to Oxford or Cambridge, and be accepted to do a postgraduate degree in two years instead of three. For anyone who has encountered some of these scholars, there is no arguing the fact that they received the best education that Britain provided for all her subjects within her Empire. Chinua would soon prove that he belonged to this group of Renaissance men, when he switched from one Discipline to another, and excelled in it.

Getting to the College, Chinua registered for Medicine. However, it did not take long before he realized that his fate did not lie in medicine? He spent a very frustrating freshman year planning his switch to the Arts. He had to find some rational explanation to present to all who would feel disappointed in his decision. That wasn't the only problem facing him though. He had to convince the University authorities that he could handle the requirements for the Arts. After all, his entrance examination result showed that he had not done as well in the Arts as in the Sciences. Furthermore, if he succeeded in switching, there was still a major obstacle. He did not do Latin at the secondary school. Therefore, London University, the parent of Ibadan College and the degree-granting Institution would not allow him to do Arts without any background in Classics. Fortunately for him, that same term, London University agreed to suspend the requirement for Latin. The rationale was that English was a second language to the colonial subjects. Chinua was so delighted with the news that "I just stopped paying any attention to what I was doing and began to plan how to switch. Then I found it was going to be difficult." He went to the Dean of Arts who wasn't pleased at all with the idea. He was skeptical of Chinua's ability to do well in the Arts. "How do we know you are going to do well here?" asked the Dean. He brought Chinua's result to show him, in case he had forgotten that he did better in the Sciences. "So, I had to argue now that I could do it," Chinua recalled. Finally, he was able to convince the Dean that he was willing to take the risk. While all this was going on, Chinua conveniently ignored what to many people constituted the greatest obstacle -finance. The major scholarship would be taken away from him! However, the force pushing him to his unknown future was so strong that he did not think about the economic consequences of his decision. "In the end it was a very unpleasant one year. And so, I changed, minus my scholarship."[21]

Chinua did not consult members of his family or his very close friends before he made the switch. He felt they might try to talk him out of it, so he told them afterwards. His life long friend Dr. Agulefo was dismayed when Chinua broke the news of the switch in a letter to him. Agulefo wrote:

> While I was struggling to find my way in Medical school in the USA I received a brief note from Chinua one winter day. He told me he has quit Medicine and has decided to study Arts, even though it meant losing his scholarship. He said he could not stand the idea of killing and dissecting animals. I promptly replied, urging him to reconsider his stand. He did not, and the rest is history.[22]

His brother John was asked how he and the rest of the family reacted when Chinua abandoned Medicine for the Arts. He responded:

> I was pleased because one should have the freedom to choose what one wants to study. He chose English over Medicine. The family accepted it calmly and adjusted to his decision.[23]

Fully aware of the financial burden such a decision entailed, his brothers, John and Augustine, pulled their meagre resources together to support their brother. Augustine who was just beginning to work in the civil service, scraped up whatever he had, including his home leave allowance, and John also put in what he had. Chinua said, "they both contributed to pay my school fees for the first year, then I got a government scholarship for the Arts."

That anyone in his or her right mind would drop a Major Scholarship in Medicine to pursue a general degree in Arts, is mind boggling to say the

---

[21] Chinua, interview with Egejuru.
[22] Dr. N.T.C. Agulefo, correspondence with Egejuru, on his relationship with Chinua.
[23] Rev. John Achebe, interview with Egejuru.

least. How does one rationalize such an act? Among the Igbo for instance, a person who made such a decision would be most certainly considered insane, bewitched or under the influence of *agwu* - those mischievous minor spirits that specialize in inflicting mild forms of insanity on their victims. In such a case, the relatives of the victim would consult a medicine man or woman for help. Therefore, if Chinua had not come from the family of Isaiah Achebe, his relatives would have gone to a medicine person to find the cause of his unprecedented action.

Other happenings in Chinua's life would lead one to speculate that the man must be endowed with a powerful inner voice. Earlier in the interview, he had reluctantly admitted that an inner voice might have been at work when he chose his wife. It was again suggested that the same inner voice was operating when he dropped out of Medical School. He provided a different explanation:

> I think it was easier than inner voice. I think it was simply recognizing where your strength is, and not being fooled by other things, distractions. It is particularly difficult for somebody who is supposedly okay in most subjects to decide and say, this is the one I want to pursue. And in my case it was further complicated by the fact that I got a scholarship for the Sciences. I ended up in the exams doing better in the Sciences than in the Arts. I got my scholarship because of my performance in Chemistry and things like that. So, one could be misled by saying, okay, Medicine is what everybody wants to do, so I can go and do it. That's what happened. But I never went to the Sciences with the same enthusiasm that I went to the Arts. So I went for Medicine but once we began doing Physics and Mathematics at the University level, it became clear to me that I wasn't going to enjoy it at all. It was going to be too much effort to get good marks. Yes, it was both inner voice and practical common sense. I know people who would say, 'Medicine or nothing else'. Yes, if you are inclined that way that's okay. If you loved Medicine, I wouldn't argue about it. But, for me, that is not my *nature*. I could have done Medicine but I think I could have been a second rate doctor.[24]

As anyone could deduce from his explanation, Chinua is a man who thoroughly knows himself, his strengths and his weaknesses. As he would probably phrase it, he is not the type of man who would swallow *udara* seeds, knowing full well the size of his anus. No, he would not indulge in self-deception even if it would lead to a most prestigious career with enormous financial rewards. Indeed, it was the wealth associated with being a doctor that prompted his young daughter Chinelo to ask her father why he wasn't a doctor. This happened when she and her father were

---

[24] Chinua, interview with Egejuru.

discussing professions and she discovered that he had left Medicine for Arts. To her question, her father had answered: "Being a doctor is fine, but if you are thinking in terms of the money the doctor makes, it's not the right question. Whatever you do, do it very well." And that was the moment she stopped asking her father why he left Medicine, a profession that could have made him very wealthy. Chinelo talked more about the conversation she had with her father that day:

> My dad said that he could have been rich, but he also could have been unhappy. He said he wouldn't have reached so many people. It was a mission to reach people. At that point, I stopped thinking about money.[25]

Perhaps, Chinua would have made more money as a doctor; he would have made his relatives and friends very proud of him. However, he is not a man who would go against his own conviction simply to please other people. Once he is convinced of the rightness of an idea or undertaking, he stands by it. Judging from Chinua's decision to pursue what he felt was his true academic calling, one could say that knowing/being oneself and standing firm by what one believes in, come to the very top of Chinua's scale of values.

Becoming a Major Scholar, and a pioneer student at the first and most prestigious University College in colonial Africa, would get most people swollen-headed, but not Chinua. He remained the person he was prior to becoming an undergraduate. He continued doing chores that he used to do before he went to the University. His sister-in-law, Agnes Achebe recalled how helpful Chinua used to be when he came to spend his holidays in their home, "He would pound *foo-foo*, he would help out in the store selling soft drinks to people. You wouldn't hear a word from his mouth because he was reading all the time."[26]

His sisters remembered a funny incident that happened during his first holiday at home from Ibadan. A man who read about Chinua's admission to Ibadan had been longing to meet him. When he heard that Chinua was home on holiday, he rushed over to see him. When he entered the Achebe compound, he saw Chinua cutting grass. The man asked if Albert was at home and Chinua told the man to wait while he hurried away to check. Chinua ran inside the house and changed his clothes. He then came out and said to the man, "I am Albert."[27] It was a funny joke but it said a lot about the young man. It was unbelievable at that time that an undergraduate was cutting grass in the village. In fact, some parents would not allow their son to do any of the chores he used to do before he became

---

[25] Chinelo Achebe, interview with Egejuru.
[26] Agnes Achebe, interview with Egejuru.
[27] Chinua's sisters -Zinobia and Grace- recalled the incident at separate interviews.

an undergraduate. Unlike most students, Chinua did not put on airs or speak with a phoney accent to demonstrate his new status. He still went round the village to greet the people and pay the traditional respect due to village elders. Unlike most educated and semi-educated Africans, Chinua was never alienated from his people. He felt at home in the village as he did at the University campus.

CHINUA: a student in the Faculty of Arts

By the time Chinua settled down to do Arts, his first academic year was over. He went on to do English, Geography and History, but he soon abandoned Geography and picked up Religion. This time around, he was influenced by the renowned Professor of Religion, Geoffrey Parrinder. Reminiscing on the courses he took, Chinua said, "One of the most valuable things I did was Religion." And his mastery of that subject is demonstrated in his frequent quotations from and allusions to bible passages in his novels.

It took no time before Chinua started proving to all who were still apprehensive of his decision to do Arts, that he was finally in his elements. He didn't have to exert himself so much in his studies to score high marks. His way with the English language caught the attention of many. It appeared that all the lecturers in the faculty of Arts knew of Chinua and his ways with the English language. Mr. C. C. Momah, his friend and classmate at Umuahia and Ibadan said:

> There must have been three or four lecturers who at different times said to the class that only Albert writes good English. Even when he has a few points to make, he writes it in good English.[28]

Momah also recalled a poetry competition which Chinua won. The organizer came to the class and asked who Chinua was. Chinua stood up and the man told the class that he wrote the best poem. Then he read the poem which went something like this:

> There was a young man in our hall,
> Who thought because he was small,
> Should pay less, for he ate less
> Than everybody else in the hall.[29]

---

[28] Christian Momah, interview with Egejuru.
[29] Chinua's poem as recalled by Momah.

Even though Chinua knew very well that he didn't have to work too hard to excel in the Arts, he didn't play around or treat his studies lightly. Several of his classmates testified to his dedication and assiduousness, especially in English courses. One of these classmates was Mabel Segun *nee* Imoukhuede, who also became an established writer. She spoke about Chinua's academic and extra-curricular activities:

> We were rivals in English; this time I am first, next time he is first. He was a model student and took his studies very seriously. At a point we had a terrible teacher with a monotonous voice. She was teaching books and authors we didn't like; most of us abandoned the class leaving only Chinua and this woman. Chinua seemed able to accommodate her; he had the patience. Looking back at it now, I am not surprised. He had a single-minded devotion to literature.[30]

In those days, students didn't do course work. They didn't have to attend classes, they could simply go to the library to read and cram for exams. Therefore, to find a student who stuck with a lecturer whom other students avoided is evidence of that student's commitment to the subject.

Bola Ige also talked about Chinua's mastery of English.

> In class, Chinua and Mabel were really the best in English and we admired them. Even though I was a Major Scholar in Arts, I was no where near them. I could understand how he could write one or two pages for Miss Mahood and score high marks. Even in History he wouldn't write long things, always brief and to the point. In literary criticism, he and Mabel were head and shoulders above us. One thing that amazed us was that Chinua would write one or two pages either for an essay or something and he would run away with an A or a B+. I liked him because he was brilliant in English. When his novels started coming out, we were not surprised. He couldn't have been doing all he did at Ibadan without coming out the way he did.[31]

Chinua was a regular student who participated in various student activities. At one time he was secretary of the Students' Union. He was a member of the Social Club and was very well known for his expertise in ballroom dancing. The most notable position he held as a student was assistant editor of the University paper, *The Herald*. Also editing the paper were A. C. Anene, F. Ade Ajayi and Mabel Segun. At this time, Chinua and Mabel worked closely together on the paper. Sometimes Mabel would go to his room to work on the paper. And as would be expected, other students started speculating that some romance was going on between the two.

---

[30] Mabel Segun, interview with Egejuru.
[31] Bola Ige, interview with Egejuru.

From all accounts however, it appeared that the normal romantic/amorous escapades of young men, was missing from Chinua's life at Ibadan. None of his classmates had any "juicy tales" to tell about him. They all insisted that he was very calm, serious and disciplined. Despite rumours of intimacy with Mabel, Ige said:

> Chinua was too angelic for boyfriend/girlfriend stuff. The problem with Mabel was that if she liked you, she went everywhere with you. Furthermore, Mabel was already engaged to be married, so she couldn't mess around with boys.[32]

Mabel confirmed Ige's story: "I wasn't anybody's girlfriend. I was engaged and my finance had gone to England for postgraduate. That was all the more reason I wasn't anybody's girlfriend."[33]

Mrs. Christiana Amachree Graham Douglas couldn't find much to say about Chinua. She remembered that Chinua was quiet and reserved. She explained why there wasn't much to be said about Chinua: "One reason I can't tell you much about him is that he was very quiet and gentlemanly. Chinua should have been more rough with the girls, we would have had more to talk about him."[34]

Senator Frank Ellah reminisced about their days at Ibadan: "In our younger days, when you talked about going to the nightclub, you didn't talk to Chinua. He was shy, how could he talk to girls?"[35]

In spite of his quiet and angelic nature, some mischievous and bugmania students, would not rest until they had manufactured some scandal involving Chinua and Mabel. The editors of the students' tabloid, *Bug*, were desperate to taint the names of Chinua and Mabel. They invented and published in the *Bug*, a telegram purported to have been sent to Chinua by Mabel. The message read: "Nuachi come at once, dying of love. Lemba." Though both names had been anagrammatized, anybody could tell they meant Chinua and Mabel. It was further alleged that when Mabel saw the caption in the much-feared *Bug*, she collapsed. According to V.C. Ike, this incident led to the banning of the *Bug* for a while. Commenting on the incident, Mrs. Segun said:

> In those days, people were very primitive. They didn't know that a boy and a girl could work together. I used to go to his room, and we worked on *The Herald*. This led to students saying he was my boy friend, it led to cartooning us *Nuachi* and *Lemba*.[36]

---

[32] Bola Ige, same interview.
[33] Mabel Segun confirmed Ige's story in a separate interview.
[34] Christiana Amachree Graham Douglas, interview with Egejuru.
[35] Frank Ellah, interview with Egejuru.
[36] Mabel Segun, interview with Egejuru.

By the reckoning of Ben Uzochukwu, "Albert was quite a popular figure and most of the girls had a crush on him. He was a moderate in the field of boy/girl relationship."[37]

Chinua was finally asked point blank, "What was your problem with girls, why couldn't you talk to them when you were a young man?" He replied:

> Of course, I talked to girls, but I had no girlfriend if that's what you mean. The person who came closest to that would be Mabel because she would come to work with me on *The Herald* which we edited. And there was really nothing going on.[38]

Apparently nothing happened till he left the University and started working. Momah joked about Chinua's "uneventful" life as a bachelor:

> To my shame I cannot recall any girl I would have associated him with until his wife. I can't recall when he was up to anything or he must have done it so cleverly that I missed it. He wasn't into playing around, I will almost swear for him though it's a dangerous thing to do.[39]

But then, as if to mock all those who only saw him as a quiet and peace loving gentleman, Chinua took part in an act that made his fellow students see a hidden side of him- outward expression of anger. Both V.C. Ike and Mabel Segun narrated the incident. Four new girls from the eastern region of the country had just arrived at the University bringing the population of female students to fourteen. These four girls had a secret meeting during which they nominated one of them as representative of the female hostel. They submitted the name to the Administration. When the other girls heard about it, they were very angry. They went to the head of the University, Kenneth Melanby, and asked him to cancel the nomination. Their request was granted. However, Bola Ige and a few other trouble-shooters wouldn't let things be. So, they started writing nasty things about the four girls in their tabloid, *Sword*. They posted copies of the *Sword* in the dining hall bulletin board. Other students kept tearing down the posters. The authors finally wrote a terrible one and locked it in a glass case in the dining hall. When Chinua and a few others saw this, they went to the kitchen, took an axe and hacked open the glass case. They tore off the paper and threw it to the floor and stamped on it. Recalling her reaction to Chinua's participation in the scandal, Mabel said:

---

[37] Ben Uzochukwu, interview with Egejuru.
[38] Chinua, interview with Egejuru.
[39] Christian Momah, interview with Egejuru.

I was shocked because I really liked Chinua and I didn't expect him to do that kind of thing. I was a bit hurt because I had been the butt of most of these articles, but Chinua didn't take an axe to defend me. Why should he defend these girls? So, I wasn't happy.[40]

Chinua might not have been very vocal in student union activities. But he subtly participated by putting his linguistic talent to use. He was known to come out with most of the definitions used in the *Bug*. As Ige put it, "There was no way you could be in the University in our days without being active." Given their intellectual level, the students were very aware of the political situation of their country. For instance, during the Enugu coal mine massacre, students demonstrated and passed various motions condemning British policies in Nigeria. In addition, the students sensed and resented the arrogant attitude of their British lecturers who taught them European history and literature that were often irrelevant to their time and circumstance. These lecturers and professors didn't even try to hide their feeling and conviction that "these native boys would not amount to anything."

Throughout those years of ferment, Chinua, like most of his classmates, was able to combine with ease, extra curricular activities and academic work. He did not have to over exert himself to write the best paper in most of his classes. In 1953, he successfully completed all requirements for the BA and graduated in the Second Division.

It was a surprise to Chinua's classmates and lecturers to see his name in the Second Division. They had all expected him to come out in the First. In fact, authorities at Ibadan contested Chinua's placement and tried to convince London University to change the placement. But London refused and the placement stood. It would be left to future events in Chinua's life to prove that examination is not a true test of knowledge.

---

[40] Mabel Segun, interview with Egejuru

4

Work experience

One thing that came up before Chinua went home on holiday was an attempt by Professor Welch, to get him into Cambridge University on an exhibition scholarship to do a post-graduate degree in History. If this had worked out, it would have been a repeat of his original major scholarship to Ibadan. An exhibition scholarship is given to the best of the best. It not only covers all expenses, but it puts the student in a class by himself. Chinua was not accepted. Although he was not given any reason for the rejection, one could assume it was because London University had placed him in the Second Division in his B. A. degree examination result. Professor Welch, like other teachers of Chinua, knew he was definitely a First Class material. Hence, he not only encouraged Chinua to apply to Cambridge, he sent in the application on Chinua's behalf. He was so confident of his student's ability that he didn't think his examination result would be an obstacle. But, the authorities at Cambridge thought differently. Chinua would make a joke of Cambridge's rejection of him forty years later! In 1993, he was invited by Cambridge University to deliver their annual Ashby Lecture at Clare Hall. In his introductory remarks, Chinua said that he wondered if the authorities hadn't made a mistake, after all, the lecture was a scholarly event. And since by Cambridge evaluation he was not scholarly material, why is he invited to deliver a scholarly lecture?[1]

Chinua went home on holiday without any definite idea of what to do for a job. This was not unusual at that time because there were more jobs than graduates. As Chinua put it, "We just took things easy in those days because we knew there was no problem, jobs were everywhere." While he was enjoying his holiday, his friend, James Ezilo got a job at the Merchant of Light, a private secondary school at Oba near Onitsha. Ezilo asked him what he was doing for a job and Chinua told him that he was doing nothing. Ezilo told him that the principal of Merchant of Light, Cannon Mgbemena, was looking for

---

[1] Chinua, interview with Egejuru. He made reference to the joke he made at Cambridge when he was invited to speak there in 1993. However, Ezenwa Ohaeto gave full coverage of the joke in his book, *Chinua Achebe*, 1997,pp.51-52.

someone to teach English. Furthermore, Ezilo disclosed the salary he was being paid and advised Chinua to ask for more. He knew the principal was desperate to get graduates to teach in his school, because, having graduates on his staff would facilitate accreditation for the new school. Chinua recalled: "So, I went there and sort of demanded five hundred and forty pounds per annum as against five hundred and seventy pounds, the highest administrative scale."[2] The principal was not allowed to pay that much. However, he wasn't going to lose the opportunity of getting his school accredited. Therefore, he devised a way to move figures around. He paid some of the money as allowances and in the end it added up to what Chinua had asked for.

Before the end of 1953, Chinua started teaching at the Merchant of Light Oba. He shared quarters with Ezilo and one other teacher. He taught English, particularly Phonetics and English literature. One of his students then was Ben Ogbogu of Ogidi, who would become a policeman for some years before he later became a very prosperous businessman. Chief Ogbogu gave a graphic description of their young tutor who dressed in khaki shorts, short sleeves, suede shoes and socks, occasionally a tie. He was cool and spoke in measured tone. He didn't shout or flog anybody. He gave a lot of homework and was strict in his marking. Above all, "He has such a melodious voice that compels you to do something." According to Ogbogu, Chinua's level-headedness and quiet disposition endeared him to students and tutors alike.

Although Chinua's stay at the Merchant of Light was very brief, it was still a very important landmark in his life. For the first time in his life, he was out on his own. There was no parental supervision and there were no University authorities monitoring his movements in and out of campus. In short, he was fully responsible for himself and his actions. Equally important was the fact that he became a "master", responsible for two houseboys, Dickson Odukwe and Kenneth Udo. Dickson, a self-employed, fifty-five year-old man, described the kind of relationship the boys had with their master:

> He doesn't know that this is a houseboy or this is a master. He embraced us like his own blood relatives, not like hired servants who, when they break something, you beat them. He used to cook for us who were supposed to serve him.

Dickson was asked if their master flogged them as other masters did their servants. He laughed and replied:

---

[2] Chinua, same interview.

Has he spoken loud enough let alone scolding and flogging you? He does not know how to flog. *O nwelu aka izizi*, he's very tenderhanded. Our relationship wasn't the type in which the boy runs away when the master is coming. When he is angry because you destroyed something, *O wusa iwe*, (lays the anger down) before he speaks to you.

He was further asked if girls visited Chinua as they did other tutors. He replied:

> He was not like those young men chasing after women. We did not see that in him. I cannot remember what I would call a weakness in his character and I cannot invent any now because I am an adult.[3]

Incidentally, Dickson confirmed what other employees who worked for Chinua nearly forty years after him said about their former employer. From the earliest beginning in his position of "master", there was absolute trust between master and servant. More importantly, there was not that traditional division which places the master or employer above the employee. With Chinua, there is only a levelling; there is oneness and embracing of another human being as a blood relative. Dickson fondly recalled his reaction when Chinua was about to leave his job at the Merchant of Light, " I wanted him to take me with him." When Dickson finished school and was looking for a job, Chinua wrote letters to him and advised him about various jobs and what he needed to do to get into them. Chinua maintains his interest and concern for those he had close association with in the past. When he got married, he introduced Dickson to his wife saying, "this was my first wife before you, he took care of my house."[4] Like other employees of Chinua, Dickson cherishes the time he spent as Chinua's houseboy.

Nigerian Broadcasting Service

Teaching at the Merchant of Light did not last long for both Chinua and his friend James Ezilo. James soon left the school and went to Cambridge for postgraduate studies in Mathematics. Chinua who hadn't looked into any other job openings was very surprised when:

> Out of nowhere, a letter comes to me from the Nigerian Broadcasting Service; just goes to show what I mean by jobs lying

---

[3] Dickson Odukwe, interview with Egejuru.
[4] Dickson Odukwe, same interview.

around. And it was the controller at Enugu saying that they were considering people for senior service positions in broadcasting.[5]

The controller asked Chinua if he would like to come to Enugu to see him, or if he preferred, he, the controller, would come to Onitsha to see him. Chinua asked him to come to Onitsha. In the end, Mr. Elphik came to Onitsha to meet with Chinua. This preliminary interview took place at NBS' little studio at Onitsha. Mr. Elphik was quite impressed. He recommended that Chinua go to Lagos and meet the Director of NBS. Mr Elphik was also present at the second interview. However, to Chinua's surprise, Mr. Elphik didn't say anything throughout the interview, only the Director was asking the questions. The interview went well because the Director seemed pleased with Chinua's performance. He in turn arranged for Chinua to go for government civil service interview. As Chinua was leaving the office, Mr. Elphik followed him to give him some tips on how to conduct himself at the civil service interview. One of the suggestions was that Chinua should wear a tie, because he appeared too casual during his interview with the Director. Considering it a good advice, Chinua bought a tie for the interview. The team that interviewed him was so pleased that one of the Directors asked Mr. Elphik, "where do you find these boys?"

Chinua would later find out that it was Professor Welch who recommended him to NBS when they went to Ibadan University College to recruit new graduates to fill positions that would soon be vacated by expatriates after Nigeria's impending Independence. "So, that's how I got into NBS after about eight months of teaching at Merchant of Light," Chinua concluded.

Chinua got into NBS without any clear idea of the job content; he did not receive any job description. Therefore, when he reached Lagos, working and training went simultaneously. As he recalled, it was then that they decided he would be better in the production line rather than in general administration. He was finally placed in the Talks Production Department which he found very interesting. It meant reading and writing, editing scripts, producing speakers, all the spoken word program apart from news. He said, "I found that quite interesting, really up my line. It was the kind of thing I found ultimately helpful, dealing with dialogue for instance."[6]

In Talks Department, his immediate boss was Mrs. Angela Beattie. While an assistant to Mrs. Beattie, Chinua learned on the job. He learned the professionalism that went into setting other people's ideas in proper order. He observed that first time guest speakers just assume

---

[5] Chinua, interview with Egejuru.
[6] Chinua, same interview.

there's no difference between written and spoken language. They just write what they are used to writing and think that that would do. Michael Olumide, a retired senior NBS official and a colleague of Chinua's, shed some light on what was going on at NBS at the time Chinua joined them. The Organization was still experimenting with various programs, trying employees at different assignments. Olumide said:

> Because he was in broadcasting, one would have thought he would have gone into the News department. He had this good command of language, but he was in Talks Department. He would fit into the News Department but he wouldn't go anywhere near it.[7]

Olumide and other colleagues were disappointed with Chinua's placement at the job. They felt he was underutilized but Chinua himself was quite content to be where he was.

In 1956, Chinua was sent for further training at the BBC staff school in London. The four months course was offered to broadcasters from various parts of the British Commonwealth. As fate would have it, Chinua took the manuscript of *Things Fall Apart* with him. He eventually showed it to Gilbert Phelps, a novelist and one of the teachers at the BBC staff school. Phelps read the script and told Chinua that it was a good novel. Phelps was eager to submit it to his publishers for evaluation, but Chinua refused. He needed to do more work on it. At the end of the course, Chinua returned to the Talks Department and continued producing the Talk Show. It is an understatement to say that Chinua's budding writing career benefited a great deal from his editorial experience in the Talks Department. The encouragement from Phelps, the extra writing sessions at the BBC training school, the editorial work he did in the Talks Department, all helped him do an extensive revision of the original manuscript of his first novel. Finally, he typed the manuscript and sent it to Phelps to find a publisher for it. Looking back at what that novel has become, one cannot believe that some other publishers rejected it. Those publishers were worried that their readers would not buy a novel written by an African. Fortunately, Alan Hill of Heinemann Publishers got hold of the manuscript and the novel was finally published on June 17,1958.

As with his teaching job, his tenure at the Talks Department wasn't going to last very long. Nigerian Independence was fast approaching, expatriates were leaving and positions were opening up everywhere. A few months before the publication of *Things Fall Apart*, Chinua was transferred to Enugu, where he would take up the position of Controller. On reaching Enugu, Chinua moved into number three Park

---

[7] Michael Olumide, interview with Egejuru

Lane at the Government Reserved Area of town. One of his co-workers, and the man who would soon replace him as the Controller at Enugu was Sam Nwaneri. He talked briefly about Achebe's time as the Controller at Enugu:

> We all knew him as an intellectual, but he interacted well with us. I knew him as a conscientious worker who did his job efficiently. At board meetings, he was always saying funny things. He had a tremendous sense of humour that was very infectious.[8]

Interacting well with people who work with him or for him, is one of Chinua's admirable qualities. His colleagues and subordinates at work testified to his cooperative spirit, and they talked especially of his very humane treatment of those working under him. He was needed to fill some other position at his job. The result was that his job as the Controller of the Eastern Region lasted barely two years. NBS once more was looking for a Director of programs in Lagos because the expatriates were leaving after Nigeria's independence in 1960. The establishment was planning to launch an overseas program; something that would later become the External Service of Radio Nigeria. The position was given to Chinua, and he became the first Director of the new Department. At this time too, the name changed from NBS to NBC-Nigerian Broadcasting Corporation.

Chinua then launched what became known as the Voice of Nigeria. According to Michael Olumide, Chinua was one of the people who formulated the Department of External Service of Radio Nigeria and he pioneered it. He saw the Department well established by the time he was forced by the Nigerian political crisis of 1966 and 1967 to abandon broadcasting. Olumide recalled the impressions the NBS authorities had of Chinua when he joined them, and also what the Corporation benefited from him:

> With his quiet disposition and unaggressive nature, we didn't think he had any specialty until he began to write. It was after *Things Fall Apart* that we realized we had a special person working in broadcasting with us. He was very self- effacing when he came in. He didn't push himself. He would talk at meetings only when he was invited to and he always spoke with clarity, not really his diction, but his ideas were always very clear. He was an idea's man, to that extent, he was able to manage a big division. He got the concept of broadcasting, and he ran the department extremely

---

[8] Sam Nwaneri, interview with Egejuru.

well. His talents were sign-posted by some of the things he did. In broadcasting, we talk of dreamers, this was Achebe's specialty.[9]

In effect, NBC was a shield behind which Achebe sheltered while he worked on his real calling. As it turned out, he published his first four novels while still employed by NBC. Inevitably, this rubbed off on the Organization as Chinua became world famous.

In addition to the ample time his job afforded him to engage in his writings, he enjoyed exciting assignments that involved extensive travelling to different parts of the country. On one such occasion, Achebe, Olumide, a few other Nigerians and an English man from the BBC, were to travel down the river Niger and follow it to where it empties into the ocean. They were to report on their adventure down the Niger, the people living along its bank, their culture and so on. Olumide reminisced on this adventure:

> We set out on a great fanfare. After a day we ran aground and nothing could move the boat. We were stranded for three days! We were killing our chicken one by one; we were running out of food and water. Eventually, we crawled back to Warri on a canoe, paddling upstream against the current. We came back physically in tact.[10]

Recalling the same incident, Chinua brought his legendary humour to bear:

> I was the officer commanding the expedition. Looking back at it, it was like a dream, we could have come to harm. And then the hunger we endured when we abandoned our ship! And the whole purpose was to make recordings of the music of the riverine people along the Niger, and we got some. I put together a program on that journey which was broadcast.[11]

Because Chinua was very efficient in whatever he did, he seemed to be saying to his employers, "I dare you to find me a job I cannot do efficiently." Therefore, NBC seemed determined to keep moving him from one position to another, in an obvious attempt to find some job that would effectively tap his talents. Consequently, he was soon alerted to the search for a Director General for the Corporation. Said Chinua, "I specifically refused to apply." His writings have made him famous by now and he had to deal with the demands of celebrity. As he put it, "I was in demand on other fronts, so I got a fellowship from the Rockefeller Foundation to travel." He chose to explore parts of East

---

[9] Michael Olumide, with interview.
[10] Olumide same interview.
[11] Chinua, retelling the same "expedition" incident with Olumide.

Africa and South Eastern Africa. While he was in East Africa, he received a cable from NBC saying that the post of Director General was available. They wanted to know if would like to be considered. He wrote back and said he didn't want to be considered. And so Chinua remained the Director of Nigeria's External Broadcasting Service-Voice of Nigeria, till the outbreak of the Nigerian civil war in 1967.

Chinua was asked if he would have remained with NBC if the war had not erupted. He replied:

> I don't really know quite frankly. I was coming to the end of my interest I think. I doubt that I would have stayed on and retired from NBC. Because, having gone up so quickly and so fast, and sort of seen the various sections of broadcasting, I don't think I would have stayed there much longer. Because I had seen what I wanted to see and my interest was not to get a job in which I had to retire. My interest was to find something challenging and interesting and perhaps different from time to time. So the problems of Nigeria just coincided with my need to move, and I had to move when it became impossible for me to live in Lagos because of the pogroms, the killings.[12]

Running back home

The massacre of Igbos was no longer confined to the North. It had spread to the Western Region and to Lagos. Many highly placed Igbo civil servants were killed or forced to flee back home to the East. Unlike many other Igbos who made haste to rush back home, Chinua, in his undying optimism for Nigeria becoming a great country, remained calm and hoped that things would soon calm down. He continued going to work until he was told that he was specifically being targeted by Hausa soldiers.

Chinua recounted the unnerving situation and narrow escape from marauding soldiers:

> One Sunday afternoon, we were at home, Christie, Chinelo, IK and I. The phone rang. It was one of the announcers on duty. He told me that some Hausa soldiers were looking for me. They wanted to know which was stronger, my pen or their gun. He said they seemed drunk. I was just confused. I called Victor Badejo and told him what I heard. He asked where I was and I told him I was at home. He said I better take my wife and kids and go somewhere else. He has heard too, so he said I should leave. I put my family in

---

[12] Chinua, interview with Egejuru.

the car and we drove off to the Director of British Council, Frank Cawson, an old friend, recently transferred from Ghana to Nigeria. Frank, who had a slipped disc, was lying on the floor on his back. He called the driver and told him to move out his car from the garage and put mine in to avoid detection. We didn't know then, but we found that those soldiers left NBC and found where I was supposed to be living in Milverton road. When they got there, they saw Ezeoke's kids and they asked them where the Achebes were. They pointed out where we lived but I don't know whether they went there.[13]

Chinua and his family stayed at Mr. Cawson's house and he continued to attend work at NBC from there. Things were getting worse. Victor Badejo called one day and told him it was much too dangerous to continue going to work. At that point, he decided to send his wife and children back to the East, to Port Harcourt where Christie's relatives lived. Because there were so many roadblocks and killings of Igbos all over the country, it was safer to travel by boat. He took his family to the mariner where they climbed on to an over loaded deck. To his horror, Chinua heard the Yoruba onlookers jeering, "Let them go! *gari* go cheap now." After three days, under the most trying of conditions, Chinua's family safely reached Port Harcourt.

Despite the threat to his life, Chinua was still hoping that things would get back to normal. Things only got worse. Relatives and friends in the East were worried for his safety. They were sending messages and asking what he was still doing in Lagos. Then one day, he and Victor Badejo ran into each other while they were out on a stroll. Victor was surprised that Chinua was still hanging around in Lagos. So Victor said to him, "life has no duplicate." Still, Chinua did not rush back to Cawson's house to pick up his things and leave. What finally pushed him to go back to the East was when someone called Frank Cawson's house asking if Chinua was staying there. Chinua was at work and when he came back Mr. Cawson told him about the call. At last Chinua and Ume Ezeoke decided to drive home together in two cars. Chinua got ready and at the appointed time, he drove to Ezeoke's house only to find that Ezeoke had left the night before.

Chinua left for the East alone. Fortunately, there were no incidents, no police checks until he reached Benin. There, a massive roadblock was mounted and there were police officers from the East. Several cars lined up for clearance. When it was Chinua's turn, they asked for his ID and "I showed them and they exclaimed. So, that's how I escaped."

---

[13] Chinua, same interview.

Despite the threats to his life and his obvious narrow escape to the East, Chinua seemed to be in denial that the Igbos were no longer tolerated in other parts of their country. However, a new job assignment by the military government of Eastern Region, awakened him to the bleak reality of the moment. In his typically humorous manner, he recalled his surprise at the type of job he was offered:

> When I came to the East, what did I know? First, the Public Civil Service Commission interviewed me as an Easterner coming back. They made me Resident Officer Class Two. They had that designation but it couldn't be Resident but the equivalent. There was no province to govern, so it was just a way to say 'I find you a job,' They suggested that I go to the University of Nigeria Nsukka on secondment from the government of Eastern Nigeria. That's how I joined Nsukka as a Senior Research Fellow before the civil war.[14]

This job came to an abrupt end when the civil war erupted. Nsukka sector was not only destroyed but it earned the sordid reputation of being the area where Achebe's good friend, Chris Okigbo, the poet, was killed at the war front. With Nsukka University gone, Chinua like other Igbo patriots had to work for the new Republic of Biafra.

---

[14] Chinua, same interview

5

Working for Biafra: the challenge

As he said earlier, Chinua's interest in employment was not in getting a job from which he would later retire. He preferred "something challenging and interesting and perhaps different from time to time." One could say that his teaching and broadcasting jobs were indeed, different and interesting. However, they were not challenging enough to fully utilize his talents. This is supported by the fact that NBC kept moving him from one position to another. He was already coming to the end of his interest in broadcasting, when a veritable *deus ex machina* - the Nigerian civil war, dropped into his laps. It was unfortunate that the challenge Chinua longed for, came literally in the form of his country's first civil war. He would have to work much harder than he did for his high paying and interesting jobs. Indeed, his payment for the work he did for Biafra, would be the untold drawn out suffering and constant narrow escapes for him and members of his immediate family.

True to his self-effacement, Chinua down played the enormous role he played during the war. He was asked what he did when his post of Senior Research Fellow suddenly ended with the fall of Nsukka and he said simply, " I did other things during the war." He was quite reluctant to talk of those other things. But it was easy to learn from those close to him, the type of things he did. His sister Zinobia recalled how Chinua was called away just before Christmas.

> During the war we lived at St. Philip's. One day, soldiers rushed into our house; they were looking for Chinua. We went and consulted him. He asked us to bring the soldiers because Ojukwu wanted to send him somewhere on an errand. He said he would go. I asked him if he was not going to stay for Christmas. He said, 'the land is in turmoil, what's Christmas?' He said he had to go and make a speech somewhere. It was around 23/24 December.[1]

---

[1] Zinobia, interview with Egejuru.

Although Chinua would not use the term ambassador or diplomat to describe his role, he was truly an ambassador at-large. He visited foreign countries in Europe and Africa on behalf of Biafra. His mission was to persuade some of these countries to recognize Biafra as a country. We know for a fact that some African countries like Tanzania, Ivory Coast and Gabon openly recognized Biafra and some European countries gave covert moral support and humanitarian aid to Biafra.

Those who worked with Chinua saw him as the brain behind Biafra's Think Tank. However, it was with great reluctance that he responded to the question, "Is it true that you were the leader of Biafra's Think Tank?"

> Basically yes; during the final years, may be the last year of the war. Ojukwu invited me and told me he wanted to set up a National Guidance Committee. He wanted me to be the chairman. The idea of the committee was to provide a philosophical, ideological base for the struggle. I said ok, the only modification was that I rejected the secretary he wanted me to work with. I told him whom I wanted- Emmanuel Obiechina. Ojukwu appointed everybody else and people in his cabinet. It was a high powered body, including people like Justice Aniagolu, Professor Ndem of Political Science at Nsukka and several other intellectuals. But to say they were the thinkers of the Biafran revolution is not correct, because, by the time this was being done, Biafra had more or less flopped. It was too late. Still, it was an interesting exercise. We wrote the Ahiara Declaration, and it was not entirely what we wanted. We wrote it in a kind of struggle with Ojukwu; we put this, he removed that. In the end it was a hodge podge of ideas and not as clear as I would have wanted. I could see Ojukwu's problem; some of the people on the committee were very right winged and there were some very left winged like Nzimiro. It was a balancing act to get something that would declare where we stood, why we were fighting, what would happen at the end if we won, how the ordinary people would be affected. Ojukwu had to copy the glamorous thing in the style of Nyerere's Arusha Declaration. This is where the notion came to him, so he was seeing himself at that particular time in a kind of revolutionary mood. I remember he had a photograph taken of him dressed like Castro. So when you talk about ideological thing for Biafra, I had to hesitate, there's a lot of playing with things. But there were some of us who were very serious and committed to having a clear notion of why we wanted to break away from Nigeria and what the ordinary Biafran had to gain, for they were suffering so badly now, and for what purpose? And when Ojukwu read the Declaration, it was such a resounding success (despite the compromise). It was read at a church (to avoid air raid) at Ahiara. It was as if the whole Biafra was assembled there. And I was hovering around to catch what the people were saying or their

reaction. There was just jubilation. I heard someone say '*o di ka si gbabia agbaba*,' it sounds like music you dance to. Then the fellow added '*a ga emekwia eme*,' would it be carried out? People were happy and skeptical, and that was the last gasp of resistance from Biafra. After that, things went rather quickly.[2]

Before his appointment as chairman of the National Guidance Committee, Chinua was invited by Dr. Ifegwu Eke, the Commissioner for the Ministry of Information to join his team. There he found that Dr. Eke and his team had been playing with the notions of justice, theoretical things about struggle and so on. When Ojukwu got wind of what was happening, he got concerned that the Commissioner of Information was just going on his own without permission from the leader. He then thought of bringing all these theoreticians under his control. This was in fact, how the National Guidance Committee came to be conceived. It became clear in the end that the Biafran leader was purposely setting up parallel bodies that would more or less balance each other, and leave him completely free to do as he pleased. He was known to play one body off another. For instance, if the military complained, he would tell them that they were not the government, and if the cabinets complained, he would say they didn't know how to fight. When the cabinet asked about the National Guidance Committee, he told them to come and observe their meeting. Chinua conducted the meetings while Ojukwu sat in as an observer. "We did what we could," said Chinua, " but we didn't have a chance, it was too late." It became clear in the end to Chinua and his colleagues that the Biafran leader actually didn't want anything like what the Declaration said. As Chinua puts it:

> Once he had delivered himself of this Ahiara Declaration, he found that it wasn't really what he wanted to do at all. But when he realized that people were going to take him up on that, to behave like revolutionaries, he began to arrest the very people who should be pushing this thing. So, to my greatest shock, I returned from one of my trips abroad and Obiechina came to me and said that Nzimiro had been locked up. The next day I went to see Ojukwu and when I mentioned it, he picked up the phone and called the inspector general of police and asked him what Nzimiro was still doing there, 'I want him released,' he said. And that was that.[3]

Throughout the time that Chinua talked about the National Guidance Committee, and the drafting of the Ahiara Declaration, he

---

[2] Chinua, same interview.
[3] Chinau Achebe, interview with Egejuru.

stressed the point that it was a group effort. However, some of the members of that committee provided a clearer picture of Chinua's role in that "interesting exercise", as he referred to it. Ikenna Nzimiro, Professor Emeritus, at the University of Port Harcourt, was the first to give a first hand account of the workings of the National Guidance Committee. At first, Nzimiro had no official status in the Directorate, probably because everyone knew him as a radical who took critical views of whatever was said. He attended their meetings any way, "they couldn't tell me to get out. That's how I met Chinua," he said. Nzimiro was politically more experienced than most of the members of the National Guidance Committee. Besides, he had a rich background in Labour Movements. Therefore, he would confidently point out to the Committee what he felt was wrong with some of their ideas. Nzimiro said:

> Even though I was left winged, Achebe supported me as a human being and he saved me twice from being killed. After that, I saw myself coming to their Tuesday meetings. One day I got angry and returned to Oguta. Achebe talked to them and asked them to bring me back. He asked them to listen to me, so they sent Ekwensi to come and get me back. I came back and joined in the struggle. I became a member of the National Guidance Committee. Three of us - Chinua, Obiechina and I stood as a block against the rest.

Within the Directorate, a socialist group was formed with Nzimiro as the secretary and Chinua made sure that this group was never disbanded because useful groups were disbanded at the whim of the leader, while useless ones were set up. Achebe encouraged Nzimiro and cautioned the Biafran leader against witch hunting. Nzimiro recalled:

> Each time Ojukwu asked Chinua to give me up he refused, because Chinua admires honest people. At one point Chinua ordered that a splinter group that was formed at the instigation of the leader be disbanded. This was the type of decision that left the Biafran leader helpless.[4]

Nzimiro said that even in such crises as distributing products manufactured by Biafrans like soap, petrol, kerosene, salt and so on, it was Achebe's paper on Social Justice that guided them. Chinua had said that the Ahiara Declaration was based on Social Justice, but he gave no indication that he had written the paper from which Ahiara Declaration was drawn. When the NGC told Ojukwu that Biafra was

---

[4] Prof. Ikenna Nzimiro, interview with Egejuru.

losing the war and that they should start asking questions, it was Chinua who asked the questions -is this a revolution? For whom is it? How do you go about it? And since Chinua was asking the questions, everybody listened.

Professor S. J. Cookey, former vice Chancellor of the University of Port Harcourt, was in the Biafran Cabinet before the creation of the National Guidance Committee. He shed more light on the objectives of the Committee and Achebe's role in it. He defined the Committee's objective as "providing an ideological basis for the existence of Biafra, crystalizing ideas that were not foreign to our people." Commenting on the choice of Achebe as the chairman of the Committee, Cookey said:

> I believe the reason for choosing him as the chair was his close contact with Igbo culture, and because of his credibility. Everyone knew he was not given to rashness. He had his feet firmly on the ground. He could be counted on to be practical rather than dramatic. As a person, he hasn't lost touch with reality; he does not have his head in the clouds. He generates interactions which people find constructive and useful.

Cookey explained in detail how opinions and ideas were thoroughly debated to arrive at a consensus or a crystallization of an idea. He regretted that the Ahiara Declaration was rushed to meet a target date. According to him:

> One cannot say that that was the best that could have been produced. Reading it today, one cannot fail to detect the attempt to have an underlying current of Africaness and Biafraness in that document. And that was a genuine contribution, in part attributable to Chinua.[5]

Obiechina, the secretary of the National Guidance Committee further corroborated what both Nzimiro and Cookey said about Achebe's crucial role as chairman of the NGC:

> You don't really know people until you meet them at close quarters and under situations of stress and emergency. These are situations that could bring the worst out of some people and the best in others. Working in the secretariat with Chinua during the civil war, was such a moment for me.

The above was Obiechina's preamble to his assessment of Achebe's role during the Biafran crisis. Like most people, Obiechina knew

---

[5] Professor Cookey, interview with Egejuru

Achebe through his works and had met him in person a few times before the war. However, he really didn't know Achebe the man, until fate threw them together to work as a team. Obiechina explained:

> What brought me very close to him was his commitment to the interest of the masses. Even in that state of emergency, there were reckless people who were hell driven to foster their own personal interest and comfort. But Chinua and a few others like him banded together and worked themselves to exhaustion trying to find answers to problems ranging from high diplomacy to how to grow vegetables for the starving masses. Chinua's integrity was the driving force behind the National Guidance Committee. Under Achebe's leadership and inspiration, the committee gave very good advice, even though its advice was not always taken.

The committee, according to Obiechina, gave thought to every conceivable human problem that confronted a beleaguered people, and Chinua was always at the helm in all situations. He always brought forth the most pragmatic ideas, things that would really save lives. Those working with him would often ask one another, "How did he just resolve this issue? Where did he get this inspiration from?" Sometimes his ideas would appear common but when you look at them closely, you would notice that they had been distilled from a lot of deep thinking; he's mulled over the problem.

One of Chinua's qualities that impressed and sometimes shocked people was his ability to remain cool and unflustered even in the most stressful of conditions. Not known for broad gestures or histrionics, his calm disposition served him extremely well during his leadership of the NGC. Obiechina also praised Achebe for his role in literally saving the lives of people who had some rough edge of officialdom. Chinua was able to stay the hands of executioners because of his powerful voice of moral authority. Obiechina commented:

> When you have cultivated that ability to speak the truth all the time and to stick to what is humane and morally sound, people come to trust you. People in Biafra trusted Achebe and the NGC he directed turned out to be the conscience of the Biafran movement, to be the body whose ideas were taken seriously by the Biafran people. The people believed because Achebe would not lie or deceive and so the committee he chaired was trusted.[6]

In addition to chairing the NGC, Chinua was also much involved in the Directorate of Culture. This was something that emerged from

---

[6] Prof. E. Obiechina, interview with Egejuru.

Ojukwu's notion of letting the international community know that Biafra had something of cultural value to offer. There was a Biafran theatre, there was a culture council that met to discuss literature and celebrate life. According to T.C. Nwosu, "Achebe was instrumental to the founding of the Manuscript committee, the quintessence of what was happening in Biafra." Among members were Achebe, Ekwensi, Glory Nwonodi, Gabriel Okara, Onuora Nzekwu and Nwosu. With the war raging, this committee was busy trying to set up a publishing system to bring out the best that was intellectually being produced in Biafra. The whole idea was to harness the creative energy and to give the people the feeling of being alive and carrying on normal creative activities. Nwosu said:

> That was how we survived for three years. Achebe perhaps may not know the extent to which he contributed. He's a man who would set something going and then withdraw. He's not the one who would take credit for his initiatives.[7]

Many other people who worked at close quarters with Achebe made the same remark -about his reluctance to accept credit for his initiatives and contributions. Nwosu was right, for each time it was suggested to Chinua that he was the brain behind some venture he would protest and say, "No, not really" and he would give a lengthy history of the venture to prove that it was not one person's idea.

---

[7] Dr. T.C. Nwosu, interview with Egejuru.

6

Picking up the pieces: University of Nigeria Nsukka

Nsukka was the first strategic town in Biafra captured by the Nigerian soldiers. Because of that, it suffered more devastation than most places. Those who witnessed the destruction used words like dilapidation, shambles, desolate and forlorn to describe the campus of the University of Nigeria Nsukka. As one campus resident put it, "The very physical environment was enough to discourage positive action, the campus was a centre of demoralization."

Chinua was among those who helped to put the University back together. He at once saw the state of Nsukka campus as a challenge, a situation requiring leadership intervention. He saw the urgent need to give people back their initiative and optimism, so they can recover their voice.

Like other Igbo intellectuals, Chinua recognized that Nsukka University was the intellectual centre of the Igbo and that it held the key to reinvigorating the spirit of the people. It was from that centre that they would get back the confidence they needed to deal with the enormous problems of post war period. It was Obiechina who told the story of how Chinua went about the business of reconstruction that had to be done at various levels of the University:

> Chinua called a meeting to restore morale to the environment. Under his chairmanship we decided on a strategy. We were to become the voice and conscience of the community at Nsukka. We were to become the group to ginger up action, because people were afraid to do or say anything critical about things going on, or try to straighten things out.[1]

The first positive and concrete action was starting *Nsukkascope*, a kind of house journal, published on a quarterly basis. Chinua was the chief editor and Obiechina the associate editor. The objective was to "knock people hard" with the intention of helping them recover their

---
[1] E. Obiechina, interview with Egejuru.

initiative. The editors saw the need to empower the people. They had to reassure the people that though they lost the war, they were not disgraced. They were very provocative in the way they presented issues. They soon constituted a pressure point on the government of East Central State. Before they knew it, reprisal came very swiftly from the government. They sent a contingent of mobile police force to Nsukka to arrest the "creators" of *Nsukkascope*. They took away and detained the circulation manager - Ikenna Nzimiro, his assistant Okechukwu Emodi and some members of the board like, Inyang Ete and Mrs. Efiong. They did not dare go to Chinua or his associate editor Obiechina, but these two went to the police to protest. There ensued a real show of force. The police tried intimidation but that couldn't work on the editors, "Certainly they could not intimidate Chinua," said Obiechina. When the police saw that detention didn't stop the publication, they tried to seize the journal, but they only succeeded in forcing it to go underground. With the help of students and staff, the editors continued production and distribution. Indeed, forcing the journal underground seemed to work in its favour. Now the circulation became nation-wide. It reached places like Lagos and the North. Igbo people in other parts of the country read it and drew strength from it. It was also at this time that Mamman Vatsa, the soldier poet from the North, read the journal and became aware of what was happening in that part of his country. He also became aware of the caliber of men who edited the journal and those who contributed articles. That exposure would eventually bring Vatsa into the community of Nigerian writers. He would become close to Achebe, Soyinka, J. P. Clark, T. C. Nwosu and others. After a while, there was nothing else the government could do than to let *Nsukkascope* be.

The most prominent target of the journal was the University administration itself, particularly the Vice Chancellor, Kodilinye, an anglicized Igbo man, who unashamedly renounced and denounced all things Igbo. Kodilinye was literally imposed on the faculty and staff of Nsukka University by the Nigerian government. As Nzimiro put it, "They brought Kodilinye to come and humiliate us. He wanted to change Nsukka to Oxford and Cambridge, to set up Colleges. *Nsukkascope* published Kodilinye's stupidity."[2] While his faculty, staff and students were wallowing in misery, squatting in makeshift shelters, the vice Chancellor enjoyed the comforts of carpeted and air-conditioned rooms in his house and office. He was more interested in importing expatriate employees rather than absorbing the teaming competent Igbo intellectuals. It was this type of insensitivity and other blatant abuses by the vice Chancellor that *Nsukkascope* exposed.

---

[2] Interview with Nzimiro

Because of the relentless attacks on Kodilinye, the editors of the journal became his arch enemies.

Despite the hardship and the frustration of working under a hostile and insensitive vice Chancellor, Achebe continued in his goal of rehabilitating the community at Nsukka morally, spiritually, intellectually and artistically. Thus, while *Nsukkascope* was busy hitting people hard to straighten them out, Achebe launched *Okike* (Creativity), a new magazine to give vent to the pent up creative energy of the war survivors. Discussing some of the enduring things he founded, Achebe said of *Okike*:

> At the end of the war, I felt we needed a magazine. Because, all around me were people who had this strange experience of the war, writing about it, talking about it, new poets, new novelists, new ideas. Why don't we have a magazine for them? and that's how *Okike* came to be.[3]

After listening to the testimony of those who worked with Chinua during the war, one is then able to understand the extent of his dedication to the physical and mental well-being of his fellow human beings. It is then that one realizes that Chinua had mulled over the idea of starting a magazine even before the war ended. Therefore, the genesis of *Okike* went back to the time when he formed the manuscript committee of the Biafran Cultural Council. From that time on, Chinua had been carrying in his head this idea of Creativity, as a counter to destruction. Obviously, what delayed his starting it earlier was lack of finance. Then came the incredible and unexpected financial intervention from his former teacher and friend, Ulli Beier.

Responding to inquiries regarding his relationship with Chinua, Beier told the touching story of how he raised money to help some of his friends who had become destitute after the Biafran war:

> We had no savings, but we had stored in London, a collection of Nigerian paintings that we thought we would never want to part with. Under the circumstances it seemed absurd, even immoral to hang on to them. We sold the entire collection to a wealthy art collector in London called Ella Winter. He gave us three thousand pounds for it. We divided the sum up and sent some amount to all the friends we could reach, to help them over the first difficult days. We had heard from various sources that Chinua was very depressed and so we sent him a few hundred pounds, suggesting he use some of it to start a literary magazine.[4]

---

[3] Chinua, interview with Egejuru.
[4] Ulli Beier, correspondence with Egejuru, on his relationship with Chinua.

Soon after the war, Beier visited Nsukka. During a reception in Beier's honor, Chinua told his colleagues the role Beier played in the history of *Okike*. Obiora Udechukwu, recalled the reception in these words:

> Chinua doesn't hesitate to tell you how things started. For example, we had a reception for Ulli Beier and Chinua told us how Ulli sent him three hundred pounds at the end of the war to start something out of the ashes of the war. He doesn't hesitate to tell you the contributions of others towards a valuable venture. There are some who would claim all the credit.[5]

If those who worked with him at Nsukka hadn't talked of the crucial role Achebe played in literally giving people back their lives, one would not have known that part of his history. The only thing he said in connection with Nsukka was:

> When the war ended, I went to Nsukka for two years and when it was clear to me that nothing in particular was happening, I then said I was leaving. I was tired of this and that, so I came to America, still as a Senior Research Fellow. So, it was in the USA that I actually began my first teaching as opposed to research.[6]

University of Massachusetts at Amherst

In 1972, Achebe joined the faculty of the English Department of the University of Massachusetts at Amherst. He held the post of Visiting Professor. His going there came as a result of meeting Harvey Swados in Biafra. Professor Swados was a faculty member at Amherst. He was among a delegation of writers from the United States who had gone to Nigeria to write about the war. He had obviously discussed the possibility of teaching at Amherst with Achebe. Getting back home, Swados made the suggestion to his colleagues in the English Department and they supported him. Consequently, they persuaded the University to bring Achebe for a couple of years.

Achebe's presence at Amherst soon drew the attention of journalists and scholars who came in droves for interviews. With that type of attention, the people at Amherst realized that he had another profession and political life going on; they were not just giving him a place of refuge. From then on, they made a real effort not to demand that he be

---

[5] Obiora Udechukwu, interview with Egejuru.
[6] Chinua, interview with Egejuru.

involved in the pedestrian mundane life of the University. When he was on campus however, he attended faculty meetings.

Perhaps, if his now famous lecture on Conrad's *Heart of Darkness* had not been published, people outside Amherst would never have known the impact of Achebe's brief stay in that University. Indeed, that lecture would overshadow everything else including two years of invaluable teaching and the distinction his presence bestowed on the campus. In the words of Professor Michael Thelwell, a faculty member, "That lecture became the single most important thing he did there that has a lasting historical resonance, to be for ever associated with Amherst." It was Dr. Thelwell and Dr. Catherine Innes who revealed some of the unpleasantness Achebe had to put up with at Amherst, especially after the controversial lecture that dealt a crushing blow on antiquated experts of *Heart of Darkness*. Achebe had no idea that the University of Massachusetts was provincial. The result was that he felt like an exile. In addition to receiving much less compensation than his reputation and stature should have commanded, Achebe received little respect from professors and students in the English Department. They were overtly hostile in their attitudes towards all things African. The narrow minded scholars and their students in turn had no idea that the man in their midst had a reputation for putting all petty minded people to shame and in their place. Commenting on Achebe's wonderful teaching and his incredible self-control, Dr. Innes said:

> One of the things that struck me was the way he handled the often-unthinkable racism of students and fellow colleagues, although he could be very strong in his comments on racism. In his classes that I attended, the students asked quite appalling questions about cannibalism; they read the books as if they were anthropology rather than literature. And Achebe was always incredibly patient. He took time to explain things to students without making them feel foolish. Some of the colleagues would often say things which were unthinkable. For instance, at a dinner party, the host who was seemingly friendly with Achebe and his wife, blurted out what he thought was a good joke; he was going to have African native girls for all the lecturers. Achebe just looked across at his wife and raised his brows. There were several other insults which lesser humans would not have tolerated, but Achebe is so secure in his own self worth that what unhinges ordinary mortals leaves him unruffled.[7]

With the black community at Amherst, the situation was different. According to Thelwell, African Americans thought of him as an elder

---

[7] Prof. C. L. Innes, interview with Egejuru.

brother. They respected him, they didn't presume. He was very cooperative in whatever was asked of him. Said Thelwell, "Whenever we had a function in Africa house he would be there. Even though he had been brought by the English Department, he made it clear he wanted to be a part of the black community." This "bonding" with the black community at Amherst showed the depth of his commitment to the black race. For, the type of behaviour African American students at Amherst exhibited when Achebe met them in 1968, would have been enough for any normal person to avoid having anything to do with them a second time. At that time, Achebe was touring some parts of the U.S. He graciously accepted an invitation from Thelwell to attend a social event to which African American graduate students were invited. Thelwell made the mistake of not introducing Achebe who was already seated before the students walked in. The students got into a political argument. They started hollering at each other and totally ignored Achebe. He had to leave without addressing them. Describing Achebe as a man who carries himself with consummate grace, Thelwell recalled this incident with deep regret, saying, "He thought he was coming to address the black community but the students misbehaved and he withdrew graciously. It was partly my fault that I didn't introduce him first."

With all the effort needed to work in a hostile environment, Achebe was still able to summon enough composure to edit *Okike* magazine right there at Amherst. Understandably, he could not handle all the editing alone. Therefore, he invited Dr. Innes to work with him as an associate editor. Innes was only too happy to accept, after all, "He was largely responsible for my getting the job at UMASS," she said. Innes worked on the magazine for two years. She commented on Achebe's treatment of those who worked with him:

> I was always struck with the kind of courtesy he had towards the workers-male and female. He always treated people with great consideration and respect. That was something not always true of either American or African men that I had met. He always listened to other people's views. He was very much aware whether people were being overworked or underworked.[8]

The lukewarm reception at Amherst was reinforced by the fact that the University made no effort to keep Achebe when the more sophisticated University of Connecticut made him an offer to join them in 1975. Their offer of a big house and twice the salary at Amherst was "the kind of offer that should have been made to him in the first place,"

---

[8] C. L. Innes, same interview.

said Thelwell. Achebe told the authorities at Amherst of the offer from Connecticut; he had hoped they would match it, they did not. In 1975, Achebe joined the faculty of the University of Connecticut at Storrs. In July of the same year, a military coup toppled the regime of Yakubu Gowon in Nigeria, and ushered in the popular but ephemeral rule of Murtala Mohammed. With the assassination of Mohammed, Obasanjo came to power. Then, there followed a massive purging of the country of abusive government officials. Kodilinye was removed from Nsukka and James Ezilo, became the vice Chancellor. With the changes in the country, lecturers at Nsukka became bold and wanted to know why their valued colleagues were not in the country to continue the work of restoring the University. Achebe was flooded with letters in which some people at home were asking "why is he not here, why is he in America?" Although Achebe had just joined the faculty at Storrs, the political development in Nigeria would force him to cut short his stay at Storrs. More pressure was put on him when his friend Ezilo started writing and making him offers. Consequently, he decided to spend just one academic year at Storrs.

Return to Nsukka

In his off-handed manner, Achebe summarized his return to Nsukka:

> I finally returned and joined the English Department at Nsukka. This time around, the work at Nsukka was more interesting. We had an interest in getting the place going. My friends were running the place. But again, there was the movement thing for me. I never planned to be in any particular place forever. There was always the possibility of something else.[9]

Achebe did not elaborate on his teaching or administrative duties at Nsukka. His colleagues and students would fill in the gaps. One of Achebe's students at Nsukka was Ada Udechukwu. She gave an insightful evaluation of Achebe as a teacher:

> From the first day, he established a kind of atmosphere that made the students want to excel and do their very best. He demanded from his students, a certain seriousness to work. He expected us to go and look for things for ourselves. It was no longer a question of taking notes, there were no notes. He didn't even speak in a way to allow you take notes. We started with short stories to novels. There was no longer a noticeable structured teacher/student demarcation.

---

[9] Chinua, interview with Egejuru.

We were there to discuss and everybody's opinion was followed. He expected a certain quality of work, but expected it in a different way than most of the students were interested in doing. He was a hard grader; there were three A/Bs the rest were Bs and Cs. To get an A from him was quite an achievement.

On a more personal note, Ada spoke of Achebe's influence on her. It was Achebe's course that exposed her to the greater body of African literature, critical essays and other writings. Ada said:

> The impact of his mind and his approach to things were things that I treasure. The example of his person, someone with integrity, security, that's what I came away with. Only a handful of teachers made such an impact on me that after ten years I can't forget what I was taught. It has certainly helped in molding me to the person I am and my own approach to literature. I see him as a kindred spirit because these things are important to me.[10]

While carrying full teaching loads, travelling within and outside the country to give lectures, Achebe still devoted a great deal of attention to *Okike* magazine. He was specifically grooming future editors. As Obiora Udechukwu put it:

> Chinua is one who recognizes that you cannot do something alone. He also recognizes that young people will grow up and take over. He gives you responsibility and the opportunity to prove yourself. He fans out work to people. With him, everybody contributes.[11]

Among those he groomed to be future editors of *Okike* were Obiora Udechukwu and Osmond Enekwe. Udechukwu recalled the casual handing over of the magazine to him and Enekwe in 1986. Chinua simply called them and said to them:

> I have been editing *Okike* since 1971; I have done enough. You should now take over the editorship. Work out the modalities and tell me what you want to do with the magazine.[12]

Always mindful of others' needs and because of the exigent nature of the situation, Achebe agreed to be the Chair of the English Department for the 1979-80 academic year. This arrangement made it possible for his colleagues, Professors Obiechina and Nwoga, to pursue some much needed scholarly activities in the United States. Within the

---

[10] Ada Udechukwu, interview with Egejuru.
[11] Obiora Udechukwu, interview with Egejuru.
[12] Chinua, as recollected by Udechukwu, in the same interview with Ejeguru.

short period of his chairmanship, he perceived more keenly the deteriorating standard of education at the University level. He wanted specifically to do something about the substandard English written and spoken by students majoring in English. As a result of his concern over deplorable standards, other lecturers started getting more serious with their own lectures and grading standards. According to Ada Udechukwu, "He tried to create in us an awareness of studies at the University level. I know it disturbed a lot of people. For me, it was like a breakthrough." Ada told the story of a female student who never cared to study but expected to pass her courses any way. That student failed Achebe's course. Then she went back and studied the assigned texts. When she took the exam again she passed. She and others like her were forced to recognize that one could still find some lecturers in Nigeria who enforce quality education and would not compromise their integrity to please anybody. For Achebe, every incident is an opportunity to teach some lesson, directly or indirectly.

In addition to running *Okike*, teaching and administering the English Department, Achebe also served various functions at the University. He was the chairman of the Ceremonials Committee, a very demanding position that entailed organizing Convocation ceremonies as well as composing and reading citations on recipients of honorary degrees. Because of the respect he commanded at all levels, he was constantly called upon to mediate or settle disputes between faculty members and the administration.

With the incredible heavy schedule he was carrying at this time, he still found the energy and time to attend and make speeches at international conferences. In March 1980, he attended the Writers' Week in Adelaide Australia. He gave a lecture on some aspects of African literature -myth, symbol and fable. He also read from his poems. The reading provided an avenue for a brief comment on clash of cultures. It also led to references to African and Australian colonial experiences.

Hardly getting any break from the Australian trip, Achebe went off again to attend the African Literature Association conference in Gainesville Florida, USA in April 1980. It was there that the historic meeting with James Baldwin took place. Anyone who was there, would never forget the euphoric feeling of the conferees as the two literary giants started their Dialogue. In his opening remark, Baldwin made the memorable comment that history never intended that Africans on both sides of the Atlantic should meet. However, Africans have defied the odds and obstacles of history, and Baldwin and Achebe finally met after four hundred years. The deafening applause that followed Baldwin's moving remark, was cut short by a mysterious voice that intercepted Baldwin's speech through the microphone. It was an electrifying and embarrassing moment that threw the memory back to the savagery of the Ku Klux Klan of the Jim Crow America. "I am coming up there Mr. Baldwin...we can't stand all this kind of stuff going on," said the intruder. Fortunately, the powerful moral voice of the two giants silenced the intruders. Baldwin boldly told them that he was going to finish his speech, "And if you assassinate me in the next two minutes, it no longer matters what you think." Baldwin further rubbed it in by telling them that the doctrine of white supremacy had run its course. It was Achebe who said the last words to the intruders, to the effect that Americans should be ashamed because they do not know how to laugh at themselves.[13]

Needless to say, the kinship felt by the two writers blossomed into friendship. To commemorate this friendship after Baldwin's death, Achebe was given Baldwin's briefcase by the latter's family. When he was asked to comment on the gesture by Baldwin's family Achebe said:

> The meeting was something that should have happened long before but it didn't. Neither of us was in control of our lives, so our paths did not cross. But if you look at how it did, through the instrumentality of a Sri Lankan professor who had invited Baldwin to the conference, and as things turned out, other people thought we should continue the dialogue. And the University of Massachusetts was going to do that. Anyway, from then on, we got on very well and it seemed we had known each other for a long time. He had this prophetic saying which seemed really biblical. It was when he first read *Things Fall Apart* in Paris. He said that he immersed himself in the story of these people whom he knew nothing about and whose culture he had no knowledge of, but he recognized every one in it.[14]

In 1981, Achebe made one of his most valuable contributions to Nigerian literature. In the middle of that year he organized a convention of Nigerian Authors. From that convention the Association of Nigerian Authors was born. However, he was quick to limit the credit due to him as the originator of the Association. He explained:

> There was something they had in Lagos before the war- Society of Nigerian Authors- they used to meet every Friday. But at the end of the war, some of the writers were not even on speaking terms. It all depended how one felt or how one fared during that crisis, on

---

[13] Words of James Baldwin and Chinua, as recollected by Egejuru who was in the audience.
[14] Chinua, interview with Egejuru.

whose side you were, and so on. There was this terrible division which we had not known before and it seemed to me we had to heal the rift, bring the writers together if they were going to survive.[15]

At their first meeting at Nsukka, Achebe, in his address, expressed the fears he had for the writers' survival in Nigeria. He had a premonition that there was something very dangerous looming for writers. Incidentally, he wasn't the only writer who felt this danger. He recalled that Saro Wiwa had mentioned it in his book. And being very much aware of what happens to writers in many parts of Africa, Achebe felt that writers must have one front, so that they could give mutual protection to one another. At the close of the convention, the Association of Nigerian Authors was officially inaugurated and Achebe was elected the President.

Although he was willing to serve his country and the world, Achebe longed to give more time to his writing and to his editorship of *Okike*. This desire coupled with his practice of never staying in one job for too long, he decided to take an early retirement from the University. He communicated his wish to the University soon after launching the Association of Nigerian Authors. At the end of 1981, he effectively retired. He still lived on campus because his wife was a faculty member in the Department of Education.

---

[15] Chinua, same interview.

7
Retirement years: 1981-1990

Retirement did very little to afford Chinua the extra time he needed to devote to his writing and to *Okike* magazine. He travelled extensively outside the country. He went to give lectures at conferences or make speeches at graduation ceremonies or to receive honorary degrees and other distinguishing awards.

He equally focused attention on Nigeria's social and political problems. He did not only speak and write about them, he actually joined a political party. In the end, the retirement translated into ending his official employment with the University of Nigeria Nsukka. For, soon after that, he accepted short-term appointments, ranging from two months to one academic year, in Universities in Canada and the United States.

In 1982, the tenth anniversary of *Okike* magazine was celebrated. It was an occasion to let the literary public learn of the various accomplishments of the magazine. It was at that occasion that Achebe told the story of *Okike* - its conception as a valve to let off the creative steam that built up during the Biafran war. He also told the story of its coming into being, made possible by the generous donation from Ulli Beier. Other contributions came from the Ford Foundation, and from Nigerian donors like the then vice President of Nigeria, Alex Ekwueme, and Arthur Nwankwo, the proprietor of Fourth Dimension Publishing Company. In addition to serving creative artists, *Okike* started an educational supplement to handle production of instructional materials. As if that weren't enough, the committee launched another journal, *Uwa Ndi Igbo*, charged with collecting and transcribing works of non-literate Igbo minstrels. Ten years after a slow start, *Okike* accomplished more than its creator had anticipated. This was possible because Achebe was fully in charge, and as Obiora Udechukwu observed, "Achebe recognizes that when you are an artist, many people come to contribute to what you are doing." Thus, his effective leadership and cooperation from his colleagues made *Okike* flourish in Nigeria where most projects never celebrate a first anniversary!

With *Okike* firmly established, Achebe felt the need to direct his attention to national issues. 1982 was a crucial year for politicians because there was going to be an election in 1983 to choose a new government. There followed a mushrooming of political Parties, out of which emerged five Parties. Achebe started studying various manifestoes with some interest. In the end, he seemed to have found a kindred spirit in Aminu Kano, the leader of People's Redemption Party. Both men felt a strong commitment to the fate of the common man. In addition, they shared a similar vision of an egalitarian society directed by enlightened and morally upright leaders. At the invitation of Aminu Kano, Achebe made the unexpected political move of joining the People's Redemption Party in 1982. His decision stunned those who did not understand the depth of his commitment to the socio-political well-being of all Nigerians. It also surprised those who did not know the extent to which Chinua had won the respect of many Nigerians. His brother Augustine who understood why he would make such a drastic move said:

> He is not a politician by nature, but when he believes in something, then there must be something there. You see how Aminu Kano came all the way to solicit him to join his Party. Chinua joined that Party because he thought they could redeem the country or rebuild it for the better. But things didn't go as he anticipated, so he left the Party.[1]

On the other hand, when his friend, Ben Uzochukwu was asked if Chinua had ever done anything out of character he said:

> Chinua joining a political Party was something out of character. He is a man of conviction; nothing would push him into politics. So, when he joined the PRP, I said, 'Chinua it's unlike you.' So, something must have pushed him into it.[2]

Another friend who found Achebe's political move unusual was Arthur Nwankwo. He could not understand why "a Professor of literature with a secure tenured job came to my office one day and told me that he has decided to join the PRP after studying the manifestoes of all the political parties."

For those who knew the seriousness of Achebe's efforts to better the lot of the common man, his political move was just the type of response he would give to the political situation of Nigeria of the early

---
[1] Augustine Achebe, interview with Egejuru.
[2] Ben Uzochukwu, interview with Egejuru.

1980s. The excesses of Shagari's government far exceeded those of Nanga's government in *A Man of the People*. Something desperate needed to be done to prevent a total collapse of the political machine. It was this need to "save" the people that pushed Achebe to join the PRP. It was simply an act of protest.

Obiechina who was also a member of the PRP explained the rationale for their joining the party:

> We did not join PRP because we were hungry for power. It was a counter weight to the people in power, to articulate the interest of the masses, to show what could be done. The PRP was not a Party of power. It was a Party of conscience, of empowerment of the masses at the grassroots. There was Aminu Kano who had no money but moral authority. His manifesto was empowerment of the masses. His position was that which all those who loved the people identified with. We just wanted to show that we identified with this movement. Chinua did not expect to win election and become president.[3]

Still commenting on the intentions of the People's Redemption Party, Bola Ige humorously said:

> PRP was a Party of protest. Aminu Kano, even if he were the Prime Minister, he would still carry a placard against his own government. Both Wole and Chinua joined the party to make a point. They would like the Nigerian government to understand that the country has a number of people who know how things are done, and would want to see things done the right way. They would also let it be known that Nigeria can afford a few mad people, because you need to be a little mad to live in Nigeria.[4]

That Achebe and Soyinka should identify with a political Party that expressed a genuine interest in the ordinary citizens, was the most reasonable response from two intellectual giants who have done much to promote the welfare of their fellow citizens. Discussing his motives for joining the PRP, Soyinka said: "I wish that more of us would go there and be politicians. I joined Michael Imoudu's wing of the PRP to give them the needed boosting and strength."[5] However, Soyinka wondered what Chinua was doing in Aminu Kano's Party. Eventually, he found out why Chinua joined Aminu's Party. It happened when he heard Chinua in an interview explaining his reason. It all started at a

---

[3] E. Obiechina, interview with Egejuru.
[4] Bola Ige, interview with Egejuru.
[5] Wole Soyinka, interview with Egejuru

conference in Addis Ababa when Chinua listened to Aminu speak about his role in stopping the Nigerian government from using weapons of mass destruction against Biafra. Aminu seemed deeply concerned about the plight of Biafran children. From Aminu's speech and demeanour, Chinua remarked that he was a compassionate person. Furthermore, Aminu was well respected for his overt espousal of equality for all in the country. He was known to champion the cause of justice for the common man. Therefore, Aminu's rooting for the masses was bound to attract Chinua who shared similar sentiments.

Whatever private motives existed for the individual members of the PRP, their remarkable gesture brought a ray of hope to Nigerian politics. For the first time in Nigeria's political history, intellectuals like Achebe, Soyinka, Obiechina, Akpan, Ikoku and others ventured into politics with the best of intentions to effect positive changes in Nigerian politics. Unfortunately for them, their dream of showing their compatriots that clean politics was possible in Nigeria did not come true. Their dream seemed to have symbolically died with Aminu Kano in April 1983.

With Aminu's death, his wing of the PRP faced a crisis of restructuring. Achebe, whom Aminu had appointed his deputy, was now offered the leadership of the party. He could not be persuaded to accept. Instead, he agreed to become the national deputy vice President, while Hassan Yusuf became the national President. However, Yusuf was too weak to handle the unruly northern members who now viewed the PRP as their private tribal Party. Without Aminu, the PRP was embroiled in personality conflicts. This was made worse by a resurfacing of Igbophobia among some northern members. After a meeting during which the altercation got very ugly and almost out of hand, Achebe left the PRP for good. His political idealism was just too fragile for the deep-rooted tribal divisiveness and power hungry profligates.

The fact that Achebe could not stick it out with the PRP should not lead one to conclude that, "He does not know the intrigues and banalities of politics," as one of his friends claimed. Achebe and his fellow intellectuals can certainly play the game of politics in a decent society but not in a jungle that goes by the name of Nigeria.

Whatever grounds Achebe lost in his efforts to send a strong message to his compatriots through his participation in politics, he regained with the publication of *The Trouble with Nigeria* in 1983. Here, Achebe turned the eyes of Nigerians inward for self-examination. And in his unmatched ability to crack jokes with the most serious and painful of issues, Achebe cast the problems of Nigeria in a hilarious mode. Instead of fuming at those who remorselessly and continuously abused the country, the reader ends up enjoying the sarcastic humour directed at the villains. In this tiny booklet, Achebe shows that he is not afraid of anyone. What is more, he can subtly insult you to your face with his jokes. It was no longer the question of allusions and subtle nuances, he charged head on at the powers that be of Nigerian politics. He indicted the sitting President and the fathers of Nigerian politics. He made it clear that their failure in leadership was the root cause of the country's socio-political malaise. He did not spare the people either. He accused them not only of conniving with, but also admiring their tormentors. The book also offered him the opportunity to lionize Aminu Kano whose vision for Nigeria, though unrealized, still made Nigerians aware of alternatives to corruption, injustice and dehumanization of citizens by their leaders.

1985 was a very important year for Achebe. For one thing, he started working again on his manuscript of *Anthills of the Savanna*. In the same year, Nsukka appointed him Professor Emeritus. This would entitle him to all the privileges of a full professor without the accompanying obligations of teaching and research, though he could do either at his own choosing. From his secretary, Esther Ogadi one learned how Achebe underutilized his privileges as Professor Emeritus. Esther noted:

> Chinua is not for 'this is my right or this is my left'. As Professor Emeritus, he is entitled to two secretaries or two typists. Yet, when he had excess typing to be done, he hired an extra hand and paid the cost. I reminded him of his right to two typists but he reminded me that the University knew what his rights were and should give him those rights without his fighting for them.[6]

Another notable happening in 1985 was the annual convention of Association of Nigerian Authors. It was hosted by Major General Mamman Vatsa, in Abuja. Vatsa belonged to the class of new writers that ANA gave support and encouragement. According to Arthur Nwankwo, "When Achebe saw the late Mamman Vatsa's manuscript, he said he should be encouraged." It was this advice coming from the President of ANA that made T.C. Nwosu decide to publish Vatsa's poems. Nwosu described the meeting at Abuja as "A telling point in ANA's history. We had a most successful convention in Abuja, made possible by Vatsa; over three hundred people attended." This was a major victory for the Association and its founder because at that time there was a prevailing feeling that the military was anti-intellectual. It was believed that soldiers could and should not aspire to intellectual

---

[6] Esther Ogadi, interview with Egejuru.

attainment. On the literary scene therefore, Achebe united Nigerian authors through his launching of the Association of Nigerian Authors.

A few days after this historic convention in December 1985, a situation that tested ANA's ability to offer protection to its members occurred. Vatsa was allegedly involved in a coup plot to overthrow the government of President Babangida. Vatsa and nine others were arrested. Understandably, members of ANA were anxious for Vatsa's safety. The Association pleaded desperately with the government asking for a fair trial for the accused. The plea fell on deaf ears because the trial was held in secret and the accused men were condemned to death. Because of the situation, J.P. Clark travelled to Abeokuta to talk to Soyinka. They both consulted Chinua and the three of them made a last ditch effort to get Vatsa released. They went as a team to see Babangida and plead for Vatsa's release. After waiting for nearly a whole day, they met with Babangida who promised to do everything he could to get Vatsa released. Soyinka reminisced on that day:

> We had lunch to celebrate; we had a marvelous time for Clark and I had not talked for years. It was like a reunion, we recaptured old times. A new relationship started and we spent hours together. Chinua was *en pleine forme*. We agreed to meet again and make plans for the future, to have regular meetings.[7]

Alas! The following day, March 5, 1986 it was announced that Vatsa and those accused with him had been executed. So much for a President giving his words to three world famous writers from his country.

Achebe stepped down as the President of ANA in 1986. He had announced at the Abuja convention that he would not seek re-election at the end of his five-year term. By the end of the year he also handed *Okike* magazine over to Osmond Enekwe and Obiora Udechukwu. Even as he gracefully relinquished these positions, offers for new positions and speaking engagements were pouring in from within his country and from overseas.

He accepted the position of pro-Chancellor of Anambra State University of Technology. Soon after becoming the pro-Chancellor of ASUTECH, Achebe received a most prestigious, non-academic appointment ever. He became the President General of Ogidi Town Union. What is very unique in his assumption of this office is that he did not contest for it. Other people would spend millions of naira vying for that position. In Achebe's case, his transparent honesty and integrity compelled his townsmen to recognize the prophet in their midst.

---

[7] Wole Soyinka, same interview.

Several Ogidi people repeated the story of how the famous Ndichie, the ruling council and king makers of Ogidi literally begged Chinua to assume the position and help save Ogidi. His friend from elementary school days, Dr. Agulefo remarked that Chinua was already a national and international figure before he was invited by Ogidi Town Union to become its President. The Union saw the danger of disharmony and disintegration facing the town. Ndichie invited him to the palace of Igwe Amobi VI where they made the offer to him. At that meeting, Achebe in his humorous way told them that he did not possess a red cap, implying that he had no *ozo* title and that he was not initiated into any masquerade cult. They reassured him that titular trappings were not necessary. The town was in desperate need of his service. As the provost of Ogidi Town Union phrased it: "Ogidi needed a man of truth and honour, a man who does not look at people's position or wealth to pronounce the truth as he sees it."

The same provost gave a detailed account of what happened when Chinua assumed the presidency. According to him, many people had lost interest in attending meetings. He recalled that during the presidency of one particular fellow, people were physically dragged into cars and brought to the meeting. People were kidnapped to the meeting. But in Chinua's time, there was no such thing. People came on their own and the hall was always full. During his address, Achebe explained to them that forcing people to attend meetings was counter-productive. It was better to have fewer committed people. When there was anything to be debated, everybody was given the chance to speak. In the end, the President would tell them what he felt should be done. Most of the time his suggestion was accepted without opposition.

The new President was soon faced with machinations of self-serving individuals who stood to lose from changes and projects meant to benefit the whole of Ogidi. Chief Ben Ogbogu gave an example of one proposed project that was squashed by a handful of people obsessed with local politics. Chinua had explained to Ogidi people that they needed a modern market. He had even solicited funds from a Foundation in the United States for the project. A lawyer went to court to get an injunction restraining Achebe's administration from building the market. "There lies the trouble of Ogidi, people living in the past while Achebe lives in the future, concerned with progress and development of Ogidi,"[8] commented Ogbogu. Regretting his uncle's non-confrontational attitude, Tochukwu said, "If he were a trouble maker, with his powers he could subdue his opponents and do what he wanted to do. But he listened to the people's views." In addition to the market, he also planned for a big library at Ogidi. Achebe's next door neighbor, an octogenarian made observations

---

[8] Chief Ben Ogbogu, interview with Egejuru

about his young neighbor's commitment to the welfare of Ogidi people: "What I know him for is *idozi obodo*, working to make the town good. He wants peace and justice in the land. He laid out plans for Ogidi which is still hanging."[9] The old man prayed that God should bring Chinua home so that he could bring down the plans still hanging. The added responsibilities of Ogidi Town Union would have provided a good excuse to cut down on other engagements. Instead, Chinua delegated most of the administrative duties of Ogidi Union to his vice President. This allowed him to face other engagements in his state, the country and in the international community.

The most important happening of 1987 for Chinua was the publication of *Anthills of the Savannah*, a novel that had been in the making for about twenty years! In this novel, Achebe laid out in a parabolic mode, the confusing and irresponsible military governments of present day Africa. Another important event was the death of Awolowo, one of the fathers of Nigerian politics. Chinua soon got himself entangled in the politics surrounding a proposed national funeral for Awolowo. Never afraid to confront the political powers that be, Achebe spoke out as the only dissenting voice in the proposal for a national funeral for Awolowo. Naturally, a few people knew that Achebe's reasons for opposing the proposal were well founded. Yet none had his guts to stand up and state their discontent. People were stunned but impressed with Achebe's stand on the "Awolowo debate." Several of those interviewed made reference to it as an example of Chinua's show of courage. Michael Olumide said, "When Awo died, Achebe was the only one who had the courage to remind us that we might be over idealizing Awo. He made us stop and think. One didn't see him as representing Igbo views alone."[10]

Achebe returned to Amherst for the 1987/88 academic year. This time his visit was arranged by the Institute of Advanced Studies in the Humanities and the Department of Afro-American Studies. James Baldwin was among the writers expected to be at Amherst for the same program. More importantly for Achebe and Baldwin, they were to resume the dialogue they started at Gainesville Florida in 1980. Unfortunately, the long anticipated reunion never took place.

Baldwin died in Paris in November 1987. A memorial service was held in his honour at the University of Massachusetts at Amherst. Achebe delivered a moving eulogy during which he recalled how he first met Baldwin through his writings, and then physically at the African literature conference in Gainesville. The year at Amherst was as busy as his other years. He taught courses in African literature and

---

[9] Okonkwo Agu, interview with Egejuru
[10] Michael Olumide, interview with Egejuru

conducted seminars for faculty. He travelled to other institutions in the US giving lectures or readings from his works. He also participated in conferences and other literary callings in Nigeria and other parts of the world.

A moment of embarrassment which only Nigeria is capable of staging, occurred in January 1988, when the convocation of Lagos State University was cancelled a day before the scheduled date. Achebe had already arrived on campus before the embarrassed vice Chancellor came to tell him of his problems. He revealed that there was a great opposition from the Yorubas against the inclusion of Achebe among those to receive honorary degrees. That was the most demonstrative way for the Yorubas to register their anger over Achebe's opposition to a national funeral for Awolowo. With that single act, the Lagos State University confirmed some of the things Achebe had been criticizing his country for- crippling tribalism and lack of seriousness of purpose.

Back at Amherst, Achebe continued to carry out his duties as a Visiting Professor of Afro-American Studies. At the same time, he toured other institutions in the United States, giving lectures and readings. He was interviewed by Bill Moyers and thus joined the list of writers and humanists who appeared on Moyer's Television Series, *A World of Ideas*. He travelled to other parts of Africa and to Europe, responding to various invitations. It was earlier in the year, while he was attending a Writers' Symposium in Dublin Ireland, that the *Irish Times* called him, " the man who invented African literature." Achebe has told the story several times, of how he quickly disclaimed the designation and the reason he did so. He took that opportunity to educate the world about Mbari institution and the communal nature of art among Igbo people.

1989 opened belatedly with the celebration of *Anthills of the Savannah* in Nigeria. The same occasion saw the launching of Chinelo Achebe's first work, *The Last Laugh and Other Stories*. In reference to this occasion, Chinelo was asked if her father's fame was a burden to her as a writer in her own right. She said it was more of a challenge than a burden to her. She added:

> That's not to say that I don't think much of my ability to write. Like father, like daughter. But I think he is in a class of his own. Somebody flatly told me that I could never write like Chinua Achebe. I don't think I can, there's only one Chinua Achebe.[11]

1989 was also filled with domestic and international travels for various engagements- to receive awards, deliver lectures, and give interviews. Organizations continued to impose offices on him. For

---

[11] Chinelo Achebe, interview with Egejuru.

instance, he was elected the first President of Nigerian chapter of PEN international. Commenting on this, Theo Vincent said: "When we made him President of the Nigerian PEN, he had narrowly missed the presidency of PEN international. Making him President was not by design, he merited it."[12] The least his compatriots could do to show their appreciation for all he had done for them, was to lobby for him to be the President of PEN international, but failing that, they elected him, even in his absence to be the President of their local chapter.

One of the highlights of 1989 was the publication of the first issue of *African Commentary: A Journal for People of African Descent*. Again, it was Achebe who initiated this noble venture. He outlined its goals and objectives in the foreword to the maiden issue. Alas! This noblest of dreams soon vanished after a couple of issues. When he was asked about the journal, he could not hide his disappointment with what happened to it. He lamented the demise of the journal in these words:

> That one is a very painful story for me, because that was a dream that had every possibility of being realized. It failed at a time I had the accident and I was more or less forcibly removed from the scene, and people who should have carried on, seemed to have their own agenda and that went completely astray.[13]

---

[12] Theo Vincent, interview with Egejuru.
[13] Chinua, interview with Egejuru.

8

1990: Turning Point

1990, the ominous year that would alter the course of Achebe's life started quite normally with three months of visiting professorship at Dartmouth College, from January to March. From Dartmouth, he travelled to other places for various assignments. In January, he appeared in the London Weekend Television's South Bank Show. As an introduction to his own lecture, he talked of his recent participation in Ireland's celebration of one thousand years of the founding of the city of Dublin. The program he appeared on was titled, "Literature as Celebration." He found that title very applicable to his lecture: "African Literature as Celebration." He then used the Mbari tradition of Owerri Igbos to explain the significance of the title of his lecture. Achebe found the Mbari phenomenon a very useful metaphor in his attempt to help the West understand not only the Igbo concept of art but also the black man's generosity of spirit. Because, through Mbari, the people celebrate every presence in their society. And celebration in the context of Mbari does not mean only praise and approval of good happenings but also of bad and unfortunate happenings in society. Soon after this lecture, he flew back to Nigeria in February for the symposium held at the University of Nigeria Nsukka to celebrate his 60th birthday.

The University of Nigeria at Nsukka had hosted innumerable conventions, conferences and symposia that brought scholars from different parts of the world. But no previous scholarly gatherings at Nsukka could be compared in any way to the symposium held there from February 11 to 15, 1990. It was organized by the late Edith Ihekweazu, Dean of Arts and Professor of Modern Languages. The symposium titled, "Eagle-on-Iroko, Chinua Achebe at 60", was staged in February to avoid conflict with events by other groups celebrating the same birthday whose actual date, November 16, was still several months away.

Participants in various disciplines of the Humanities came from different parts of the world. There were also diplomats representing countries from Europe, the United States, Canada, Britain and some other countries within the British Commonwealth. The sheer number of high-powered intellectual and artistic minds from all the continents underscored the powerful symbolism of Eagle-on-Iroko, beauty and strength fused into one. The support from Nsukka University in cash and kind, plus the enthusiastic response from Nsukka and the international communities, spoke loudly of the respect and appreciation Achebe receives from his home and abroad. The Association of Nigerian Authors was well represented. They took the opportunity to present Achebe with their first Triple Eminence Award. Inside Nsukka town, there was a celebration within the celebration during which a major street -*New Market Road*- was renamed *Chinua Achebe Avenue*. Some friends and colleagues who could not be there physically, sent papers to be read or some other message or gifts. The gift that caused the most stir was a white ram sent by Wole Soyinka. The gift of a ram is a very symbolic Yoruba way of showing respect to a great man. This ram played the role of a messenger-dove; it wore round its neck a piece of paper on which Soyinka wrote his congratulatory message to Chinua. The ram was slaughtered and barbecued as a final offering at the close of the symposium.

For those who did not witness the events marking the occasion, the word symposium, would only connote presentations and discussions of papers on Chinua Achebe. But this was no ordinary symposium, it was more of a festival of the arts and culture. Numerous papers were presented and plenary sessions were held, but the most exciting events were the masquerades, the traditional and modern dances, performances by traditional minstrels, theatrical performances by professional groups and the finale dramatic staging *of Arrow of God* by the Drama Department of the University of Nigeria Nsukka.

The celebration of Eagle-on-Iroko was a fabulous news item that participants would carry to distant lands. For the honoree, the entire event was certainly one of those occasions during which one could not find the mouth with which to speak because the heart was overflowing with joy and gratitude. Achebe's entire family was completely overwhelmed and his daughter Chinelo expressed the feeling of the family: "So many people came from far and wide to celebrate and venerate him, it was a very humbling experience for us."[1]

After the celebration, Achebe went back to Dartmouth and finished his short appointment. He had two weeks free before he would move to the next appointment at Stanford University in California. But he would not rest easy in those two weeks if he did not rush back home to Ogidi to preside over an important meeting of the Town Union. Now serving a second term as the President, he continued to push for a number of changes aimed at restoring some of the traditional ways of

---

[1] Chinelo Achebe, interview with Egejuru.

doing things in Ogidi. The most thorny of the issues was how to choose the Igwe, the overall ruler of Ogidi. The change called for rotation of Igweship, to end the monopoly of that office by one specific family or kindred. This suggestion angered the Ndichie, who had been picking and choosing kings for years, without regard to traditional protocol. The present Ogidi people, especially members of Achebe's age grade did not want Ndichie to continue choosing Igwe for them. They argued that the responsibility of choosing a ruler lay with the entire Ogidi population. It was to see this very issue resolved in favor of the general public that Achebe decided to run for a second term for the presidency of Ogidi Town Union. He wanted the people to choose between his progressive ideas and Ndichie's antiquated ways. Ndichie presented their candidate, but he lost miserably. Chinua was re-elected by a landslide. It was thus crucial for him to rush home from the United States and confront a disgruntled Ndichie over the sensitive issue of Igweship. He knew how important his presence was for the success of any meeting because, "every time he wasn't there, the meeting will have no head." Therefore, it was a veritable act of courage and devotion to his people that made Chinua risk a journey from the United States back to Nigeria, barely a month after the celebrations of Eagle-on-Iroko.

He successfully presided over the meeting during which the heated topic of rotating the Igweship was reopened. Tempers flew as the Ndichie vigorously defended their proscribed traditional role of kingmakers. They were quite vociferous in demonstrating their disappointment in the President whom they had virtually begged to take that office. All the progressive elements of Ogidi were horrified even frightened by the unexpected reaction of the Ndichie. It was quite a revelation because people from Ogidi and beyond assumed that everybody in Ogidi loved Chinua. In fact, his friend, old man Johnson Okudo spoke of him in terms of *Olisa e nwee ilo* -God has no enemy. As for Achebe, it was just a meeting like all other meetings where people disagreed and shouted at one another. So, he left Ogidi for Nsukka from where he would return to the United States.

The accident

On the morning of March 22,1990, Chinua and his son Ikechukwu, left Nsukka for Enugu airport. From there, they would board a plane to Lagos, and from Lagos, Chinua would catch another plane for the United States while Ikechukwu would catch a plane to London. For the trip from Nsukka to Enugu Chinua rented a station wagon from a company called *Land Flight*. He had rented from this company on a number of occasions, an indication that he had received good services from them. The company's driver came and picked Chinua and his son from their home at the University campus. The two passengers made themselves comfortable in the back seats and the driver took off.

The ride was quite smooth and soon Chinua dozed off. As soon as they passed the Awka campus of Anambra State University of Technology, at a spot uninhabited by people, it happened! The axle broke in two. The car somersaulted several times before it landed on Chinua who had been ejected during the somersaults. Meanwhile, his son who was trapped in the car, realized what had happened. He started calling and looking for his father in the car; he didn't find him. There was so much dust and heavy smell of petrol that Ikechukwu got frightened. He continued frantically calling his father. He recalled:

> I was thinking the car would burst into flames. I kept calling him. Then I realized he was not in the car. I managed to get out of the car, then I saw him under the car.[2]

Several motorists stopped to help lift the car. One of those who stopped was a lecturer at Awka College of Education. It was the lecturer's station wagon they used to carry Chinua from one clinic to another, in Awka. The longer they searched for doctors, the worse his condition became. There was no choice but to go straight to the University Teaching Hospital Enugu. As soon as they moved, the car broke down. Everybody came out to push the car. While they were struggling to get the car moving again, message was sent to the Teaching hospital to alert them about the patient on the way.

As fate would have it, one of the orthopaedic doctors at the hospital was Dr. J. U. Achebe, son of Chinua's brother John. He was contacted and informed that a relative of his was in a car accident. They didn't tell him who it was. When he came and saw who it was, he was devastated. Speaking of his reaction to the accident he said:

> Apart from the shock, I now have insight into what relatives of patients go through. When I saw him, I knew what would happen. I asked why this should happen to him. He just lay there with his eyes closed. When he opened his eyes he said, *'o bu olu ekwensu*, it's the work of Satan.'[3]

But Satan was bound to lose because "God fights for him as his name says. His name is working and God performs," said Chinua's brother John. When the patient was finally brought in, the scene at the

---

[2] Ikechukwu Achebe, interview with Egejuru.
[3] Dr. John. U.D. Achebe, interview with Egejuru.

hospital was like a disturbed anthill. Messages were dispatched to relatives at Ogidi and Nsukka. Within hours a huge crowd gathered. Everyone was anxious to see the patient. Soon, Achebe's personal driver Reuben arrived from Nsukka. He would have to fight his way through the dense crowd to reach the family. Describing the crowd Reuben said, "The whole world was there *neshi onwu ihu ya*, risking even death to get a glimpse of him." The team of doctors, nurses and other health workers at Enugu, toiled continuously for forty-eight hours to stabilize the patient. Thus, the miracle of saving Chinua's life started with the initial spectacular handling at Enugu hospital.

The hands on deck were not only of the team at the teaching hospital. Starting with those who arrived on the scene of the accident to the health team in Paddocks England, hands stretched from Nigeria to England! Among the hands that stuck out were those of Professor Ejike, the vice Chancellor of Anambra State University of Technology. From the moment he received news of the accident, Ejike started making the necessary contacts to get the most sought after expert in spinal injury in England. Ejike's daughter had a similar diagnosis some years back, and she was treated at Paddocks hospital in England. Thus Ejike's contact with the specialist, Dr. H. L. Frankel, facilitated Achebe's admission to Paddocks hospital. What's more, immediate funds were needed in cash and kind and Prof. Ejike appealed to his University for help. The British Council was most co-operative, even the British Airways flight was delayed until Achebe was flown from Enugu to Lagos. They worked together and moved the patient out in record time. The doctors in England commented on the excellent job done by the initial handlers, and the record speed with which the patient was moved from Nigeria to Britain. Commenting on the crucial role of Ejike and his team, Chinelo Achebe said:

> He was the one person outside the family who took over the situation. This man didn't rest until he got him out of Nigeria. The British Embassy cooperated. The plane had to wait for him.[4]

As for Ejike's comment on his role, he said it was merely providential that, because of his daughter's case, he knew the best facility and how to go about getting there on time. In a truly Igbo mindset, all who saw Chinua hours after the accident, said that his name rose to the occasion and fought for him. Ejike said, "If his *Chi* had not been there, things would have been worse."

---

[4] Chinelo Achebe, interview with Egejuru.

9

The Paddocks Hospital: a miraculous recovery

The Paddocks Hospital is located in Princes Risborough, Buckinghamshire in England. At the time of the interview (1995) Paddocks was about twenty years old in its present form and status as the best facility for the treatment of spinal injuries in England. Before this time, it had been accepting patients from all parts of the world. The first international patients were the casualties from the Arab/Israeli war of 1967. With all its fame, the physical appearance of the Paddocks belies its importance. The whole facility is contained in a small compound of three to four ordinary looking bungalows. Its secluded location and modest appearance make it the type of place Achebe would approve of. It also has an unusual and interesting history.

The Paddocks Hospital was originally a private residence. Later, it became a training centre for a company that manufactured tires. Finally, two ladies turned it into a nursing home for the elderly. At about the same time, there was an increasing demand from international patients in need of treatment for spinal chord injuries. The government hospital at Isleberg could not handle all the requests because their first priority was for residents of the United Kingdom. Since there were many domestic and foreign patients, the Paddocks Hospital was chosen to handle international patients.

There are only thirty-six beds in this hospital. It treats people with various conditions except Obstetrics, Heart surgery and Paediatrics. At any one time, they have twelve patients for spinal injury or head injury or a combination. Nine or ten of the twelve would come from outside Britain. The hospital has more requests than it can handle, so they select the most urgent cases. The director said, "we charge for our services. Anyone who comes here must have the means to pay for the services." On the average, a patient would pay about seventy thousand pounds.

The Director was asked if the hospital was swarmed with visitors when Achebe was there. He responded: "I don't recall the influx of visitors. Any patient who comes receives good treatment as an individual. Every year we have ten to fifteen people who are well known."[1]

The caregivers at Paddocks didn't know who Achebe was. One of the physiotherapists said:

> I had no idea who he was before he came here. My son went to the library to get his novel *Anthills of the Savannah*, which he enjoyed. We enjoy helping and treating people but we didn't realize then who he was and it's all coming out now. You would never have known he was an important person. He was very modest.[2]

The nurses spoke glowingly of how he conducted and presented himself:

> He is a lovely man, quiet, gentle and very private. He came daily for his exercises, he was very easy to handle. He put up a marvellous brave front; never saw him in any form of depression. We didn't notice any despair, no reaction to his situation. He didn't let us know how he felt.[3]

One therapist who seemed to have noticed Chinua's weakness in sports said of him:

> I don't think he is a sports person, but when we took him to hydrotherapy, I think he enjoyed learning how to swim without his legs. He enjoyed the warmth and support the water gave. With the type of injury and the kind of therapy needed for rehabilitation, many people lose the determination to continue. Achebe had a quiet determination.[4]

Although Achebe is now wheelchair bound, he is far from being handicapped. At the very worst, he is physically inconvenienced, to borrow Gwendolyn Brooks' expression. This is because the caregivers at the Paddocks hospital achieved their goal of making everyone of their patients totally independent. Mr. Hazley, the administrator said:

---

[1] Sam Hazley, administrator of the hospital, interview with Egejuru
[2] One of the physiotherapists at the hospital, interview with Egejuru.
[3] The nurses and physiotherapists spoke as one body during the interview with Egejuru. Each of them made a comment on Chinua's deportment.
[4] One of the therapists, same interview.

Achebe was here to gain the maximum independence for a person who had fractured his spine, and the therapists were responsible for helping him gain that independence. What we try to put across to patients is that we want them to live as normal a life as possible when they get home. It takes courage to move about in a wheel chair, so we try to help them come to terms mentally with the condition, remaining a whole human being.[5]

In addition to being able to make the various manoeuvres for getting in and out of spaces, Achebe also passed the driving test for the wheel chair bound. In fact, the way he behaved after he passed the test reassured his family that he had returned to his old self. Commenting on it, daughter Chinelo said:

When he passed his driving test, he looked downcast. He hates driving, so he was not happy to pass the driving test. He was back to his old self. That showed recovery. He is very independent. There is nothing you can do for him now.[6]

Achebe's physical as well as mental recovery, was noted by the staff at Paddocks hospital when he went back for a check up. The nurses said:

He looked wonderful. You couldn't notice he was sitting in a wheelchair. He was sitting quite normal and natural; he looked quite contented. He was coping extremely well and that's what we like to know. It has been a two-way thing. We did get through to him.[7]

Family members and close friends were asked if they had noticed any changes in Achebe's behaviour or the way he looks at life now. Responding to the question, Professor Obiechina said:

I haven't noticed any changes. I noticed instead, stronger commitments to his old attitudes. I know he cares about Nigeria as a country, he cares a lot more about the Igbos and what happens to them. This concern has been a major force in his attitude to life since the war. There has been no flagging of his commitment to the wellbeing of our people.[8]

---

[5] Mr. Sam Hazley, interview with Egejuru.
[6] Chinelo Achebe, interview with Egejuru.
[7] The nurses at Paddocks Hospital, interview with Egejuru.
[8] Prof. E. Obiechina, interview with Egejuru.

Professor Ejike did not notice any changes. During a three-hour conversation that Ejike recorded, he noticed Chinua's usual posture of hope for the Igbo. He still believes that Igbo struggle for equality in their own country should be collective. He believes that families should be points of focus.

Professor Thelwell did not noticed any changes in Chinua:

> I have not seen any changes in him. The qualities that struck me when I first met him- the grace, the dignity and wisdom of his spirit are all still there. I have never seen him step out of character. I have only seen him step more deeply into it, and nothing exemplifies that more than the extraordinary courage, fortitude and grace with which he has handled his affliction.[9]

On a more practical note, his friends, Ben Uzochukwu and Vincent Ike noted that in spite of his condition, his handwriting has not changed and his mind and intellect are not touched. Theo Vincent went to see him at Bard two years after he settled there. Vincent made the following observation:

> The accident has not changed anything. Nothing has changed from the Achebe I knew. We had a wonderful time; he laughed as usual. Anybody would have thought the accident would break his spirit. His conversations were laced with humour, especially when he made fun of people who think they are the best things that happened to the world. I was so happy to see him in his old frame of mind.[10]

If anyone outside Achebe's family should notice any changes in the man, it would have to be his life long friend, C.C. Momah who lives a couple of driving hours from Chinua, and sees him regularly. Momah made the following observation:

> He is still very much his old self, the man I knew from the very beginning. He has remained constant in his views on life. He has such equilibrium that one can't say if something has shaken him. The only change is his slowed pace which is quite normal for anyone his age.[11]

---

[9] Prof. Michael Thelwell, interview with Egejuru.
[10] Prof. Theo Vincent, interview with Egejuru.
[11] Christian Momah, interview with Egejuru.

For some years after his discharge from the hospital it was still not easy to get information from Chinua about his reaction to the accident. It was still necessary to rely on his family, his close friends and those involved in his treatment. His personal physician, and long time friend, Dr. F.C. Adi was among the team of doctors who provided the initial treatment at the University hospital at Enugu. He was by Chinua's bedside throughout the ordeal of getting him stabilized. Dr. Adi said, "I was very impressed with his ability to withstand severe pain, and his philosophical resignation of his fate to Almighty God." Later, Dr. Adi visited him at the Paddocks hospital. At that time, the definitive prognosis had been made and Chinua knew the chances of walking again were dim. Yet, "even this did not depress him much,"[12] observed Dr. Adi.

His son Chidi explaining the source of his family's strength said, "there's no secret to anything other than, when I look at him, I don't see so much as *ewo! ewo!* Look at what happened." In other words, Chinua's disposition since the accident has not led anyone to look at him with pity or downcast eyes.

Ikechukwu who was in the car with him said, "The great thing about the accident and its aftermath is the way he has taken it. He is very philosophical about why things happen, and that philosophy is rooted in the way that Igbos perceive things or view life." Like his father who likes to tell stories to illustrate his points, Ikechukwu launched into the story of his father's readings and appreciation of Gustavus Equiano's Igboness, especially Equiano's attitude to his predicament as a slave in a strange land. "That's the level at which my dad operates."[13]

Still addressing the same issue of their father's reaction to his accident, Chinelo said:

> He doesn't say much about the accident. He listens and tries to pick up things from what eye -witnesses like Ikechukwu tell him. What touched me was that this man's mind was not touched. While his wounds were still fresh, he was talking about his lectures for various occasions. He was instructing our mother on what to do about his lectures. Then I knew there was some super intelligence directing things.[14]

When Professor Thelwell called Chinua on the phone to express his sympathy and anger that such a thing should happen to him:

---

[12] Dr. F.C. Adi, interview with Egejuru.
[13] Ikechukwu Achebe, interview with Egejuru.
[14] Chinelo Achebe, interview with Egejuru.

It was Chinua who was comforting me. He was telling me how lucky he felt for being alive. Other people would be feeling a sense of outrage and injustice. It's an uncommon grace, the way he endured this calamity.[15]

His friend, Aigboje Higo noted Chinua's reaction when he visited him in the hospital:

I went to see him in the hospital. I said, 'Chinua thank God, it could have been worse.' He saw the joke. Only with Chinua could I take such liberty, not with any other person, they wouldn't see what I meant.[16]

Wole Soyinka was among the people who visited Chinua at the hospital in England. Like other visitors, he didn't notice any changes. He said that Chinua was philosophical and even brought a sense of humour to the accident. At the same time Chinua admitted to Wole that he had moments of depression, "Sometimes it's hard," he said to Wole. Though only a few words were said, one could sense a heart-to-heart communication from one brother artist to another.

Finally, Chinua responded to the question: "Do you see God working His purpose out through this accident?"

I don't think I would be the one to talk about that. The only thing I would limit myself to is that since I am still around, it means I have something to do. I would also say that there is clear indication of His Mercy in the fact that I got through a very difficult and perilous time. I am not aware of the degree of that damage, because I was not even conscious. But my family and doctors all say the deliverance was of immense magnitude. Therefore, if God did all that, He must have a reason. I don't think it is for me to say, this is what it is. But as long as I am alive and kicking, I go on doing what I think is my work. I think it will be for the rest of you later on.[17]

Clearly, one sees no sign of anger or lament. There are none of the self- pitying innuendoes. There is instead, a total acceptance of God's plans. Achebe leaves it "for the rest of you" (biographers and critics) to read meanings into his accident or evaluate its impact on him.

---

[15] Michael Thelwell, interview with Egejuru.
[16] Aigboje Higo, interview with Egejuru.
[17] Chinua, interview with Egejuru.

Sure enough, people read meanings into the accident as soon as it happened. At home in Ogidi, the people knew the identity of the Satan that overturned the car:

> It is Ndichie, *ndi ekwensu, ndi amosu*- people of Satan and witches, they are responsible for his present condition. But God did not let them succeed in killing him. He will live as long as God has planned for him.[18]

There were rumours in Ogidi that Ndichie had a hand in the accident because they wanted to stop Chinua from changing things in Ogidi. Therefore, for most Ogidi people, it was quite logical that Ndichie would want to get rid of the man whose leadership of Ogidi Town Union was threatening their position of king makers. After all, they went away from the meeting the previous day, swearing to stop Chinua and his administration from changing the traditional ways of doing things in Ogidi. Few people were surprised when they heard of the accident. Many concluded that the accident was fatal. A few bold ones went to ask Chinua's relatives if it was true that "the accident killed him." And his nephew Tochukwu said: "I avoided all those who were saying he was dead. I convinced myself that he wasn't dead. Finally, I heard he was alive."[19] For the lay people at Ogidi, the cause of the accident was quite evident. The lesson from the accident was also clear to the people, that no human can stop God's plan. Many were convinced that if Chinua had been somebody else, the outcome would have been different.

The more learned and the sophisticated had their own interpretation of the accident. At Nsukka University campus, there was a different speculation as to the cause of the accident. According to Jane Achebe, who was then working at Nsukka, people were saying that it was wrong to honor Chinua with the symposium while he was still alive. They even blamed the gift of a ram from Soyinka. They said the ram was an evil omen because Igbo people use rams for funerals, not to celebrate happy occasions. Dr. Michael Thelwell was one of the keynote speakers at the Eagle-on-Iroko symposium. When he heard about the accident, he was devastated. He wondered whether what was done at the symposium hadn't contributed to the accident. Another participant at the symposium, Professor Ifeanyi Aniebo had this to say:

---

[18] Johnson Okudo, interview with Egejuru.
[19] Tochukwu Okocha, interview with Egejuru.

If I were superstitious, I would say that as long as I live, I wouldn't want anything of that sort (symposium) done for me while I am alive. The accident turned the symposium into a wake keeping.[20]

The only person who had no illusions of the exact cause of the accident was Emeka Okocha, Achebe's nephew. Emeka said the accident affected him more deeply and personally because, he happened to be working for the company that owned the car his uncle rented. He knew the inadequacies of the company. He knew that some of the vehicles were not road worthy. But he didn't know that his uncle was one of their patrons. He left the company after his uncle's accident. He spoke bitterly against the company:

> As a member of staff, I wouldn't use their service, so, I don't see why I would allow my uncle to use their service. If only I had known he was using the company's service, I would have recommended a few things.[21]

Most of these speculations filtered to Chinua. But, it is not in his nature and upbringing to encourage superstition. Yet, he recognizes that people are entitled to their beliefs even superstitious ones. The closest he got to superstition was blaming Satan for the accident. His imagination did not stretch as far as seeing Ndichie to be the incarnation of Satan. As far as he was concerned, the meeting he presided over was like most of their other meetings. There were disagreements and shouting from opposing factions. In the end, the thorny issues were not resolved. Consequently, Chinua went away to think of more creative and productive ways of handling the sensitive socio-political problems of Ogidi people.

---

[20] Prof. Ifeanyi Aniebo, interview with Egejuru.
[21] Emeka Okocha, interview with Egejuru.

10

Bard College: the hermitage

Bard College is located in Annandale-on-Hudson, New York. Annandale is well hidden in the bowels of the Hudson valley. There is no fast way of getting there from any of the airports in New York, the nearest being Albany, about an hour's drive. The interstate freeway would take one close to Annandale. However, it takes about one hour to drive from the freeway exit to Bard College.

Getting to the College campus does not make it any easier to find Achebe's hide-away bungalow. This modest dwelling is not on any named street or drive or circle on campus. To get to it, one has to follow a narrow tree-flanked road, leading away from one of the parking lots off the main thoroughfare of the campus. This less traveled road ends at a clearing where two unpretentious houses stand side by side. The first of these looks more like an abandoned house than an infrequently occupied one. The next is a newly built house hemmed in by the forest. This is Achebe's present home, specifically designed to accommodate a wheelchair bound person. Though the Achebes moved into their house in the fall of 1990, some construction work was still going on by the summer of 1991. In addition to adding more rooms, a paved walk way had to be constructed around the house. Bard had originally planned to modify an old house for Achebe and his family, but in the end, they found it would cause more trouble modifying an old house than building a new house. Thus, a new bungalow was custom built.

Achebe's home at Bard College is a veritable hermitage. It provides the type of privacy needed for undisturbed physical and spiritual recuperation. Achebe is particularly pleased with the way that Bard handled his accommodation. Speaking about their decision to go to Bard, Achebe said:

> I find it gratifying that we were able to settle for this place. It is also in a good place, and at a time we were not looking for visitors.

Anyone who comes out here to look for us must really care about us.[1]

Obviously, some people have wondered why Achebe overlooked all the well-known and prestigious institutions to settle at Bard, a small and little known College. Asked how he came to Bard, he replied in his humorous way: "You need to see the President to find out how I came to Bard." But then he proceeded to tell how and why he came to Bard:

It came to me as a surprise. Well, I get invitations. This time, I was still in the hospital. I wasn't yet thinking of where we were going to go from the hospital. Stanley Diamond, a distinguished anthropologist, was a friend from Biafra days. He wrote me to ask how I was doing. Then he said whenever I was ready to leave, I should consider Bard because they were very keen. He knew I was going to spend a term at Stanford before the accident. And Stanford had sent someone just to say they would reschedule my visit whenever I was ready. But Bard was something else. I didn't know where it was. I may have heard the name. I didn't know anything about them, but Stanley was very enthusiastic when he mentioned it. He said the President was very eager. He was sure they would match whatever any other school would offer, including the top Ivy League schools. So I said, fine, and put it aside. But this kept coming up and eventually we said we would look at it more closely. In the end, the vice President of Bard came to England on a conference and he telephoned me.[2]

It was during that phone conversation that Achebe was told that Dr. Leo Botstein, the President of Bard, had listened to him speak during an international conference of writers and artists, held in Budapest two years earlier. It wasn't until his arrival at Bard that he finally met Dr. Botstein. Their official meeting happened at a dinner given by the President, and to which Stanley Diamond was also invited. It was at this dinner that the President retold the story of how he first met Achebe. The story became the President's welcoming speech to Achebe. "That was a surprise to me," said Achebe, because "the President is not a literary person, he is a musician, a conductor." However, from all the arrangements they made to accommodate his needs at the time, Achebe knew they were very serious.

Apart from building a new house, the arrangement for teaching was very reasonable. For the first year, Achebe taught all his courses in his house. The College provided a special van for his private use. And if

---

[1] Chinua, interview with Egejuru
[2] Chinua, same interview.

he had to be taken anywhere, the College took him there. Another very important part of the package was the provision for Achebe's wife to pursue her own professional interest at Bard. Dr. Christie Achebe is in Education Counseling. She was a faculty member in the Department of Education at the University of Nigeria Nsukka before her husband's accident. At Bard she was able to continue in her field. In the end, both husband and wife became faculty members at Bard. Chinua occupies the Charles P. Stevenson, Jr., Chair in Literature.

President Botstein made no secret of the fact that he appreciates Achebe's presence at Bard. He was asked why Bard went out of its way to hire Achebe. He retold the story of how he first met Achebe and how he thought Achebe was one of the great lights of the conference at Budapest. He had read some of Achebe's works, but it was Stanley Diamond, a former faculty at Bard, who had recommended that he invite Achebe to Bard and to offer him a position. President Botstein readily outlined some of the advantages of having Achebe at Bard:

> His literary stature with his moral authority has graced Bard. This has lent both faculty and students, a sense of their own importance and values. He has helped to elevate our sense of aspirations. He has drawn visitors and students to Bard. He has opened at Bard, a new line of intellectual inquiry into the African world. Bard now has a full line in African literature. Before he came, we offered some African literature on periodic basis. Achebe is an invaluable presence on Bard College campus.[3]

Achebe had retired from active University teaching nearly ten years before the accident. One would naturally assume that the accident would push him further back into inactivity. On the contrary, he was forced back to University teaching. He equally resumed touring the world to lecture and speak on vital issues. In fact, the only obvious change in his schedule is the reduced number of travels he makes. His family is very firm in cutting back on his travels. They are more concerned that he should start writing again. It appeared he had listened to his family's advice to take up his writing again. He picked up an ongoing project that he is reluctant to discuss with anybody. He grudgingly stated that he was working on a volume of poetry in Igbo language. His son Chidi elaborated:

> He is slow at it. His writing comes in stages, much of it is mental. He carries it in his head. He arranges everything so that when he settles down to write, nobody disturbs him and the family can function without his physical presence. It may be months and

---

[3] Leon Botstein, President of Bard College, telephone interview with Egejuru.

nobody reads it. He doesn't discuss his works with anybody. Sometimes he stays outside thinking and when you are talking to him, he would not hear. He is very fascinating that way.[4]

As he gradually resumed his writing, Achebe collaborated with a photographer to produce a book of photographs of Africa South of the Sahara. The same photographer had already completed a similar project on Egypt with Naguib Mahfouz. He approached Achebe to provide the writings to go with the photographs. Achebe felt the project was a good one so he agreed to provide some poems, essays and short stories. The book titled, *Another Africa* was in press in 1996.

It is true that Achebe's home at Bard is comfortable, but his HOME is at Ogidi. The preparations for a visit to Nigeria would take some time. He was asked, "If you go home to visit, are you sure you would return to Bard?" and he replied:

> Everything depends on other things. Obviously I cannot travel as much as I used to. But where I will be will depend on whether it is feasible for me to be there for long periods. We are certainly getting ahead with getting our place back. If it is possible, one would be there as much as possible.[5]

Getting his place back refers to his home in Ogidi. Adjustments needed to be made to accommodate his new lifestyle. His two-story house was not designed to accommodate his present condition. The experience at Bard taught them the lesson that it would be more trouble modifying the old house than building a new one. Therefore, a bungalow of two bedrooms was built next to the old house in the compound. By December 1995, the new house had been completed except for electrical fixtures and a paved walkway still being constructed around the house. As can be expected, Ogidi people held their breath as they prepared for a royal welcome for their beloved Ikejimba. And nine years after Chinua was flown out of Nigeria for treatment in London, he was physically and spiritually ready to visit home.

---

[4] Chidi Achebe, interview with Egejuru.
[5] Chinua, interview with Egejuru.

11

1999: a triumphal return

It would take Chinua nine years to get his health and his home in Ogidi ready for his first visit to Nigeria since the accident in March 1990. The preparation for this journey home (physical and spiritual) had been going on from the moment he left his country for medical treatment in England. On their part, Ogidi people had been waiting for Chinua's return from the time they got the news of his accident.

On August 23, 1999, Chinua with his family in the US went home to visit. His son Ikechukwu had preceded them from England. He had to make sure that everything his father needed for a comfortable stay in the village was taken care of. The US custom-built van and a driver specially trained to operate it were ready to drive Chinua and his entourage home from Lagos.

Chinua wanted to keep his visit quiet and private. Only his immediate family members knew the exact time of his arrival in Nigeria. However, he totally ignored or grossly underestimated the type of stir his presence was bound to cause at the airport. Besides, there was no way he could have prevented his relations at Ogidi from leaking the information about his impending return. Thus, before the formalities of arrival were completed at the airport, the news was out. A crowd quickly gathered and journalists were ready to trail him to an undisclosed (Sheraton) hotel, where the family was scheduled to spend some time in preparation for the long drive to the home town Ogidi.

Unbeknownst to Chinua, the Nigerian Federal Inspector of Police was staying at the same hotel. When the Inspector heard that Chinua was in the hotel, he made haste to go and greet Chinua. He offered to provide him with police escort to Ogidi. It was a most welcome offer because the escort would make it easier for Chinua's party to cut through the heavily jammed traffic of Nigerian highways. So, with a visible police escort, Chinua's hope of keeping his visit private was completely dashed.

They travelled in record time of six hours, reaching Ogidi around six in the evening. As they entered Ogidi, the policeman drew their attention to a white banner hanging like an arch over the road; he wondered what it was for. " Who knows what they might be celebrating at this time," Chinua commented. On closer examination, the banner read, " Welcome to Ogidi! After nine years, Ikenga Family Union welcomes you." Out of nowhere, dancers and masqueraders emerged and started to perform. Gun salutes rent the air. It was so unexpected and so moving that Chinua and his family could not hold back their tears. In the end, all his efforts to keep a low profile failed.

This was no ordinary visit. It was not undertaken simply to satisfy the need to reunite with family and friends. The primary aim for this visit was to observe a typically Nigerian Christian tradition known as *Thanksgiving Service*. It is a special occasion for a person to openly thank God for doing something very special for him or her. Therefore, Chinua's survival of a car accident called for a huge Thanksgiving Service in the proper Christian manner.

On September 29,1999, the entire Achebe clan, their families-in-law and countless friends, accompanied Chinua with his wife and children to St. Philip's Anglican Church Ogidi. Well-wishers and dignitaries from different parts of the country joined the procession to the altar for Thanksgiving. The Archbishop, C. J. Onyemelukwe presided and preached the sermon. The Bishop remarked that Chinua's coming home to give thanks to God was an exemplary gesture, because people of Chinua's fame hardly recognize the role of God in their lives. The choir of St. Philips composed and sang a special anthem for the occasion. Again, the entire service moved Chinua and his family to tears.

For Ogidi people in general, Chinua's visit was a veritable triumphal return that needed to be dramatized. Therefore, the week after the Thanksgiving Service, was marked by receptions and celebrations unparalleled in recent memory of the town. Dance groups and masqueraders competed and danced themselves to exhaustion. The crowd seemed to be in a trance as they chanted "*Ugonabo natalu* Ogidi - Ugonabo returned to Ogidi."

The visit was also timed to coincide with the annual Odenigbo lecture which Chinua was scheduled to deliver in September. Therefore, on Saturday, September 4, 1999, the stage was moved to the larger Igbo community gathered at Owerri in Imo State. There, at the imposing Mana Assumpta Cathedral of the Catholic Archdiocese of Owerri, Chinua delivered the fourth lecture in the series of Odenigbo lectures.

These lectures are unlike any other in Igbo land because they are delivered in Igbo language. The radical but very laudable idea of addressing an academically distinguished audience in Igbo came from the founder of Odenigbo lectures, the very Reverend Anthony Obinna, the Catholic Archbishop of Owerri Archdiocese.

Chinua was received at the Villa Assumpta by a distinguished crowd of Igbo people from all over the country and from overseas. As he approached the podium in his wheelchair, he was greeted with a sustained thunderous applause. The atmosphere was charged with Igbo pride and enthusiasm. It was very obvious that no Igbo person was more qualified than Chinua to speak on the present state of Igbo language. He also spoke on the sensitive topic of the fate of Igbo people in Nigeria. Chinua's lecture was titled: *"Echi di Ime, Taa bu Gboo*-Tomorrow is Pregnant, Today is yet Early." It took only a few words of his opening remarks for the audience to notice that the sixty-nine- year- old novelist has not lost any of his boldness and vigour.

He immediately unleashed his cutting criticisms and condemnations of various groups in the audience. He started with the traditional chiefs. He castigated them for their deplorable and unpardonable betrayal of Igbo dignity and pride. On the pretext of speaking for Igbo people, the traditional chiefs had committed the shameful act of going to plead with the late dictator, Sani Abacha, to continue his oppressive rule of the country.

Next, he turned to Igbo politicians whom he vehemently denounced for their selfish and reckless abuse of office. Like the traditional chiefs, Igbo politicians had sold their souls to the devils of Nigerian corrupt politics. In their bid for crumbs of the "National Cake" falling off the table of northern politicians, Igbo politicians eagerly licked the boots of northerners to whom they played second fiddle. In his typical display of courage, Chinua accused Igbo politicians of being responsible for marginalization and misrepresentation of Igbo people in Nigerian affairs. He charged the politicians of tarnishing the memory of their forefathers whose traditional politics was rooted in democracy. He made no attempt to hide his disgust and contempt for current Igbo politicians whom he blamed for causing the horrible condition of the Igbo as second class citizens in their own country.

On the other hand, Chinua commended Dr. Alex Ekwueme, the former vice President of Nigeria's defunct second civilian government. By Chinua's estimation, Ekwueme seemed to stand by democracy and thereby retained his identity as a true son of Igbo.

Chinua spent a great portion of his time reminding his kinsmen where the rain of disunity started to beat them. He traced it to the early white missionaries and early Igbo clergy and scholars. As a team working under Archdeacon Dennis, the group had worked together to create for the Igbo nation, a lingua franca known as Union Igbo. This Central Igbo, as it is sometimes called, was concocted from myriad of

Igbo dialects. Although the intention of the creators of Union Igbo was highly commendable, the result, according to Chinua was fairly disastrous. Instead of serving as a unifying force, Union Igbo served to alienate the Igbo from their true language. Chinua maintained that this language which he termed "Dennis' Mix" (after Archdeacon Dennis, the British missionary who spearheaded the Union Igbo experiment and translated the bible into Union Igbo), produced speakers who are neither English nor Igbo.

The entire lecture was intended as a wake-up call to the Igbo race. Since the end of the Nigerian civil war, the Igbo seem to be heading towards self-annihilation in their reckless abandon of their true Igbo character. To remind them of what he meant by a great Igbo personality he drew from his literary masterpiece, *Things Fall Apart*. Okonkwo, the main character of that novel, was a quintessential Igbo man who would rather commit suicide than compromise those qualities dear to the Igbo. Okonkwo was strong, fearless, industrious, truthful and above all, a self-made wealthy man.

Although he spoke in Igbo, Achebe made sure to couch his message in proverbs, the most cherished Igbo traditional discourse. "*Echi di Ime*, tomorrow is pregnant" and no one is certain of the outcome of a pregnancy. Nonetheless, " *Taa bu gboo*, today is early enough to rectify the errors of yesterday," he told them. Therefore, they must start today to teach the Igbo language to the young at all levels of education. In that way, they can once more inculcate Igbo values, morals and ethics in future generations of Igbo people.

Owerri people showed their appreciation with the usual elaborate traditional Owerri dances. In place of masquerades, they had traditional wrestling for which Owerri is known. The Achebes were very pleasantly surprised by the level of preparedness and efficiency of Owerri people. His son Chidi remarked:

> His lecture at Owerri paralleled his lectures overseas. Everything was done as it is done overseas. People were there on time. There were ramps wherever daddy was supposed to go. The entire event was so highly organized that we wondered if we were still in Nigeria.[1]

One of the highlights of his stay at Ogidi was the visit of the governor of Anambra State to Chinua's compound. The sight of Chinua moved the very sensitive governor to tears. Both men talked of the destiny of the Igbo and what needed to be done to restore the people's confidence in their elected officials. At the end of the governor's visit,

---

[1] Chidi Achebe, interview with Egejuru.

he announced that the road leading to the governor's residence at Awka had been renamed Chinua Achebe Road.

Finally, Obasanjo, the President of Nigeria sent a letter inviting Chinua to Abuja. Chinua accepted the invitation to the surprise of many who do not really understand him. There were lavish lunches and dinners thrown in his honor. During his visit to Abuja, journalists had the opportunity to ask him if his acceptance of Obasanjo's invitation meant giving his stamp of approval to the new Regime. Chinua told them that writers never give stamps of approval, they call a spade a spade. "So far we are heading in the right direction, that's all I can say for now,"[2] he told them. He wanted to let the press and the people know that democracy is the answer for Nigeria.

What would become the crowning moment of Achebe's visit to Abuja came when the President announced that Chinua was the first winner of the National Creativity Award. This award carries a cash prize of one million naira (roughly $10,500). Chinua was completely surprised by the announcement. He had heard of the proposal to create the Award but he remained skeptical of its actualization. Thus, as he thanked the minister of Culture, who handed him the award, Chinua confessed that the award appeared to be "fiction" to him.[3] That this award came to fruition was a surprising indication that, the new government might be serious in its intentions to make things work in Nigeria. In fact, this award was like a repeat of what happened in 1979 when Chinua became the first recipient of Nigeria's highest civilian award -the National Merit Award.

The entire visit home was memorable for Chinua, his family, his friends, Ogidi and Igbo communities and indeed, for Nigeria. As he told an enthusiastic crowd at the Lagos airport, Chinua went home "to touch base with my country and test the ground."[4] It was of the utmost importance for Chinua to make contact with his homeland before the close of the millennium.

After so many emotionally charged reunions with his relations, friends and former colleagues, Chinua and his family left Ogidi for Lagos en route to the U.S. But the Ogidi people had not finished with their celebrations. The Lagos branch of Ogidi Town Union was determined to stage a special send-off celebration for Chinua. They had rented a hotel for the occasion, the dancers had practiced extensively. But Chinua and his family were really worn out by all the celebrations.

---

[2] Chidi Achebe summarized his father's words during interview with Egejuru.
[3] Agence France Press posted the information on the Internet. It reported Achebe's visit to Abuja on September 14, 1999.
[4] The Associated Press lifted the information from *The Guardian* newspaper of Wednesday, August 25, 1999. It posted the information on the Internet.

Besides, Chinua had given the driver the day off, so there was nobody to take him to the hotel. The people would not be discouraged. They quickly changed plans and got permission to perform right at the hotel where Chinua was staying. Chinua was particularly moved by this last show of appreciation of him by his people. Despite the physical exhaustion, the entire visit was emotionally and spiritually satisfying.

On September 27, 1999, Chinua returned to the United States. He is making plans for his eventual return to his country.

Part II

...Chinua and his measure...

12

A family man first and foremost

Perhaps it was God's plan that Chinua had to be sent to Enugu by the Nigerian Broadcasting Service to become the new Controller for the Eastern Region. For, it was there that his path would cross with that of the woman who would become his wife and soul-mate. Miss Christie Chinwe Okoli, of Umuokpu in Awka, a student at the University of Ibadan, went to do her vacation job at NBS, Enugu. It was at work that, a strictly business matter, brought her and Chinua together. The circumstances of their meeting, their courtship and eventual marriage, point to the workings of an inner voice that directs Chinua in matters of grave importance. It has earlier been suggested that this inner voice was at work when Chinua changed his major from Medicine to Arts. This same inner voice told him that he had found his future spouse. When he was asked how he met Christie, he answered:

> We just happened to be at the same place at the right time. That was it. It was nothing so exotic as your parents finding somebody. Actually, she came for vacation work at NBS from Ibadan and I had nothing to do with hiring her. It was Sam Nwaneri's job as head of regional programs. It was Nwaneri who came to tell me that one of the holiday people said that her salary was less than what was paid to another worker in another section. Nwaneri said that this person wanted to come and tell me about it.

"This person" was Miss Christie Okoli. She came and complained about unfair treatment of her and a fellow student from Ibadan. Chinua described their coming to him as "a joint delegation" and "they had a good case. There was a disparity and that was straightened out."

This might seem like a minor incident, but it reveals Chinua's passion for fairness and justice. This casual business meeting with Christie would gradually lead to acquaintanceship, to courtship and finally marriage. Chinua was asked: "Did your inner voice tell you that Christie was the right girl for you?" He replied:

Yes, I think a lot of what happened to me, (whether you call it an inner voice) I would say there was something like inner voice. You followed what you thought was right or good or just or valuable.[1]

Chinua listened to his inner voice but his close friends were a bit nervous when they realized that he was really in love with Christie. They had some reservations about his choice of Christie. V.C. Ike recalled how he and some other friends reacted to Chinua's courting of Christie:

> There was nothing any one of us had against her as a wife. The only thing was that there was somebody else, an undergraduate who was friendly with Christie. We really wondered whether Christie was taking Chinua for a ride, because she seemed to be very much attracted to the undergraduate. And for me, I rated Chinua much higher, not just because he was already a graduate and had published his first novel, but I knew his ability and the kind of person he was. We really thought it was a pity if Chinua was said to be competing with this undergraduate. But obviously he knew what he saw in her; not that we didn't see anything in her, pretty, lively, pleasant, good schools, good home background. But we just didn't want Chinua to be wasting his time if this thing wasn't going to lead to marriage. But Chinua stuck to his gun and later they got married. Looking back on it now, we were certainly wrong and Chinua was right.[2]

Mrs. Ethel Momah who is one of Christie's best friends also recalled Chinua's courting of Christie:

> Chinua was coming from Lagos to chase her and she kept running. We used to get angry with her for giving him such a tough time. Chinua must have known what he saw in her. And now we see the hand of God in it.[3]

There might not have been anything "exotic like your parents finding someone for you," as Chinua stated, yet he knew that tradition demanded the participation of his parents in the traditional protocols of marriage. Therefore, he told his people that he had found a girl for himself. His sister Zinobia recalled: "He didn't ask us to look for a wife for him. We were at Enugu and Christie's father was there too, so when Chinua declared his intentions to marry Christie, we started visiting

---

[1] Chinua, interview with Egejuru
[2] V.C. Ike, interview with Egejuru.
[3] Ethel Momah, interview with Egejuru.

them." As the courtship continued at Ibadan and Lagos, the traditional marriage protocol was carried out in the village by Chinua's family.

A couple of years after the initial meeting at NBS, Enugu, Chinua and Christie had a Christian wedding on October 10,1961 at the Chapel of Resurrection, University of Ibadan. His friend C.C. Momah, was the best man while Sam Nwoye was chairman at the reception. Normally the wedding takes place at the groom's hometown or the place of his employment. However, Chinua is often more interested in the practical rather than sentimental side of things. He didn't see the need to go back to the East when the bride and groom were in the West. And if one insisted on the sentimental, Ibadan was sentimental enough, after all, he and Christie graduated from Ibadan. Besides, a number of their classmates were working in Ibadan and Lagos, and many of them trooped from Lagos to Ibadan for the ceremony.

The newly wed settled in a nice house on Milverton Road Ikoyi, Lagos, the exclusive residential area for expatriates and local senior civil servants. Chinua continued with his busy schedule at NBC, and Christie worked at the Ministry of Information. With their wedding, they fulfilled part of the traditional expectations for adults in Igbo society. Just under a year after the wedding, on July 11, 1962, the birth of their first child, Chinelo brought the ultimate fulfillment of the couple as parents. With the birth of their daughter, they acquired a new identity among the village folks, especially among children who now called them mama Chinelo and papa Chinelo. And even when her siblings came along, Chinelo remained the identity of their parents. As an adult and a mother herself, she recalled the privileges she enjoyed as the first child. She had the feeling of being important because "when people came to the house, they would first ask about me. As the first child, you are always known."

Marriage added another dimension to Chinua's responsibility. He now has to navigate between his job of Director of External Broadcasting at NBC, his writing, and his role as husband and father - head of household. How does one divide one's attention between numerous and equally valued responsibilities? Striking a balance between his job, his writing and his family would constitute a great challenge not only for Chinua but for Christie as well. He would need her understanding and cooperation to strike that balance. And she gave him both. Christie quickly realized that much of her husband's time would be taken up by his job and his writing. She adjusted to the situation very early in their marriage. She took care of the house and the children while her husband was often away, attending to his job and his writing.

Mrs. Achebe was reserved and quite reluctant to speak about her relationship with her husband during the interview. For her as well as her husband, their relationship is not one to be captured in words. She subtly gave a hint of their relationship by pointing out the architecture of their house at Bard. "Look at this dark and gloomy interior," she said, " Imagine a couple who don't get along, cooped up in this place in dreary winter!"[4] And one could see that the physical stress that this house was capable of inducing was enough to send any other couple at each other's throat. In other words, if she and her husband didn't have a special rapport, they couldn't live peacefully in such a depressive environment. Though she wouldn't elaborate on their relationship, one understood her reluctance after listening to her friends, her children and her husband talk about her role in the marriage. If she were to speak of herself the way others spoke about her, anyone would say she was just blowing her trumpet.

All four children were interviewed in different locations but they all sounded as if they had rehearsed their responses to the question: "How would you describe your parents' relationship?"

Chinelo gave the following response:

> From what I have seen, they complement each other, they are great supporters of each other. For instance, during the war, he was away most of the time. But she had the sense of what and who our father was, and what he was doing and why. Between the two of them there is a lot of respect. On my mother's part, she believes in him totally and he believes in her. I don't think my father's success is primarily due to his incredible extraordinary talent. A lot of his success comes from being married to this woman and he is very aware of it. She never spends time defending what she does. She is so supportive of him. She has forsaken so many things she could have become to be with her husband.[5]

Chidi was interviewed at Bard and he probably gave the definitive description of their parents' relationship:

> When they are together, the way they converse, one could see they are soul mates; you and me against the world, that kind of relationship. Many of their friends say they are very quiet, they don't stir. The reason for that is this soul mate thing, they are very content.

---

[4] Mrs. Christie Achebe, though unwilling to talk about her relationship with Chinua she gave this hint in a conversation with Egejuru
[5] Chinelo Achebe, interview with Egejuru.

To illustrate how much their father values and appreciates their mother, Chidi related what their father did at the wedding of his sister Nwando. At some point during the feasting, the father of the bride had to give some words of advice to the newly wed. Chinua spoke at length on husbanding to his son-in-law, Chukwuma Ekwueme. However, when it was Nwando's turn to listen, her father said: "I have only one thing to say, just be like your mother." Chidi also repeated almost word for word, what Chinelo had said about their mother's role in their father's success:

> One very important thing I think should be emphasized is that a large part of Daddy's success is a result of the type of wife he has. I am not saying he is not talented or that he wouldn't have become famous. But I am convinced that because of our mother, he has gone further than he would have. This is because they have this special relationship.[6]

Chinua is always cautious, and he is even more reluctant to talk about his relationships with family members. He had earlier warned: "There is something about our relationships which is difficult to put in words, because we are not word people in talking about relationships." The subject of his relationship with his wife had to be approached with caution and so the question was put this way:

> "Your children said they had never seen you and their mother in a fight, physically or verbally, is that true?"
> "I think that's a difficult thing to talk about. I prefer not to turn this relationship into clearer words because it is something of great value."
> "Your son Chidi called you and Christie soul mates, can you comment on that?"
> "Soul mates, yes. I think there are so many ways I feel blessed and very fortunate that it is she rather than anybody else. But that doesn't mean we have never disagreed, that's nonsense. We have, because we are not one person. We are two people, in fact, very different in many ways. But somehow we get on well, and if we disagree, we try to limit the disagreement and attempt to work things out. I have no reason not to do that because my parents were like that."[7]

Chinua's relationship with his wife is much more than getting along and limiting disagreements. There is much unspoken love that is very

---

[6] Chidi Achebe, interview with Egejuru.
[7] Chinua Achebe, interview with Egejuru.

obvious to a third party. One of Chinua's colleagues said: "Chinua loves his wife to the point of stupidity." Their friend Momah feels that Chinua and Christie are more than soul mates. What comes across to their friends is a total giving of one to the other. They have complete trust in each other to do what is best for the family. As the children testified, their father left the job of disciplining and running the house to their mother, because he believed in her. Because of her efficiency in taking care of her family, Christie's praise name is *Odozi Ngwulu*-custodian of the homestead.

Christie is known to be very meticulous about food, and very creative in using locally grown produce, especially beans. Her practicality is legendary among their friends. She makes her own drapes from locally manufactured cloths, and she pours her energy into gardening. On the whole, Chinua and his wife are very stable in their marriage. They have become a model of good family to their friends. Above all, they are a normal couple and they truly love each other. They have disagreements like normal couples. It is important to note that Chinua gave credit to his own parents for their influence in the way he interacts with his wife, as well as the way they raised their children. He in turn is a model for his own children. His son Chidi said he would follow in his parents' footsteps:

> Growing up, I have been trying to recollect how my parents live their lives, to remind myself when I become excessive in anything, that this is not the type of behavior my parents would show under that circumstance.[8]

The subject of disciplining children is one that often tears parents apart, because they can't agree on a definite plan. How did Chinua and Christie deal with this popular problem? Again, the children articulated their parents' approach. Ikechukwu described his parents' method:

> Their approach to child raising is basically putting a collective front. There is no way you can appeal to one and the other backs down. No, you cannot break that barrier. Even if one does not feel the way the other feels, they still will present the common front. Yet, they have different approaches. The one I would say that talked to us and enforced this discipline was our mother. It is our mother who tells us, don't do this. She is the main influence in our lives because our father is so busy.

---

[8] Chidi Achebe, interview with Egejuru.

Ikechukwu was further asked, "Did your parents ever flog you children?"

> Of course, we were flogged well well. But it was mainly our mother who flogged us. Our father doesn't know how to flog. I don't remember being flogged by him. He believed very strongly in the program of discipline our mother instituted for us. He liked to stand back and watch while our mother told us what and what not to do.[9]

All the children made fun of their father's weakness in enforcing corporal punishment. Chidi recalled a day his mother sent him to his father to be flogged. After he received the few taps on his behind, he ran into his room to laugh.

When asked if her father ever flogged her, Chinelo said: "My father cunningly left that to my mother." She recalled an incident similar to Chidi's, when her mother told her that her father was going to flog her.

> I was very happy to hear that my father was going to spank me. He put me over his knee and gave me some slight taps and I started laughing. My mother took over and flogged me.

Chinelo conceded that her father chose no occasion to discipline. She recalled one day she slammed the door after he had cautioned her not to disobey her mother.

> He came back to my room and spoke to me in a stern voice and that scared me more than spanking. He said to me, 'don't ever do that again.' I was shocked, therefore, that worked.[10]

Nwando, the last child stayed longest at home before she left in her second year at college. She said her father never spanked her. She remembered that if they did something bad and were reported to their father:

> He would look at us and sigh. Then he would ask, 'why did you do that? Don't do it again. After that you just go into your room ask why you did it. He does not raise his voice. That sense that he is disappointed in us is what does it more than scolding.[11]

---

[9] Ikechukwu Achebe, interview with Egejuru.
[10] Chinelo Achebe, interview with Egejuru.
[11] Nwando Achebe, interview. With Egejuru

Other forms of discipline were also applied. Quite often a child can be "banned" from doing her or his favorite thing. For instance, Chinelo was often prohibited from borrowing books from the library or from friends, and she couldn't stand that for one week! When asked what parenting lesson she learned from her parents, Chinelo said: " I will try to discipline my daughter just like my mother did. When mother says come in at 4 p.m. you better come in at 4 p.m."

In addition to discipline, there was the need to provide emotional support for the children. Since the husband was very busy writing or travelling, one assumed that his role in the daily caring of the children was not met or was very limited. Yet, from the children's testimony, they did not suffer from an undue deprivation of fatherly presence. Chinelo said:

> Even though he traveled a lot, we didn't have that feeling of not having him around, because when he came back, he was very much around. He used to tell us stories at bedtime. When I fell asleep he would carry me upstairs to my bed. I remember that sensation of being carried up, he was way up there. We loved that holiday feeling that every one is home.[12]

Each of the children was asked to recall his or her earliest memory of their father doing something for them or with them. Chinelo went back to when she was about two years old. She saw a television commercial on a Parker pen writing on its own. She asked her father to get her that pen. She waited everyday for him to return from work, then she would ask if he had bought the pen. One day her father watched the commercial with her. The next day he bought the pen. She recalled: "I took the pen and started writing but I didn't know what I was writing." The grown up Chinelo finally understood her father's action: "Instead of my father putting me through the agony of explaining TV tricks, saying next time and for ever, he bought me the pen. I stopped bothering him."

Ikechukwu, had a different and very touching early memory of his father doing something for him. It was during the Biafran war. Ikechukwu was ill for about three or four days. Finally his father decided to take him to some health facility even though there was no car to get there. He remembered:

> My father was carrying me on his back for many miles. I felt I was quite heavy for him. So, after some time he put me down and I walked for a short distance, then he carried me again. I knew we

---

[12] Achinolo Achebe, same interview.

were going to a hospital or clinic. I don't know exactly what health facility it was. But that's my earliest memory.[13]

Chidi recalled sitting in a circle with his siblings listening to their father as he told and retold stories of the trickster tortoise and other animals. What Chidi enjoyed the most during his pre-school years at Amherst was being picked up from the nursery school by his father. They both routinely went to lunch at the cafeteria on campus. Unlike their mother who insisted on a balanced meal and one desert, "Daddy would allow you an extra desert like ice cream," said Chidi. Laughing as he looked back at that time, Chidi admitted that, "Daddy spoilt us a bit in a loving delicate way."

One ritual Chidi disliked was going with his father alone every weekend, to their village. "I hated going with him to Ogidi every weekend," he said. As an adult, Chidi now understands why his father literally dragged him to Ogidi:

> He wanted me to learn of the culture. He wanted it so badly that I sort of rebelled. I believe I was going through that phase of childish resistance.

Chinua helped his children cultivate a love for reading. Chidi recalled being assigned a book to read each week, but then he started reading the newspapers and magazines laying about their living room. When his daddy noticed this interest, he started subscribing to various magazines. Chidi reminisced:

> I loved reading the newspapers, and I read all the magazines. Now I know it was Daddy's way of tricking me into reading and loving reading.[14]

Chinua himself had on a number of occasions, made reference to the deal he made with his youngest child Nwando, to get her to attend nursery school when they were at Amherst. Apparently Nwando resisted being taken to this nursery school called "Living and Learning." Her parents didn't know why she didn't want to go to that school. They knew she enjoyed listening to stories, so her father promised to tell her stories while driving her to and from school. During the interview, Nwando told the whole "untold story." She had her first traumatic exposure to American racism at that school. There

---

[13] Ikechukwu Achebe, same interview.
[14] Chidi Achebe, same interview.

were only two black children at the school, Nwando and an African American child who didn't look black to Nwando because he had blue eyes. When Nwando realized that they were not treated like the other kids, she reacted the only way she knew how: "I stopped speaking English and just spoke Igbo. They spoke in English, I responded in Igbo." Then the teachers complained to her parents. That was how her parents found out what was happening. They told the teachers that she had been learning both languages and could speak both. In the end, the problem was somehow solved.

Nwando heard more stories than her siblings because she stayed the longest with their parents. "Most of my memories are stories," she said. Before going to bed at night she listened to stories. She liked especially those with songs and refrains that she could join in singing. Very often her father read to her. When the stories failed to send her to sleep, her parents took her for a drive and told her stories until she fell asleep and they put her to bed.

Chinua did not only tell stories and read to his children. He took very active part in toilet training. When the family returned to Nigeria, Nwando was about six years old. She recalled her father's role in her life at that time:

> My memories were also of stories and of my dad tucking me in at night. He used to come and get me up at night to pee three or four times. If he didn't come, I would pee in bed. He used to carry me to the bathroom.

As a teenager, she noted how deeply her father cared about being there when his children needed him. She was seventeen when her appendix was taken out. That day, her father cancelled his trip to be by her bedside. She said:

> When I woke up, his were the first pair of eyes I saw by my side. I was struggling and they were holding down my legs. So he has always been there for me.[15]

At the time when it was not fashionable for an African man to "stoop" to such "effeminate" chores as toilet training and story telling, Chinua took time with each of his children and carried out those chores. By so doing, he spent priceless quality time with his children. From the testimonies of his children and their relatives, Chinua did not treat his children in ways that made them feel special or different from other

---

[15] Nwando Achebe, same interview.

children. Tochukwu gave an example of how his uncle sent his children to Enugu, where they lined up for hours to get application forms for one examination or the other.

> Yet, this man can drive to the exam office and take as many application forms as he wanted. He can have them bring the forms to his house. But he will not use his position that way. He will send his children to suffer like others. He wants each man to make himself.[16]

Unlike many Africans in their social class, the Achebes hardly use househelp. This is not because they have anything against it. In fact, they once had uniformed stewards, and gardeners. They had also lived with a number of their relatives who helped with housework. But all the paid or unpaid helpers were treated like family members. As Ethel Momah observed," Christie is very considerate of those who live with her. She gives her servants the opportunity to rise in life." Most of their relatives who served them, have been helped to come to the United States to study. On the whole, house help "is something we don't depend on," said Chinua. Even with his limited mobility, Chinua and his wife have continued to do everything by themselves. Christie does most of the housework and tends her garden and lawn. Chinua still helps with some chores.

When he was a child, Chinua often heard his mother say: "Any woman who leaves her children and sends only the servant to do chores and run errands, is raising the servant." Because of what Chinua learned from his mother, he made sure that he and his wife involved their children in house chores and in that way they raised their children instead of their servants.

Ethel Momah shared her observation of the Achebe family:

> If you see them in a family setting, you will enjoy them more. Even in cooking, all the children take part; everyone has a function to carry out.[17]

In the way that Chinua and his wife handled their children, one noticed a balancing of firmness and gentleness, love and care of one's children. Chidi spoke of their father's love for them:

> My father is very good to us. There's nothing we ask that he wouldn't do for us. My mom used to tease us by saying 'if I want

---

[16] Tochukwu Achebe, interview with Egejuru
[17] Ethel Momah, interview with Egejuru.

anything, I tell him it is for you people.' That's why we are in a hurry to finish our studies so we can start giving back to our parents. At this stage we should be the ones doing things for them, that's what we are looking forward to.[18]

One of the commonest causes of conflict between parents and children is in choosing fields of study and careers for their children. The Achebes didn't have to deal with this type of conflict because they allowed their children to choose their own fields of study and careers. Ikechukwu observed that when it came to issues of studies and careers,

> Our father doesn't like to be obtrusive. He doesn't like to make statements or say things that would sway you one way or the other. He believes very much that development for each individual is different. But if you ask him what he thinks about what you are considering doing, he will answer you and give you all the directions which he feels a father should give his son.[19]

Ikechukwu started out with Political Science and Literature, but he ended up doing a doctorate in History at Cambridge. Chidi said he unconsciously tried to run as far away as possible from his father's field. Therefore, he went into Medicine. Chidi added:

> Even in this medicine I am doing, he asked me, 'are you sure you can do it? It's not an easy ride!' He knows that when you get into what you want to do, you will do well, and he will support you.[20]

Speaking about their mother, Chinelo said:

> Like my father, she doesn't impose her views. Especially now, she lets me be my own person. Ikechukwu is doing his own thing, so is Chidi. Nwando is grown, married, going to conferences. We are just living normal lives.[21]

That Achebe's children are living normal lives is due to their upbringing. As his son observed, Chinua puts much of his energy into his family. Thus, he is successful in separating family and business. When his children were younger, he shielded them from his fame and public glare.

---

[18] Chidi Achebe interview with Egejuru.
[19] Ikechukwu Achebe, same interview.
[20] Chidi Achebe, same interview.
[21] Chinelo Achebe, interview with Egejuru.

Nevertheless, it was inevitable for the children to sense or notice that there was something different about their father. For instance, when young Chinelo noticed the frequency and number of journalists, pressmen and foreigners who came to see her father, she sensed that her father "was a little different from other people." Likewise, a grown up Ikechukwu realized that "our father *bu onye n'ewu ewu* (famous) in a real sense."

The children were asked if they didn't sometimes think about their father's fame; if it didn't get into their heads. Chinelo responded, "The way he carries himself at home doesn't give us the opportunity to think of him in that way." Ikechukwu noticed that their father's fame drew attention to the family. After a while, they accepted the fame as real and learned to live with it. "I personally cope with his fame by his own example," said Ikechukwu. Chidi equally admitted: "We know our father is very special and blessed. Sometimes, we are frightened by the way people view him. But we know he is very human." Nwando also feels that her " father's success is a blessing from God, and if you recognize that this unique gift is coming from God, it is easier to deal with. I learned to take it in stride."

Naturally, there were some instances when Achebe's children had to identify themselves for one reason or the other. In some of those instances, they were treated either as royalty or as impostors. By following their parents' example of not letting fame get into their heads, they forced people to recognize them as fellow human beings.

Some of Chinua's friends look at him as a good model for parenting. They comment on his relationship with his children, especially with his oldest son. Ejike noted: "Chinua's relation with his son is enviable. To be on the same wave length with your son is not common."

Since Chinua doesn't like to talk about his personal relationships, or his role in the family, one had to rely on the testimony of his children and close friends. It was his son Ikechukwu who shed light on his father's attitude to family. Looking back at his earliest memories of his father's interaction with his nuclear family, Ikechukwu stated:

> His family is central to his life as a man and it is very strong. Children and wife are very important to him. And if there is anything that could hurt his feelings deeply, it will be something that threatens his family, because that's where he puts most of his feelings and energy. His extended family is equally important to him. So, I see him as a family man first and foremost. When you look at him, you know he is your father, and that's it. That's the way he comes across, simply by separating family and business as

much as possible. He makes a lot of sacrifices for his family without talking.

Ikechukwu also confirmed what his father had implied when he stated that asking him to name his favourite novel was like asking him to name his favourite child.

> I really don't believe he has a favourite child. He navigates among his children, encouraging strong points in each of them. The same can be said about my mother.

Chinua and his wife made sure they grounded their children in Igbo culture. For instance, in most African families living in Europe, Canada and the United States, their children born in these foreign countries, do not speak the African languages of their parents. Indeed, most African children who live in urban cities of Africa do not speak the native tongues of their parents. This is not the case for the Achebe children. Ikechukwu said:

> When we were at Nsukka, they spoke Igbo to us. There was no need to discontinue when we came to America. They told us we were strangers in America and we would have to go home. Telling stories to us in Igbo was very important to them, because Igbo tradition and culture were important to them. We were supposed to know our culture.[22]

As if to demonstrate his commitment to Igbo culture, Chinua performed a very fatherly act of initiating his sons into the Ogidi masquerade cult. "He made a point of initiating us into *Mmanwu Ogidi*," said Ikechukwu. "He believes we should be a part of it." This was something that Chinua's own father, Isaiah Achebe could not have tolerated let alone done for his own sons. It was much later that Isaiah saw the need for culture and tradition.

It is an understatement to say that Chinua's family is very close. We often hear people say "it's a close family", implying that closeness in a family is rare. Nwando finds it funny when people say that a family is close. To the Achebes, family means being close.

"To us, there is nothing that seems too close. That's just the way it has been." said Nwando. However, as with most families facing one crisis or another, the family of Chinua Achebe has become much closer since his accident. They have had their priorities juggled. To the entire family, their father's recovery remains a miracle and a second chance at

---

[22] Ikechukwu Achebe, same interview.

life. Therefore, they are making the most of the time they can spend together. For instance, as soon as Chidi and Nwando heard of their father's accident, they dropped out of school for the rest of the quarter and flew to England to be with their parents at the hospital.

And how does one speak of a wife leaving everything to stay by her husband's bedside from the time she heard of the accident to the time he was discharged, months later? Mrs. Achebe did not just sit by her husband's bedside, she actively participated in the nursing care, and sometimes she had to interfere with some treatment procedure. There are very few women with promising careers, who would abandon everything to be with a sick husband. Most wives or husbands would be content to let the health care givers do their job, while they paid visits to the sick spouse.

Speaking about the impact of the accident on the family, Chidi said:

> It was emotionally painful for the family to watch him go through nine months of therapy and rehabilitation. Since his recovery, we have had time to reassess some of the things one feels to be important. For instance, you take for granted that your father is alive and available whenever you need him. Since the accident, we have started to understand that everyday is a blessing, that's the way we look at him now. He is extremely special and valuable to us. We can't even begin to talk about how we would bend backwards to do things for them. That's part of the reason I rush down here any time I have a break from school.[23]

The same is true for the rest of the children. Hardly a month after her wedding, Nwando was back with her parents at Bard. "What are you doing here soon after your wedding?" she was asked. "Well, there was one week left of my vacation before I got married, so I have come to take it." Chinelo had her wedding in her parent's home at Bard. She came back there to have her first child. Her parents were the first to hold the baby and name her, before she received the rest of her names from her paternal grandparents in Nigeria. Chinua named the baby Chinwe, in honor of his wife, and Christie named her Buzochochukwu -seek God first.

Equally important to Chinua is his extended family. No one seemed to have any negative things to say about him as a brother or an uncle. His siblings described him as the peace-loving man who eschews trouble. "*O daa acho okwu* -he does not look for trouble," they repeated over and over again. And when the accident happened, they all felt it was unfair that such a thing should happen to Chinua. They

---

[23] Chidi Achebe, same interview.

would easily have changed places with him. His brothers, Frank and John broke into tears at the thought of Chinua dying before them. "What I am begging God is that I should not be the one to bury Chinua. He should be the one to bury me," said his brother John in between sobs.[24]

John's prayers that Chinua should bury him were answered; John died in March 2000, roughly seven months after he and Chinua were reunited at Ogidi in August 1999. He was the only sibling who had not seen Chinua since the accident in 1990.

Commenting on the unexpected death of his brother John, Chinua said:

> He seemed to have been waiting for my return. I was told that he kept asking, 'when is he coming, when is he coming.' And he looked quite well when I saw him.[25]

Chinua's nephews spoke of him in glowing terms. Oyibo Achebe said this of him:

> His sense of family is very keen. He used to spend his vacations at home to be with his parents. Now, he keeps the memory of his parents alive, he talks about them a great deal. It's a real privilege to be associated with him.[26]

Oyibo also related his experience at the secondary school. Just because he was an Achebe, he enjoyed certain privileges and other students courted his friendship. "Being his relative is a challenging role" he said, "But also a badge of honor which you have to wear with pride."

Jane Achebe experienced the challenge of being Chinua's relative. When she arrived at the secondary school where she was supposed to teach biochemistry, the principal reassigned her to teach literature when he learned she was Chinua's niece. She admitted that, "It has been more of an advantage being related to him. People attend to you when you mention that name."

Tochukwu remembered his uncle's visits:

> Whenever he visited us we were very happy, and we tugged at him. That relationship continues and there is nobody in the family who does not like him. When I was in secondary school he helped me a

---

[24] Rev. John Achebe, interview with Egejuru
[25] Chinua Achebe, telephone conversation with Egejuru.
[26] Oyibo Achebe, interview with Egejuru.

lot. Sometimes I would go to him at Nsukka for pocket money and he would give me. He did this for everybody, not me alone. He helped our most senior brother to go to the U.S. He still gives money to our mother from time to time.[27]

Another nephew, Emeka Okocha, gave an example of how Chinua meticulously followed what went on in the lives of his nephews and nieces. At one point, Chinua had seven nephews at the University of Nigeria, Nsukka. Emeka said:

> He could locate everybody's room in different buildings. He would come and look for us in the hostel. So, through him, some of us became famous. Once he came to see four of us together and the people around were excited for us and that boosted our morale. I cannot ask for more. He has been the shinning star in our family and the family has so much love for him.[28]

Dr. John Achebe also talked about his uncle's interest in his nephews and nieces:

> His interest is in school and hard work; he looks at results and report cards. He caught it when I dropped from a better position, and he reminded me that I did better previously. He praises you for doing well and points out your poor performance.[29]

Like his sister Jane, Dr. John Achebe faced the challenge of being Chinua's relative. He was compelled to read *Things Fall Apart* because a teacher wanted to hear of Chinua's background. He admitted that his uncle's name rubbed off on them positively.

Professor Nnaemeka Ikpeze recalled his childhood memories of his uncle:

> He used to spend holidays at our house. He would chop firewood, pluck feathers off chicken and clean the chicken for stew. He taught me to take cod liver oil to strengthen my bones. He used to give us kids treats like biscuits and lumps of sugar, and he used to carry me on his bicycle. Even when I was in the secondary school he wrote me letters. In one of his letters he enclosed ten shillings as pocket money. He assured me that if I didn't get a scholarship for University he would pay my school fees, but I got a scholarship.[30]

---

[27] Tochukwu Achebe, interview with Egejuru.
[28] Emeka Okocha, same interview.
[29] Dr. John U. Achebe, interview with Egejuru.
[30] Nnaemeka Ikpeze, interview with Egejuru

It wasn't only by giving them material gifts or inviting them on holidays that Chinua helped his extended family members. Without exception, they all acknowledged the power of his name. "His name opens doors", said Nnaemeka. And Tochukwu said, "It is fantastic being his relative. I am well received all over Ogidi because of Chinua. With his name alone I can gain admission to any family or function."

Ernest Achebe is Chinua's cousin. Ernest is blind and he referred to Chinua as "the eye with which I see." Ernest also recalled that Chinua spent some holidays with them when he was in school. Chinua helped him get into the school for the blind. When he graduated, he got a job as an artist in the broadcasting establishment. "My relationship to him helped me in my own career," he said.

Chinua's sisters-in-law, Mrs. Agnes Achebe and Mrs. Lucy Achebe sang his praises. Agnes never had cause to complain about Chinua. She has never known him to say no to a request and he buys her the best of presents. "I pass on the way with his name", she said. "When I am introduced, people ask, 'is it Chinua's Achebe?' and I proudly say he is my husband. He is my pathfinder. I take Chinua as my younger brother, not as a brother-in-law."

Mrs. Lucy Achebe developed a special relationship with Chinua when he was still very young and before his brother John married Lucy. Probably because of that and his attachment to his brother John, Chinua spent most of his vacations with sister-in-law Lucy and his brother John. Lucy said:

> He is not the type that sneaks around and sniffs out how you live with his brother. I cannot think of any time that Chinua wronged me. I feel quite happy to be associated with Chinua. There are advantages in being related to him, but sometimes I don't know whether it is advantage or responsibility.[31]

She narrated her experience when a white man suddenly appeared at the school where she was teaching. She was whisked into the white man's car to show him round her kindred. Nonetheless, she enjoys the privileges of being related to Chinua.

Chinua and his family are devout Christians. Some people would say that's how it should be, considering the background and upbringing of Chinua. It is assumed that one who is brought up in a devout Christian household as Chinua was, automatically remained a devout Christian. But we know that it doesn't always work out that way. Some of Chinua's relatives were aware of the possibility of his losing faith

---

[31] Mrs. Lucy Achebe, interview with Egejuru.

when he joined the civil service. His sister-in-law, Mrs. Lucy Achebe remembered: "When he was employed at NBC, we were afraid for his faith because civil servants are taken to be heathens. But he didn't lose his faith." On the other hand, his brother-in-law, Dr. Sam Okoli wondered if Chinua's concept of the white man had affected his Christian faith. Dr. Okoli said:

> I think his original Christian ideas have changed. The way he treated the missionaries in his novel gives me the impression that he has no regard for the Christian religion.[32]

Indeed, many readers of *Things Fall Apart* came away with the same impression as Chinua's brother-in-law. The reality is that Chinua never lost his Christian faith. If anything, he has maintained a close walk with God. Just as the accident brought his family much closer, it also brought them all much closer to God. His miraculous recovery from the injury made his family juggle their priorities, not only in their relationship with one another, but in their relationship with God. If they had any doubts of God's presence in their lives, the accident reassured them. The accident became a sort of litmus test for the name, Chinualumogu. Therefore, God came to fight on his behalf. As an eyewitness to the accident, Ikechukwu had this to say:

> When I look back, I thank God and that's the only sentiment that comes to me, just thanks, because to survive being crushed under a car, is a great thing. So, I am very grateful to God.[33]

Referring to the source of their spiritual strength during the trying period of their father's hospitalization, Chidi said: "We turned to God and the scriptures." He talked about an incident in which someone had asked their mother, "What makes you tick?" and their mother replied, "Nothing makes me tick, God ticks me."[34]

Friends of the Achebes marvel at the way Christie handled the entire situation of her husband's accident. Not many people would understand what it takes to care for someone in a wheel chair. Yet, Christie carries on as if she had been preparing for this "new" lifestyle all her life. Her friend, Ethel Momah said, "Christie is not an angel, but all she has been through since her husband's accident brings her nearer to perfection." Both her children and her friends are certain that her faith in God helps her cope with the situation. She leads her family in

---

[32] Dr. Sam Okoli, interview with Egejuru.
[33] Ikechukwu Achebe, interview with Egejuru.
[34] Chidi Achebe, interview with Egejuru.

their close walk with God. Chinua with his household remains loyal to his Christian upbringing. He and his family are practicing Christians and their spirituality is genuine.

An oral biography a

Isaiah Okafor Achebe, Chinua's father
Courtesy: Rev. John Achebe

Janet Nwanene Achebe, Chinua's mother
Courtesy: Rev. John Achebe

Original compound of Isaiah Achebe at Ikenga Ogidi; known today as "The Headquarters" and occupied by Frank Achebe (first son) and his branch of the Achebe clan.
Photo by Phanuel Egejuru, 1995

*Rev. John Achebe, (Chinua's elder brother whom
he served as a houseboy)*
Photo by Phanuel Egejuru

An oral biography

Mrs. Zinobia Ikpeze (Chinua's elder sister who was his wet-nurse – like a mother to him)
Permission by Mrs. Z. Ikpeze

Photo by Pahnual Egejuru

f   Chinua Achebe: pure and simple

Adrian Slater (Chinua's English tutor at Government College, Umuahia)
Photo by Phanuel Egejuru, 1995

Chinua's Matriculation at University College, Ibadan, 1948

Chinua Achebe: pure and simple

University Herald Editorial Board, 1952-3, from left to right, Chinua Achebe, Chukwuemeka Ike, Mabel Segun, D. Oforiokuma, Agu Ogan and Akio Abbey
Photo with permission of Chinua Achebe, courtesy of Indiana University Press

An oral biography

Send-off picture for John Munonye, 1952. From left to right, Achebe, Adi, Munonye, Ezilo, Nsolo
Courtesy of John Munonye

j   Chima Achebe: pure and simple

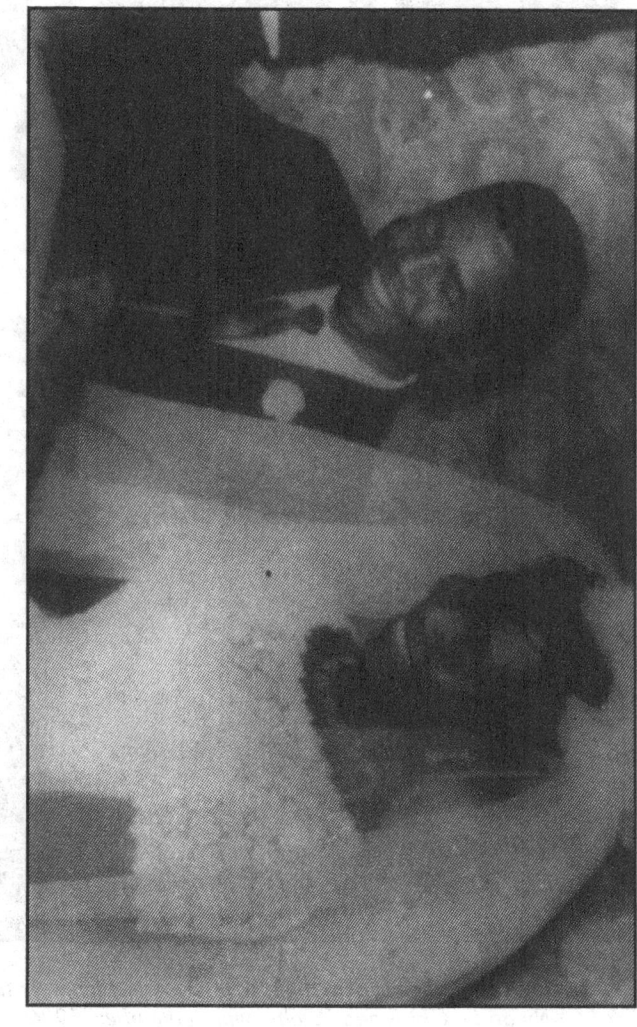

Chinua and Christie signing the Marriage Registry in the Chapel of Resurrection, University College Ibadan, September 1961

Photo with permission of Chinua and Christie Achebe

Chinua and Christie Achebe on their silver wedding anniversary with Nwando, Chidi and Ikechukwu, September, 1986
Photo: Mike's Photos, Nsukka, with permission of Chinua Achebe, Courtesy of Indiana University Press

1 Chimua Achebe: pure and simple

Chinua's compound at Ikenga Ogidi
Photo by Phanuel Egejiuru, 1995 with permission of Chinua

An oral biography iii

Inside Achebe's compound, newly built, wheelchair accessible bungalow next to the old two story building

Photo: Phanuel Egejuru with permission of Chinua Achebe

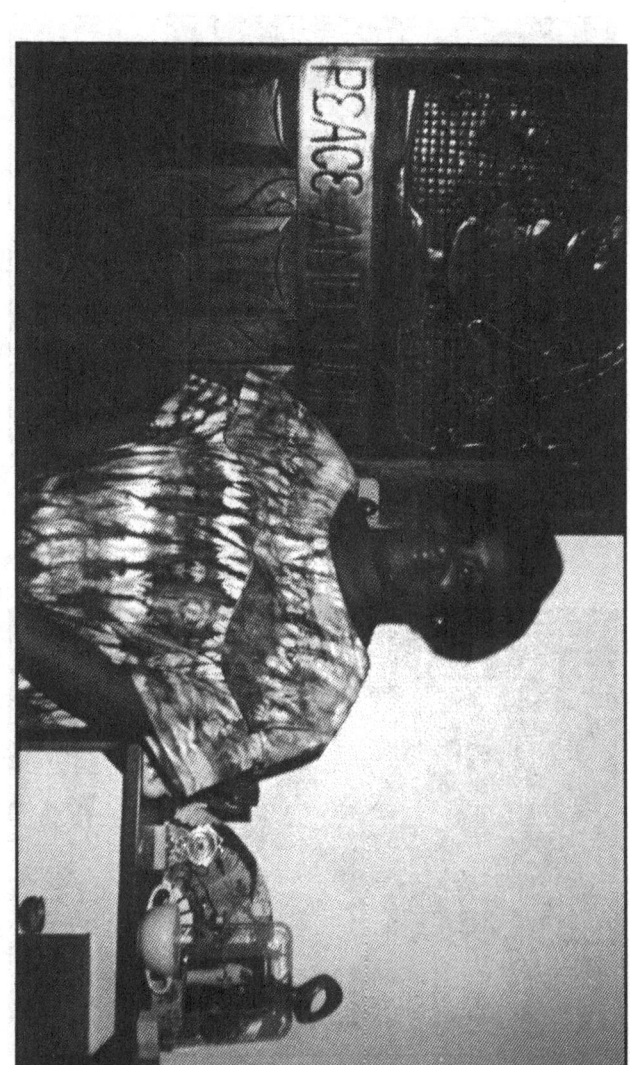

Chinelo Achebe-Ejiunyitchie, Lagos 1995
Photo by Phanuel Egejuru with permission of Chinelo

An oral biography

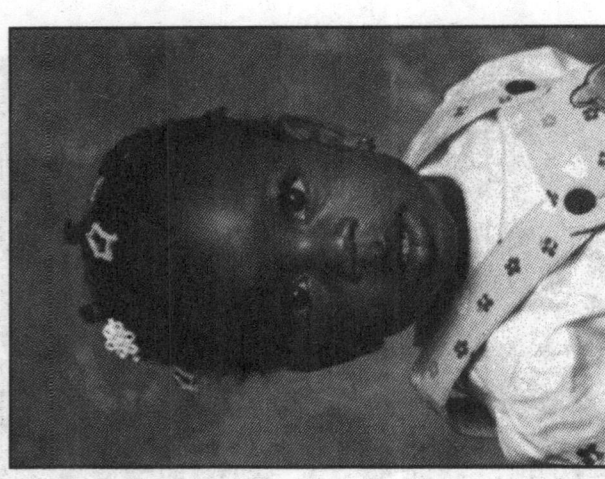

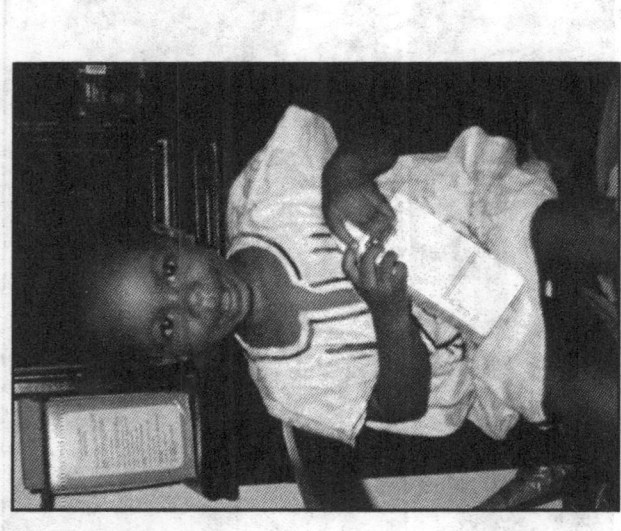

Buzodudukwu Ejunyitchie, first grandchild of Chinua and Christie Achebe from daughter Chinelo
Photo by P. Egejuru, 1995 with permission of Chinelo

Chinonyelum Ekwueme, second grandchild of Chinua & Christie Achebe from daughter Nwando
Photo with permission of Nwando Achebe-Ekwueme

p   Chinua Achebe: pure and simple

The Paddocks Hospital (Buckinghamshire, England) where Chinua was treated after the car accident in
Nigeria in March 1990
Photo by Phanuel Egejuru

Customized, wheelchair-accessible bungalow built for Chinua and his family by Bard College in Annandale-on-Hudson, NY

Photo: Phanuel Egejuru, 1996 with permission of Chinua Achebe

r Chinua Achebe: pure and simple

St. Phillips Anglican Church, Ogidi founded by Isaih Okafor Achebe
Photo by Pahnuel Egejuru, 1995

An oral biography s

Johnson Okudo (a centenarian) a.k.a Nwawuluaru. Chinua's mentor for Igbo Culture & Tradition

Photo by Phanuel Egejuru, 1995

1 Chinua Achebe: pure and simple

Chinua giving a public lecture at Loyola University, New Orleans, 1992
Photo by Harold Baquet, Loyola University

Chinua listening to a comment from the audience at a public lecture at Loyola University, New Orleans, 1992

Photo by Harold Baquet, Loyola University

Chinua Achebe: pure and simple

Chinua at an informal discussion with students at Loyola University, New Orleans
Photo by Harold Baquet, Loyola University, 1992

Chinua receives Doctor of Humane Letters from Syracuse University, 1998. From left: Kenneth A. Shaw (Chancellor of Syracuse University), Robert Fulghum, Chinua Achebe, Elizabeth Carnegie, Douglas Barclay and a member of Trustee

Photo by permission of Syracuse University, Office of Special Events, 1998

x   Chinua Achebe: pure and simple

Celebrating 40th Anniversary of Things Fall Apart
Chinua Achebe and Phanuel Egejuru, African Literature Association
Conference, Austin, Texas, 1998

Courtesy of Marie Umeh

13

Chinua: a big *alusi*

With the word, *ALUSI*, Reuben Alumona tried to capture the enigmatic nature of Chinua's personality, especially the vastness of his wisdom. For lack of a better rendition, *alusi* could be called a fetish. The Igbo people create some complicated and mystifying object that is supposedly charged with mysterious powers. They call this object, *alusi*. An *alusi* could be small or large but the larger it is, the more mysterious its nature and powers. For Reuben and perhaps for some other people, Chinua is a big a*lusi*. One may puzzle over Chinua as one does an *alusi*, but one can never figure him out. Yet, the urge persists to figure Chinua out or evaluate his character somehow.

How do we deal with the complex non-physical component known as character? We may have interviews or hold conversations with a person. However, these do not provide enough grounds for character evaluation. It takes years of association and observation to speak confidently of a person's character. Therefore, the views of those close to Chinua and those who have had long associations with him are crucial to our understanding of his character. Sometimes the views of those outside his family and friendship circles are also very important. As objective outsiders, their views can underwrite and validate the views of insiders.

Man of wisdom

Starting from elementary school through grammar school, Chinua's intellectual performance was legendary. Most of his friends back then viewed him as the wise one among them. A childhood friend from Ogidi, Dr. Agulefo said of Chinua, "He was born with God's wisdom. From our youth till today, he has been known as a man of few words. He talks much sense in a few words."[1]

---

[1] Dr. N.T.C. Agulefo, correspondence with Egejuru.

As a young man at the university, Chinua's deportment reminded his classmates of village elders. Bola Ige spoke enthusiastically of Chinua's brilliance, but he was more intrigued by his wisdom. He described Chinua this way:

> Chinua is the epitome of the deep thinker. Many of us had never thought of him as belonging to our class. He always behaved like an old man and I think he must have come before, taken an *ozo* title, died and then came back. When I read the things he writes, I wonder if he goes to the meeting of the old people.[2]

Another classmate, Frank Ellah also marvelled at the way Chinua conducted himself like an elder though he was young. Ellah said: "He had an interesting way of looking at things in a way others didn't."

It was because Reuben couldn't find adequate words to describe the totality of Chinua's wisdom, that he resorted to the *alusi* imagery. Reuben said:

> A big man is like a big *aluis*. You can't figure out Professor Achebe. If nothing else let it be his wisdom. If you put forward the left foot or the right foot, Prof. knows. Whatever you are doing and think he doesn't know, he knows. If he sends you with the car and you go somewhere else, he knows. If he doesn't tell you, it doesn't mean he doesn't know that you went somewhere else. Prof. reads people like book.[3]

Perhaps the ability to read people may count as wisdom. One thing is clear about Chinua's gift of reading people; it is different from a psychologist's reading of man or animal behaviour. Chinua's knowledge of people is purely empirical. He pays close attention to people because of his interest and concern for his fellow human beings.

To his Igbo peers, Chinua's copious and appropriate use of proverbs, is the finest demonstration of innate wisdom. The ultimate mark of wisdom for an Igbo elder is the ability to combine in proper context, all the varied elements of traditional discourse. Chinua is a sage in the Igbo understanding of that term. Sages have immense knowledge of things and they make a lot of contribution to leadership. The village sage is undemonstrative, he is sedate, deeply reflective. Chinua demonstrates his wisdom by the manner in which he uses to his advantage, knowledge that is available to all. His appropriation of Igbo proverbs is a case in point. He has the ability to use this collective

---

[2] Bola Ige, interview with Egejuru.
[3] Reuben Alumona, interview with Egejuru.

insight in defining the significance of his views. He subsequently puts these views into wider conceptualization, by drawing on collective wisdom embedded in the proverbs.

Proverbs belong to the community but a wise person like Chinua can use it to give pith to his opinion; that makes him an elder and a sage, and that is in fact, how the Igbos define a wise person. Therefore, when Chinua uses proverbs, he does invest what he says with immense authority. In the end, Chinua's native wisdom and humanity are encapsulated in the kinds of proverbs he uses in his works.

Higo believes that Chinua is endowed with a superior intelligence and innate wisdom. He went into details to explain what he meant by innate wisdom:

> I explain his innate wisdom thus: people who are thinking all the time, weighing, balancing, analysing issues and situations in their heads, come up with this type of wisdom. You don't catch them off guard. There seems to be a store of answers; they press the button and the answers come. If you ask Chinua a question, he stalls and then presses the button and the correct answer comes. If you ask him another question, he tells you two or three stories and these stories illustrate the answer he is going to give you. Chinua is a superior intelligence of sorts. All the placidity is the cloth covering a restless soul.[4]

Man of ideas

Chinua's colleagues and friends referred to him severally as a deep thinker, a philosopher, a man of ideas, and a prophet in our time. While it was difficult for respondents to pinpoint the elements that distinguished one as a philosopher or a prophet in our time, it was fairly easy to provide concrete examples of a man of ideas.

Early in his career in broadcasting, Chinua's colleagues identified him as a young man of ideas. Michael Olumide recalled that Chinua always spoke with clarity at meetings. He added:

> It was not really his diction but his ideas were very clear. In broadcasting, we talk of dreamers, this was Achebe's specialty. He was an idea's man, to the extent he was able to manage a big division. He was good in getting hold of ideas, and he ran the department extremely well.[5]

---

[4] Aigboje Higo, interview with Egejuru.
[5] Michael Olumide, interview with Egejuru.

The managing director of Fourth Dimension Publishing Co, Victor Nwankwo, had no problem proving why he called Chinua a man of ideas. It all began when the two brothers, Arthur and Victor Nwankwo, were groping and searching for an appropriate name for the their company. And in what appeared to be a normal conversation, Chinua came up with a definitive philosophy for the company. Nwankwo explained:

> He had this crisp enunciation of a Fourth Dimension philosophy that immediately did it for me. In a nutshell, the Fourth Dimension is the other dimension to make things work. It is the power of mind over material things, the sustenance of man in the use of material, money, management and progress. This is the Fourth Dimension, that extra dynamic force without which the third physical dimension would just be an ordinary inert lump.[6]

These might not be the exact words that Chinua used in expounding his Fourth Dimension philosophy, yet the very idea itself is quite unique. Just as he did it for the Mbari Club, Chinua named the Fourth Dimension publishing company for its proprietor.

It's a well-known fact that Chinua experimented with the idea of publishing when he collaborated with Christopher Okigbo to establish the Citadel publishing house in the mid sixties. As short-lived as that venture was, the fact that Chinua went into it was an inspiration to future publishers like Arthur Nwankwo. Nwankwo remarked that Chinua has never been a hesitant player in the publishing venture, because he believes that Africa should have a strong publishing house. And speaking about the board members of his company, he said of Chinua, "He alone understood the need for enormous capital investment in publishing."

Probably the first great service of Heinemann to African literature was the publication of *Things Fall Apart*. The second would be the establishment of *African Writers Series*. For the ten years that Chinua edited the Series, his name came to be very closely associated with it. When he was credited with initiating the venture, he quickly put the record straight:

> It wasn't even my idea, I was there; I had written the first book that gave this notion to my publishers who said, 'if this book is there, why wouldn't there be other books?' I was there and it was pushed to me. I did what I could for ten years.[7]

---

[6] Victor Nwankwo, interview with Egejuru.
[7] Chinua, interview with Egejuru.

African Writers Series became a profitable venture for its publishers and for consumers of African literature, because its first editor, Chinua brought his wealth of publishing ideas to the project.

Three prominent Nigerians scholars, S.J.Cookey, Ikenna Nzimiro, and E.N. Obiechina worked together with Chinua in the task of providing an ideological basis for the existence of Biafra. They had to crystallize the idea of nationhood to the Biafrans themselves. Each of the three learned men identified Chinua as the main man of ideas in their committee. They said that Chinua most often came up with brilliant ideas that other members examined, debated, and most often accepted. Nzimiro said, "Chinua doesn't say much, but he has talent for seeing things. He knows how to construct ideas, and most of the time he sees ideas and principles, not persons."[8] The end product of the National Guidance Committee's deliberations was the *Ahiara Declaration*, appropriately regarded as Biafra's Manifesto. Chinua was the main architect of that document. All three members of the committee stated that it was distilled from a paper titled, "What is Social Justice" written earlier by Chinua.

Speaking about the same document S.J. Cookey said:

> Reading it today, one cannot fail to detect the attempt to have an underlying current of Africaness and Biafraness in the document, and that was a genuine contribution, in part attributable to Chinua.[9]

Chinua always tries to limit the impact of his contributions and credits given to him. He spoke of the same document thus:

> It was a hodgepodge of ideas and not as clear as I would have wanted. And this was because we wrote this in a kind of struggle with Ojukwu, you put this, he removed it. It was a balancing act to get something that would declare where we stood, why we were fighting, what would happen at the end if we won. And how the ordinary people would be affected.[10]

Despite the compromise, the document was a resounding success. It was unveiled and read to the Biafran people, inside a church at Ahiara. That day, while it was being read Chinua was hovering at the edges of the crowd to catch what the people were saying in reaction. He noted, "there was just jubilation. I heard someone say, *'o di ka si gbabia a*

---

[8] Ikenna Nzimiro, interview with Egejuru
[9] S.J. Cookey, interview with Egejuru.
[10] Chinua, interview with Egejuru.

gbaba.'" It was not just music to the ears, it was music that invited one to dance.

John Munonye was among Chinua's friends at Ibadan and they remained friends till John's death in 1999. Munonye described Chinua as the silent one and the genius in their group. "Are you suggesting a superhuman intelligence?" he was asked. He replied:

> He is human quite alright, but when he is presenting ideas, he loses his humanity; his spiritness comes out. He is doing the world a favour by remaining the man he is; he's a philosopher, not just a novelist.[11]

While the Biafran war was raging, Chinua was nursing another idea he would put into effect at the end of the war. This was the idea of harnessing the pent up creative energy of Igbo artists. Chinua recalled what went on in his mind:

> I felt we needed a magazine, because all around me were people who had this strange experience of the war, writing about it, talking about it; there are new poets with new ideas. Why don't we have a magazine for them? I asked.[12]

And that's how the idea of *Okike* magazine was born. Even the Igbo word, *Okike* – Creativity - is charged with cosmic overtones of imposing order upon chaos.

In 1989, Chinua was in the forefront of a select group of scholars, artists and humanists of African descent. They came up with the idea of a global black literary journal called *African Commentary: A Journal for People of African Descent*. It fell to none other than Chinua to articulate the mission of the journal. His ideas of what the journal stood for, appeared in the forward of its maiden issue published in Oct. 1989. Perhaps it was a coincidence that the journal folded up at the time Chinua had the automobile accident. It seemed that those who should have carried on in Chinua's absence had other ideas. Anyone, who had the fortune of acquiring the first couple of issues of the journal, can attest to the very high quality of articles contributed by the very best of black scholars and artists across the globe.

Perhaps, the greatest milestone in the history of Nigerian literature is the launching of a Club for Writers and Artists at Ibadan in March 1961. The founding members included Wole Soyinka, Chris Okigbo, J.P. Clark, Eskia Mphahele, Ulli Beier, Dema Nwoko, Chinua Achebe, Uche Okeke, Ralph Opara, Yemi Jaodu, and a few others. Many of

---

[11] John Munonye, interview with Egejuru.
[12] Chinua, same interview.

these members lived in Ibadan while Chinua lived in Lagos. Consequently Chinua was often absent when the others held meetings at Ibadan.

The group needed an appropriate name for their club. Soyinka initially suggested the Igbo word *ala* but he was outvoted. He then came up with a Yoruba name, *Orisun Abamoda*, which was adopted. Chinua was not at the meeting that day. J.P. Clark took the news of the name to him. Chinua objected to the name because it was Yoruba. He claimed it did not represent the entire country. Then Chinua called Ulli Beier on the phone and suggested the name *Mbari*, an Igbo word! At a meeting in Clark's office, Beier told Clark, Soyinka and Okigbo that Chinua had come up with the word *Mbari*. It was in that office that the four men decided to adopt *Mbari* for their Club's name. So, there was Chinua objecting to a Yoruba name, yet suggesting an Igbo one. Soyinka said, jokingly, "there was a conspiracy because it was very undemocratic."[13]

Recalling how they were groping about for a name for their club, Beier said,

> Wole suggested *Ori Olokun*, but I felt it didn't roll over the tongue fast enough. But when Chinua said '*Mbari*,' I knew immediately that this was it, and in my enthusiasm, I found it easy to persuade the others.[14]

Why didn't other members of the club object to the word *Mbari*? Could it be that the others were more liberal in their views? Could it be that they found *Mbari* the most appropriate name after Chinua expounded on the significance and depth of its meaning? Whatever their reason, Chinua's *Mbari* idea stuck, even as it collided with his own sense of fairness. And as if in conscious justification of his choice of *Mbari*, Chinua has continued to couch most of his lectures on African concept of art, in the *Mbari* tradition. Just as he appropriated the communal wisdom of Igbo proverbs, to create a specific mode of narrative discourse in his novels, he has created out of *Mbari*, the powerful metaphor of acknowledging and registering every presence in human society.

In the same way that proverbs provided him with the means of exposing a wide range of African philosophy, *Mbari* provided the platform for exploring the Igbo concept of art. Chinua is not the only Igbo person who knows about *Mbari*. In fact, he probably wouldn't have seen any *Mbari* exhibit if he had not spent his final year of primary school at Nekede. Chinua's part of Igbo land did not have the

---

[13] Wole Soyinka, interview with Egejuru.
[14] Ulli Beier, correspondence with Egejuru.

Mbari tradition. It was purely by chance that Chinua found himself in Owerri and then the *Mbari* tradition. However, it would take a man of Chinua's depth of thinking to reach back into his childhood, retrieve and propound a concept that would affect how the world thinks of Igbo art. Though Owerri people no longer observe the *Mbari* tradition, they know the significance of *Mbari*. Yet, they were not the ones to articulate the complex meaning of *Mbari*. It was Chinua who did it.

Through *Mbari* art, the community documents old and incorporates newly occurred events. In this respect, *Mbari* is in fact, the opposite of western academy or museum whose collections remain static if not stale. It would also take Chinua to articulate the aesthetically charged application of *Mbari*, as a creative process that expresses in moulded clay, the life of the community, and thus ensures its survival.

Often and again, Chinua uses the *Mbari* analogy to demonstrate how the African acknowledges and indeed, celebrates every presence in his world. This presence, Chinua keeps reminding his readers, includes the white man with his colonial baggage.

It is true that the *Mbari* club was literally killed by the Nigerian civil war, but the idea of an association of literary artists survived and lay dormant for more than ten years after the civil war. After the war, some of the writers were estranged from one another. They all suffered from the rift created by the war, yet they seemed afraid to reclaim their previous oneness. Again, it would take Chinua to acknowledge "this terrible division we had not known before." He saw the urgent need to close that rift and bring the writers together again.

On the surface, Chinua's immediate goal was to bring the writers physically together for re-acquaintance. To this effect, he convened their first meeting at the University of Nigeria, Nsukka, in 1981. However, he had another idea and a hidden agenda. His inner vision had caused him to see that something very dangerous was looming for African writers. Therefore, he felt that Nigerian writers must have a front if they must survive as a group. Chinua said he was actually thinking in terms of a trade union to give some protection to the writers. He disclosed all this to his fellow writers when he spoke to them at that initial meeting of what later became the Association of Nigerian Authors. Today, the Association of Nigerian Authors is a very strong body that tries to protect the interest of its members.

Chinua's ideas can sometimes be challenging and embarrassing. His friend C.C. Momah and his nephew Oyibo, both talked of an incident when a brilliant idea of Chinua's caused them to sit on the edges of their seats. The incident occurred at the inauguration of *Igbo U.S.A.* in 1996. Chinua was the guest speaker. When it was time for him to speak, he started in Igbo. People thought he would switch to English shortly, but he made his whole speech in Igbo. Later, Momah asked why he spoke in Igbo when there were many non-Igbo speakers in the audience. Chinua simply answered, "It's an Igbo gathering, sometimes these things have to be done."[15] It was one of those moments when the situation dictated his choice of language. Indeed, the idea that a meeting of an Igbo Cultural Association in the U.S.A., called for the use of Igbo language, was unnerving to the Igbos who only thought of their foreign guests. Chinua's idea of speaking in Igbo challenged, if not embarrassed some of his Igbo listeners.

On a more domestic front, members of his family hail him as the one who comes up with the brightest ideas. For instance, two of his nephews talked about Chinua's great idea of getting the Achebe clan together for a historic visit to their motherland Awka, in 1985.

They bought a cow and cartons of drinks which they took to their relations at Awka. Their visit caused quite a stir in their motherland. The Awka people were jubilant that the famous writer and his brethren had come to pay homage to their motherland.

When his nephew Dr. John Achebe got married, he specifically asked Chinua to speak for the Achebe family because, "No one ever has a better idea than uncle Chinua."

When Chinua's eldest brother Frank died in 1992, Chinua was unable to attend the funeral in Nigeria. However, he wrote a short farewell letter to his dead brother. The letter was so packed with Chinua's aura and wisdom that it became the centerpiece as well as the news item that visitors carried away. Even when Chinua expresses grief, his wisdom seeps through.

---

[15] Incident recalled by Christian Momah and Oyibo Achebe, in separate interviews with Egejuru

14

A complex simplicity

Simplicity is probably the most striking of Chinua's qualities. Several people told stories that illustrate the man's extraordinary ordinariness. These were stories of how some people felt very disappointed at meeting the man in person for the first time. These people instinctively expected to find this great man decked out in glamorous expensive outfit, sitting in a lavishly laid out drawing room, or sitting at the head of the table at social functions.

Many stories were told about Chinua's disarming simplicity. The most amusing were those in which his simple appearance shocked those meeting him for the first time. V. C. Ike commented on how so many people are amazed at Chinua's ordinariness. He told the story of a Canadian diplomat's amazement at Chinua's simplicity. It was in the early sixties, Ike and this Canadian were attending the same meeting in Lagos. Their group was discussing African literature and Chinua's name was mentioned several times. Finally, the Canadian told Ike that he had been wishing to meet Chinua in person. Ike told him that he could take him to see Chinua. The Canadian didn't believe it could be that easy to just drive up to Chinua's place. There and then Ike phoned Chinua and told him that he was bringing someone to meet him. So, they set out for Chinua's place. When Ike told the visitor that they were getting close to Chinua's house, the visitor took out his comb and combed his hair. He looked into the mirror to make sure he looked his best for the great man. On reaching Chinua's house, they found him in a pair of shorts, waiting for them. Ike said, "the man was shocked, shocked by the ordinariness and simplicity of this great man he was coming to see."[1]

Chinua's sister Grace told a similar story of a young Yoruba man who was doing his national youth service in the Ogidi area. He was very anxious to meet Chinua in person. Mrs. Okocha promised to let him know when her brother would be in town. On the appointed day,

---

[1] V.C. Ike, interview with Egejuru.

the young man appeared in his best suit and waited nervously. Eventually, Chinua appeared. The young man mistook him for one of the people wishing to see Chinua. Then Mrs. Okocha came in and said to the young man, "that's Chinua." The young man exclaimed, "Is this the person?" "He was expecting to see a man dressed to kill, but he only saw a simple fellow," commented Mrs. Okocha. She gave more instances to show how Chinua has remained constant in his simple ways despite his fame:

> His relationship with those he has known from childhood remains the same. People still come to ask about him as they used to, and they would say, 'tell Albert I asked of him,' and when Albert returns, he tours the village on foot, greeting people as he used to do in the old days.[2]

Another family member who is impressed by Chinua's unassuming nature is his sister-in-law, Lucy who said:

> What impresses me the most about Chinua is, with all his greatness, he doesn't know that he is a great man at all. Any time he comes, we still converse with him and talk the same way as of old. He does nothing to draw attention to himself. God created him to be different and important but he does not brag about it nor is he arrogant about it till tomorrow.[3]

To Nigerians who associate greatness with pomposity and flamboyant attire, Chinua is a puzzle. For instance, after several years of seeing Chinua in person at conferences, Egejuru thought she had got used to the big man's habit of appearing in the simplest of clothing. Yet, she too was shocked at his damning simplicity during the Eagle-on-Iroko symposium honouring his sixtieth birthday. It happened on the evening of the last and biggest banquet of the occasion. Egejuru had spent about two hours choosing and tossing aside clothing, looking for the outfit for the occasion. But nothing in her suitcase seemed good enough for the evening. Finally, exhausted and sweating, she decked herself out, albeit, unsatisfied. Arriving at the banquet, she saw the guest of honour in a short sleeved shirt, the type that Nigerians call jumper, made of *abada* or Dutch print cloth. There wasn't even the simplest embroidery round the neckline or the sleeves. Egejuru had expected to see Chinua for once, dressed to kill. After all, it was his birthday and his moment! But he would not make any exceptions, not

---

[2] Mrs. Grace Okocha, interview with Egejuru.
[3] Mrs. Lucy Achebe, interview with Egejuru.

even for this particular birthday, attended by scholars and humanists across the globe. Chinua would not follow the specific code of behaviour and outward appearance expected of people in his class.

It is not only his clothing that testifies to his ordinariness. The way he interacts with people at any level, his habit of engaging in things we do not associate with people of his distinction, all attest to his down-to-earth personality.

Chief Ben Ogbogu told of his wife's reaction on seeing Chinua for the first time. This lady had her first opportunity of meeting Chinua when she and her husband attended the 75th birthday celebration of Chinua's late brother Frank. A big crowd had already gathered when the couple got there. Mrs. Ogbogu started looking at the high table, trying to figure out who was Chinua among the people there. When she couldn't tell which one was Chinua, she asked her husband to point him out. Her husband told her that Chinua wasn't there. A few minutes later, Chief Ogbogu located Chinua sitting among the general public, he pointed him out to his wife. She asked her husband, "why is he sitting there, shouldn't he be sitting at the high table?" Her husband suggested that she ask Chinua that question. So, he took her to meet Chinua. She just couldn't ask that question, instead she asked, "are you the Chinua I have been hearing about?" Chinua said he was. And before she knew it, she fell into conversation with him. She asked about his works, whether he remembered everything he said in each work. Chinua responded to all her questions. When she and her husband returned to their seats, she said to her husband, "Did you see how he was speaking like an ordinary human being? Is that how he really behaves?" Her husband said yes. And in a voice filled with wonder and apprehension, she said to her husband, "*agakpo kwanu nkaa gini*?" meaning, "what does one make of this type of behavior?" To this lady and other Nigerians, important people sit at the high table during social function; they must speak in a way that betrays their status, they must have an unmistakable air of importance that hangs about them. Chief Ogbogu went on to say:

> Chinua combines knowledge with humility and ordinariness. He doesn't carry himself like a man who has become the international identity for Ogidi. Yet, this is a man you will not recognize on the street, because of his simplicity.[4]

One question that interviewees were asked was "What sets Chinua apart from people in his rank?" To this question, Udechukwu answered,

---

[4] Chief Ben Ogbogu, interview with Egejuru.

"he is very simple, he does not mind his position. He mows the lawn, he cooks, does some carpentry and fixes things." He also told the story of a colleague who went to see Chinua at his house. On entering Chiuna's house, the young man saw him in the kitchen cooking. He shouted, "*Oga*, you are cooking?" and Chinua told him there was nobody in the house, so he had to cook. This man couldn't wait to tell Udechukwu what he saw and learned that day from Chinua. Finally, he said to Udechukwu, "I am living a very dangerous life. Someone who could have any number of cooks he wanted is cooking, and a nobody like me thinks I am too big to enter the kitchen."

Reuben also listed things that set Chinua apart from other big people. "He doesn't act or feel like a big man. I have never seen him wearing a tie, just safari suit. Sometimes he mows his front lawn. If you see him, you wouldn't know he's a big man."

Egejuru had her own shock about Chinua doing something considered unusual for a Nigerian man, especially a husband. Every summer, Egejuru sends fresh bitter leaves from her garden to several of her friends across the U.S. She sends some to the Achebes too. This particular time, Achebe's wife called to say she had received the parcel. Egejuru asked whether the leaves arrived still fresh. Mrs. Achebe said yes and added, "Chinua has already processed them." Egejuru shouted, "Did you say that Oga processed the leaves?" Then Mrs. Achebe explained that she's had this bad finger for some years, so she could not process the leaves. Then she reminded Egejuru: "You know we have no house help here." When she hung up Egejuru said to herself, "So, I have been causing a great man to process bitter leaves?"[5] It had never occurred to her that a Nigerian husband could do such a thing. For non-African people, it might not be such a big deal for a husband to help with housework. But for Africans, it is a very big deal froth with misinterpretations.

The Ugwoke children, who live in Achebe's premises at Nsukka, narrated their own experiences with Chinua's ordinariness.

> When we come into his house, we chat with him. He doesn't carry himself so high to show he is a big man. Sometimes he enters the kitchen to help. He eats with us. We have learned a lot from him about life. We use him as an example of humility and simplicity.[6]

Udechukwu also learned from Chinua's simplicity:

---

[5] Processing bitter leaves involves kneading, squeezing, washing and rinsing the bitter juice off the leaves, to the point where only a slight taste of bitterness is left.
[6] Ngozi Ugwoke, interview with Egejuru.

He's like a model to me. Here's a great man behaving as if he is nobody. Why then should a small person like me act as if I am the greatest thing that has happened to the world?[7]

Once more, Udechukwu captured Chinua's complex simplicity in the Igbo saying, *"anu n'ewu ewu a deju ukpa* -a famous animal does not fill a basket." In other words, a famous animal doesn't have to be huge. By the same token, Chinua doesn't need elaborate outfits and conspicuous deportment to prove his importance. Sometimes he goes out of his way to avoid being noticed. His friend Sam Nwoye said that Chinua used to put on dark glasses to avoid being identified. But Nwoye warned that his friend's quiet disposition could be deceptive because "behind this quiet façade is a man of steel."[8]

Approachable and accessible to all

It is the practice among the Igbo, to seek audience with a highly placed person, through his or her servants. It is considered disrespectful to go directly to the "big" man or woman to ask for favors. By all accounts, Chinua is a "big" man who deserves the honor of being approached through servants or agents. In fact, his sister-in-law Lucy Achebe expressed the sentiments of Chinua's admirers when she said of Chinua: " At this stage in his life, one needs a ticket to get into his house. One would be interviewed by his security guard before one gets in to see him. But Chinua is a simple man."[9] It is Chinua's disarming simplicity that makes him accessible to all. Many people expressed their surprise when they found how easy it was to approach Chinua directly. Soyinka indirectly talked about Chinua's approachable nature when he responded to the question: "Why did Obasanjo ask Achebe, instead of you the great poet, to write the words of the anthem for the Festival of Arts and Culture?" Soyinka explained: "Chinua is a very urbane person. He has this manner which is reassuring to people generally. I do not know of anybody being comfortable with me."[10] Chinua's presence does not intimidate, it rather draws one in and reassures one.

Chinua was very successful when he worked in the Talks Department of the Nigerian Broadcasting Service. This was due in part to his ability to make people feel at ease in his presence. Michael

---

[7] Obiora Udechukwu, interview with Egejuru.
[8] Sam Nwoye, interview with Egejuru
[9] Lucy Achebe, interview with Egejuru.
[10] Wole Soyinka, interview with Egejuru.

Olumide who got to know him better at that time observed: "Chinua's ability to relate to people in the flesh added color to his personality."[11] It is this same characteristic that Ifeanyi Aniebo alluded to when he described an experience he had with Chinua. The writer was invited to be the keynote speaker for African Literature Association conference in Los Angeles in 1984. It fell upon Aniebo to drive Chinua around while he attended the conference. Even though Aniebo is an Igbo man and a successful novelist himself, he still felt very nervous to drive this super icon of African literature. To Aniebo's surprise however, "Chinua made it appear so natural, I might as well be driving my younger brother. I didn't feel a looming intimidating presence."[12]

Many of Chinua's younger relatives unwittingly talked about his ability to relate to them in the flesh. For instance, his cousin Ernest said, "When I talk with him, you wouldn't know we are not in the same age group. You wouldn't know that it is a child talking with an adult."[13] His niece Ukamaka Ikpeze didn't realize that her uncle was a big man until he started travelling and bringing home, news of the Biafran war. She talked about the Achebe clan living together at their Headquarters (Isaiah Achebe's compound) after the war. Their uncle, Chinua would scold them when they misbehaved, but they still liked to spend time with him because he played scrabbles with them. "If you want to play scrabbles go to uncle Chinua; there are no words he will not get," said Ukamaka. Oyibo Achebe and Tochukwu Okocha both talked about how their uncle's fame really blew their minds when they were much younger. They heard so much about Chinua's fame that they started joking about him. They said things like, "Does this Chinua still fart?" When they heard that he travelled to Ethiopia and to Israel, they became more intrigued. Tochukwu said, "We marveled because from our knowledge of the bible, we still believed that Jerusalem was in heaven and our uncle had traveled to heaven. To us he became an exceptional person." As an adult, Tochukwu saw an uncle whose deportment belied the image of a great man they conceived him to be. Tochukwu was amazed at his uncle's down-to-earth personality. He said: " He comes to our house and we sit together and talk. I sit next to him in the car, and we drive together to Ogidi town meeting. Yet, this is a man other people struggle to get a glimpse of."[14] People assume it is natural to have access to one's relation no matter how famous the relative. The truth is that fame and fortune tend to alienate ordinary folks from their wealthy and highly placed relatives. Hence, Chinua's

---

[11] Michael Olumide, interview with Egejuru.
[12] Ifeanyi Aniebo, interview with Egejuru.
[13] Ernest Achebe, interview with Egejuru.
[14] Tochukwu Okocha, interview with Egejuru.

family members are quick to recognize that they are truly blessed to have a famous relative who remains accessible to them in spite of his celebrity status.

Chinua's friends and family members cited as an example of his accessibility, the fact that he accepted the Presidency of Ogidi Town Union. For these people, it takes a man of Chinua's intellectual maturity to summon the type of patience and tolerance needed to interact with village folks. And not only did Chinua preside over town meetings, his presence literally pulled members to the meetings. Before he became the President, many people had lost interest in the Town Union and avoided its meetings. With Chinua's remarkable ability to relate to people in the flesh, and make them feel at ease in his presence, he rekindled people's interest in their town union and they flocked to the meetings.

15

Gentle as a lamb, fierce like a lioness

It is paradoxical to find the qualities of a lamb and a lioness in the same body. Yet, as if in response to his favourite philosophy of dualism, Chinua's gentleness stands beside his fierceness.

Chinua's brothers and sisters started their reflections on their brother with, "*O bu onye nwayo. O daa acho okwu.*" Literally, Chinua is gentle; he does not look for trouble. His brother John and his sister Zinobia said they never saw him in a fight with other children. He never beat his younger sister Grace, as older siblings do their younger ones. Grace found the explanation for her brother's distaste for altercations in his name. "*Afa onye n'achojie* -a person's name seeks him out," she rationalized. Thus, Chinua leaves the fight to his Chi. Chinua's next door neighbor said, "I have never seen that young man involved in *ife n'ese okwu* -things that cause dispute." He stays clear of all conflict-ridden situations. When Chinua's former houseboy Dickson was asked if Chinua ever flogged him, he replied: "Has he spoken loud enough let alone scold and flog you? That's how his God made him. O nwelu aka izizi."[1] And a person of *aka izizi* cannot bring himself or herself to lift a hand and hit or inflict physical pain on a fellow human. This probably explains why Chinua was unable or reluctant to spank his children.

There are some good examples of Chinua's conscious avoidance of altercation or outright confrontation. Chinua acquired a piece of land at Enugu and laid the foundation for a building. Without any warnings, some fellow working for a vicious businessman went and demolished the foundation. The man claimed that Chinua had no occupancy rights to the land. Chinua took the matter to court and naturally, the case was going to drag on in the Nigerian way so as to make room for bribery and corruption by those handling the case. Chinua gracefully withdrew the case. He just couldn't be bothered with a drawn out litigation even when he was unjustly provoked.

---

[1] Dickson Odukwe, interview with Egejuru.

One cannot resist mentioning Professor Nnolim's accusation of plagiarism that threatened Chinua's reputation in the late 1970s. People continue to wonder why Chinua didn't even deign to give any response to Nnolim's allegations. In fact, some enraged critics and admirers of Chinua took it upon themselves to come to his defense. Some critics have speculated that Chinua kept silent because, giving a response would amount to lending credence to the accuser and thus dignifying his claim. Ifeanyi Aniebo who remains puzzled over Chinua's lack of response commented:

> He has not even made a comment on it. He left others to talk about it. Anybody else would have flown off his handle; and that's the difference between us mortals and Chinua.[2]

There might be a number of reasons why Chinua chose to remain silent. However, from what interviewees revealed about him, one can surmise that it is just in his nature to eschew all types of altercations. As one of his nephews crudely put it, "Chinua's non-violent nature is not out of physical weakness. It is because God created him not to be fighting or trouble shooting."

Chinua can be as gentle as a lamb, but this gentleness should never be mistaken for weakness. Theo Vincent talked about the "pairings" of Chinua's qualities: "Chinua is almost self effacing but he is not one you will put into your pocket. If you rub him on the wrong side, and he gives you his tongue, you will for ever regret it." [3]

Victor Nwankwo addressed Chinua's quiet confidence and seeming softness thus:

> He is strong in a quiet way, not boastful. He has this soft spokenness that comes across as from one who is a master. He says a few soft icy words, they are so icy you wouldn't be able to feel the cold.[4]

Chinua is generally very slow to anger when an act of aggression or insult is directed at him. But he is very swift to righteous anger when the weak are trampled upon by the strong and powerful. He is especially enraged when the people are stolen from and abused by those they put in office. As the pro-Chancellor of Anambra State University of Technology, Chinua got angry at the ways things were handled at that university. The vice Chancellor, Ejike, noted two

---

[2] Ifeanyi Aniebo, interview with Egejuru.
[3] Theo Vincent, interview with Egejuru.
[4] Victor Nwankwo, interview with Egejuru.

instances when Chinua exploded in anger during some of their meetings. "It was just like a sudden roaring of a lioness," Ejike said.[5] Chinua often comes to the defense of the weak in the manner of a lioness defending her cubs.

Many Nigerians commented on Chinua's courage in challenging authorities or entities who feel they have the right to inflict all manners of pain on the innocent and the defenceless. People cited two top examples of Chinua's display of courage. These were his publication, *The Trouble with Nigeria*, and his opposition to the proposal for a national funeral for Chief Obafemi Awolowo. In *The Trouble with Nigeria*, he took on Nigerian politicians, beginning with the doyens - Azikiwe, Awolowo, Sarduana and others, to the military juntas. He indicted them all for their reckless abuse of power and miscarriage of leadership. Even the victims, the people themselves, were equally accused of acquiescence and complicity because of their unabashed admiration for those who constantly cheated them, stole from them and dared them to complain. In this booklet, Chinua warned Nigerians not to allow a repeat of corrupt leadership in the government destined for election in late August and early September of 1983. All Nigerians, including the sitting President Shagari, heard the loud message of truth which Chinua sent the nation via *The Trouble with Nigeria*. But it was too late for the re-elected government of Shehu Shagari to heed Chinua's warnings. Therefore, the new government was barely two months in office when it was overthrown by the military on December 31, 1983. Once again, Chinua's prophetic vision of doom for the country was dramatized as it was done in 1966, shortly after the publication of *A Man of the People*.

Chinua was even more daring when he spoke out publicly against a national funeral for chief Awolowo in 1987. He played right into the traditional Igbo/Yoruba antagonism. The Yoruba people immediately saw his opposition as a collective resentment and insult by the Igbo. To make matters worse, Chinua did not choose his words carefully. "People were angry that he called Awolowo a mere tribal chief," said Soyinka. All the same, Chinua was correct when he pointed out that Awolowo never held a national office to warrant a national funeral. In effect, Chinua was truly more concerned for the people of Nigeria, who stood to lose millions of naira to politicians who would definitely exploit the occasion of a national funeral to siphon the people's money into their private pockets. Unfortunately, most Yoruba people did not want to believe Chinua's concern for the people. They attacked him viciously in their local newspapers. They went as far as accusing him of being jealous of the Yorubas because their son, Wole, had won the

---

[5] Prof. Chiweite Ejike, interview with Egejuru.

Nobel Prize in Literature in 1986. Chinua was forced to respond to the article that accused him of being jealous of Wole Soyinka. Chinua's words as Wole recollected them were, "Winning the Nobel Prize does not make Wole the *Asiwaju* of African Literature." That is to say, winning the Nobel Prize does not make Wole the Alpha and Omega of African literature. And Soyinka was disappointed that Chinua allowed himself to be drawn into the Yoruba/Igbo debate because "the heap of abuse he (Chinua) got was unnecessary," Wole thought. According to Wole, the way Chinua responded to the attacks of him in Yoruba newspapers, "is a clear manifestation of his black pull. When this black pull is probed or touched, he lashes out, and he gives it to you fine fine."[6]

When asked his views on the anti-Achebe press during the Awolowo crisis, Professor Biobaku said: "I prefer to suspend judgement because I don't have all the facts."[7] Whether Chinua was right or wrong in opposing a national funeral for Awolowo, the fact remains that, being able to go public in a controversial issue requires considerable courage in Nigeria where there is an entrenchment of culture of fear. There you have entities that intimidate people and muzzle public opinion, especially critical opinion. But Chinua dared to speak where most people, in guise of detachment, would pull out and not dare confront issues publicly.

Just as he comes to the defence of his oppressed compatriots, Chinua also challenges western perceptions and treatment of black people. Speaking about Chinua's constant defence of Africans, Soyinka said:

> I have known Chinua to be angry. I have seen the way he takes on foreign critics, the presumptuousness of foreigners who know nothing about African literature. He definitely has the same kind of intemperate approach to stupidity of that nature as the rest of us.[8]

Chinua was definitely enraged by the endemic racism he encountered at Amherst. The situation was such that his four year-old daughter, Nwando recognized that she and another black child were discriminated against at their nursery school. Chinua was obviously deeply hurt and angered by the disparagement of African peoples and their culture by white people on campus of the University of Massachusetts at Amherst. He finally lashed out in a most constructive and eloquent manner through his now famous lecture, "An Image of

---

[6] Soyinka, interview with Egejuru.
[7] Prof. S.O. Biobaku, interview with Egejuru.
[8] Wole Soyinka, interview with Egejuru.

Africa: Racism in Conrad's *Heart of Darkness.*" In a reasoned, undeniable marshalling of evidence, he delivered his lecture to an audience made up largely of English professors. Indeed, Chinua was exposing Conrad's racism, but he was also reminding or alerting Conradian scholars in the audience that they were as racist if not more so than Conrad. And speaking about the professors' reaction to the speech, Thelwell said: "You could see the growing shift beneath their critical feet as they had to rethink long standing assumptions." In the way Chinua responded to institutionalized racism at Amherst, he demonstrated an aspect of his personality that impresses all who deal closely with him- controlled rational response to provocation and injustice. Still testifying to Chinua's intellectual courage, Thelwell said: "I have never heard him raise his voice, yet he's not afraid to go against the grain, to confront the shibboleths of western intellectual arrogance."[9]

Apart from those occasions when Chinua was known to have openly expressed righteous indignation against injustice directed at defenseless groups of people, he is generally known to be very slow to anger. Most people who worked closely with him over a period of time, marveled at the level of his self control. S. J. Cookey claimed:

> In normal day-to-day interaction with Chinua, it's not conceivable that one would reach a point that would provoke a reaction in anger from him. I suspect that he is a man who is in total control of his emotions.[10]

Cookey speculated that the reason Chinua had so far managed to control his anger was "perhaps he has not found himself in situations that try men's souls." Under the very stressful conditions of the Biafran war, he never lost his cool. He was never flustered. He remained calm and determined in his search for solutions to endless and frustrating situations.

On the domestic front, Chinua is so subtle in his expression of anger that his relatives and employees are unable to tell when he is angry. Therefore, they claim they have never seen him angry. His secretary Esther said:

> When he is angry you can hardly know because he controls his anger. And when he is talking to you as a result of something that made him angry, it sounds like an advice to you. He does not give

---

[9] Prof. Thelwell, interview with Egejuru.
[10] Prof. S.J. Cookey, interview with Egejuru.

negative rules -don't do this, don't do that. He does not command, rather he advises you.[11]

Grace Ugwoke, a fifteen-year-old girl who lived with the Achebes when she was a bit younger said: "He never scolded me and even when he did so, his words came out as advice, not the type of scolding that sends shivers down your spine or the type that startles you." Chinua's nephew, Emeka Okocha racked his brain trying to remember an occasion when he saw his uncle angry. He remembered an incident which he felt qualified as an expression of anger. Emeka and a friend of his went to pay a visit to Chinua on a Sunday, but Chinua was out. Emeka found some hot drinks and helped himself and his friend. While they were drinking, Chinua came in. He did not say anything but went out again. He came back with a large quantity of soft drinks and stocked the refrigerator. Emeka concluded: "That was his way of letting me know that I was not supposed to serve myself hot drinks and beer. As a student, I should make do with soft drinks. That's when I could say he was angry."[12]

Although his sister Grace said Chinua never beat her when they were growing up, she readily admitted that he has a sense of anger and she added: "But it's the way he handles anger that makes the difference." She then gave an example of Chinua's special gift of controlling his anger. It had to do with Chinua's houseboy, Okwundu. Okwundu had travelled and spent some weeks away. The day he returned, Chinua was in the house with some visitors. The boy did not greet Chinua as one is supposed to do after a long absence. So, Chinua called him and asked, "Okwundu, have you seen me before?" Okwundu went outside again, came back inside and greeted Chinua in the proper manner and everybody laughed. It was his former houseboy Dickson, who provided the most plausible explanation for Chinua's calm and rational handling of anger. He said: "Before he responds to any situation that causes a person's anger to flare up, *o wusa iwe* -he casts anger aside."[13]

---

[11] Esther Ogadi, interview with Egejuru.
[12] Emeka Okocha, interview with Egejuru.
[13] Dickson Odukwe, interview with Egejuru.

16

A man of truth and justice

In the Desiderata, one finds this counsel: "Speak your truth quietly and clearly; and listen to others, even the dull and the ignorant; they too have their story." Chinua lives by this counsel. Many people remarked his extraordinary ability to listen patiently and give his full attention to anybody speaking to him. And when he responds, he comes across as a soft spoken, quiet man of truth, a man who listens to people with two ears. For, as Obiechina pointed out, there are people who listen with half an ear. "But with Chinua, his two ears are always alert when he is talking with you."[1]

Chinua's younger relatives marvelled at the way he listens to everyone and seems to soak in everything like a sponge. His nephew Dr. Okey Ikpeze said: "I think listening is one of his greatest attributes. He listens and takes in everything without your knowledge."[2]

Chinua prefers listening to talking. Professor Ejike substantiated this by recalling a three-hour conversation he had with Chinua. Ejike claimed that Chinua spoke to posterity in that conversation. However, "in thirty minutes he makes two or three sentences. He sits and listens with little comments like *'odi egwu* -it's frightening'."[3] Chinua listens to people because he is genuinely interested in their lives and stories. More than that, he recognizes the need of human beings to be acknowledged and respected, not ignored and despised.

Truth, honesty, credibility, trustworthiness, and reliability are just a few of the words used to characterize Chinua. Of all the words, truth was repeated most often. Ejike voiced the opinion of many people about Chinua's truthfulness:

> Being with Chinua is like a pilgrimage for someone who is seeking the truth. The type of man he is does not call black, white or tall

---
[1] Prof. E. Obiechina, interview with Egejuru.
[2] Dr. Okey Ikpeze, interview with Egejuru.
[3] Prof. Ejike, interview with Egejuru.

short. He tells it as it is. Chinua does not coat things with sugar to make them sweet.⁴

Even though Ejike and Chinua are very close friends, Ejike couldn't find adequate English expressions to describe his friend's moral uprightness. Therefore, he resorted to mixing Igbo and English words:

> Chinua is *oka ibe* – he is greater than his peers in his adherence to *Nso Ani* – sacred ordinances of the land. Chinua *bu madu gboo* – he is a man of the old. Chinua is reliable at the puritanical level. The likes of him are seen once in a generation.⁵

In Ogidi, people referred to him as "*Onye ezi okwu* -man of truth." Mainly because of his honesty and credibility, Chinua was implored to assume the Presidency of their Town Union. Ogidi people valued his service so much that they waived the traditional requirement of *ozo* title for any leader of that prestigious body. The provost of the Town Union said:

> Even though he is not an ozo-titled man, Ogidi needed a man of truth and integrity. They needed a man who does not look at people's position or wealth to pronounce the truth as he sees it.⁶

Johnson Okudo, a contemporary of Isaiah Achebe and mentor of Chinua, used one profound phrase to describe the young man: "Chinua *a buka madu*." Literally, Chinua is too much of a human being. Okudo repeated the phrase several times during the interview. He insisted: "I know him as one who obeys *Nso Ani*, above all, I know him as one who speaks the truth at all times."⁷

Like Ejike, Udechukwu was lost for words when he was asked to characterize Chinua whom he claims as mentor. And in a typically Igbo understanding of a good human being, he could only repeat: "*Madu ka o bu* – he's human." This means that Chinua combines all that is good in a human being. Udechukwu went on to compare him to an eagle that had attained the final stage of whiteness after its seventh kill: "*Ugo gbuzue, o chake*." Simply put, one couldn't improve on Chinua's completeness, a word that many people used to describe the man. To further illustrate Chinua's moral integrity, Udechukwu drew from the *ozo* institution:

---

⁴ Ejike, same interview.
⁵ Ejike, same interview.
⁶ Tochukwu Okocha, interview with Egejuru.
⁷ Johnson Okudo, interview with Egejuru.

He casts an image of an *ozo* man. He upholds the two sides of *ozo*ship -right and responsibility. Like an *ozo* man, Chinua takes the burden of his high position seriously. His position is not only for receiving privileges; it is also for standing up for what is right and just.[8]

Chinua is literally driven by a fierce sense of justice and fairness. Even as a young man, he was not afraid to stand up against the slightest form of injustice. His nephew, Professor Nnaemeka Ikpeze, recalled an incident that took place when Ikpeze was very young. Chinua was invited to a school function at Mary Mount Girls' secondary school at Agbo. Chinua took with him, his young nephew Nnaemeka. When Chinua was called to the high table, he grabbed his nephew and proceeded to his seat. He was told to leave the child because children were not allowed up there. He left his nephew sitting with the general public. A short while later, a white couple arrived with their children and they all went to sit at the high table. When nobody came to take the children away, Chinua went down and picked up his nephew to sit with him. He could not stand the blatant injustice.

It must be recalled that it was in his effort to intervene on behalf of two underpaid student workers of the Nigerian Broadcasting Service, that Chinua met his future wife Christie. She and another student were paid less than another worker doing the same type of job. After examining their case, Chinua found there was just cause for their complaint, and he made sure that justice was served.

It must also be recalled that Chinua's primary motive for writing *Things Fall Apart* was to tell the truth about Africans. After reading and listening to European stories about Africa, he realized that European "experts" on Africa had presented an unfair picture of the continent and its people. Thus, from the publication of his first novel, Chinua's literary career became one long crusade for justice for the black race.

There were several reasons Chinua was chosen to lead the Biafran National Guidance Committee. Foremost of these according to S.J. Cookey, were his transparent honesty and credibility. Cookey commented:

> It will be unthinkable to conceive that you can live with Chinua and he can be doing something behind your back, which he will not tell you up-front. In the Committee, we had divergent views on issues but everyone respected Chinua and everyone accepted his summary of the proceedings, because everyone believed he was genuine. He

---

[8] Obiora Udechukwu, interview with Egejuru

had not lost touch with reality; he did not have his head in the clouds.[9]

Furthermore, other members of the committee observed that Chinua spoke the truth all the time and always stuck to what was humane and morally sound. Therefore, their trust in him soared. His reputation as a trustworthy man spread to the common people. The result was that the committee he chaired became the conscience of the Biafran movement. The ideas that came from this committee were taken seriously. The people believed in the committee because its chairman would not lie or deceive. To have that type of confidence from those around you, that you are up to no tricks, is now a rare quality among people in high position.

As a member of the Biafran National Guidance Committee, Chinua saw first hand, how Biafran authorities abused the rights of the Biafran masses and some left wingers in the NGC. But Chinua would not stand by and watch the innocent suffer. He would frequently intervene and say: "this is not right." Ikenna Nzimiro was of the extreme left wing. His political stand was such a risky one that he became a constant target of witch-hunt by the Biafran leader. Nzimiro told how Chinua saved his life twice. "Even though I was left wing, Chinua supported me as a human being and saved me from being killed." At one point, Nzimiro went back to his home at Oguta not only because his life was threatened, but because the right wing didn't want to listen to his views, which often clashed with those of the government. But Chinua asked them to bring Nzimiro back. He told them to listen to him because he made valuable contributions to their discussions. Nzimiro said: "Each time Ojukwu asked Achebe to give me up, he refused. He was the man giving us cover, defending us and warning the leader against witch hunting."[10] In all of Chinua's demand for justice for the oppressed, there resounds the voice of moral authority, a voice so powerful that it could stay the hands of executioners.

Like so many African writers, Chinua is even more outraged by the enormous injustice Africans suffer at the hands of their own leaders. Consequently, he often abandons fiction to speak to people in the real world. Certain of the power that can be wielded by the pen and the word, he harnessed that power to fight injustice at the local and national levels in Nigeria. He harnessed the power of the pen during the physical and emotional reconstruction of the University of Nigeria, Nsukka. During that trying time, the anglicized Nigerian vice Chancellor, Dr. Kodilinye, preferred white expatriate workers to

---

[9] S.J. Cookey, interview with Egejuru.
[10] Ikenna Nzimiro, interview with Egejuru.

Nigerian workers. For his expatriate workers he provided comfortable housing with running water and electricity. He treated the Nigerian faculty, staff and students like dirt. While he lived in the luxury of carpeted floors and air-conditioned rooms, his Nigerian workers lived in shacks without running water and electricity.

Chinua constantly exposed and criticized the vice Chancellor's policies in *Nsukkascope*. Not only did he attack the vice Chancellor, he equally attacked the government of East Central State that trampled on the very people they were supposed to rehabilitate. The journal's attacks were so persistently virulent that reprisals came swiftly from the government. The police arrested Nzimiro, the circulation manager and a few others and locked them up. Chinua and Obiechina, the sub-editor, went to the police and insisted on being locked up with their colleagues. In fact, Chinua argued that since he was the chief editor, he was the one to be arrested and not the others. In the end, everyone was released. The journal went underground and continued to publish and circulate.

Justice was finally served when a new government came into power and removed the vice Chancellor. Chinua's relentless and scathing criticism of the man played a very important role in his removal. Chinua's friend, James Ezilo became the vice Chancellor. With Chinua and other dedicated colleagues, true reconstruction began in earnest at Nsukka University campus.

17

A great humanist

Probably the most problematic, if not an unanswerable question asked of the interviewees was: "Where lies the meaning of Chinua Achebe?" Various responses were given. Several respondents believe that his meaning lies in his broader concern for humanity. Some others think his meaning lies in his commitment to the welfare of the black race. Yet, another group believes his true meaning lies in his simplicity. S. J. Cookey observed:

> Chinua is first and foremost, a humanist. He is steeped in Igbo culture with its multidimensional character, the good, the bad and the ugly. And he doesn't make any apologies for that. When one applies that, one sees him transcending that Igbo culture to make him a human being, capable of appreciating the deeper, broader, more complex aspects of human culture that one sees inside of him.[1]

Chinua expresses his humanness, through his concern for and appreciation of his fellow human beings. Professor Ejike said, "Chinua has immediate belief in the goodness of man. He does not condemn anyone on hearsay. He trusts you first and then, if you betray that trust, he will cast you aside."[2]

Many people, including some of Chinua's relations, couldn't understand his choice of friends. One of his nephews commented:

> I have looked at some of his friends. I don't see anything that should bring them together. Some of them will go against the same principle for which he stands. That's something I can't explain. He is not flamboyant, but some of his friends are. He is not noisy, but some of his friends are noisy. Some are, whose family lives are not what one would expect or accept. Yet, they are all his friends. He

---

[1] S.J. Cookey, interview with Egejuru.
[2] Prof. Ejike, interview with Egejuru.

has a lot of interest in human beings, so he must find a way of relating to everybody.[3]

It took sometime for Dr. Sam Okoli to figure out Chinua's mode of thinking. He noted however, that whenever he and Chinua spent time together, they rarely talked about Chinua's books or whatever he was doing. Instead, "Chinua was often more interested in talking about issues affecting the down-trodden, no matter their race. Every people seem to relate to him."[4]

Arthur Nwankwo also stated that he has been tremendously influenced by "Chinua's concern for the poor, his egalitarian values and strivings for a just society." Without exception, everybody insisted that Chinua's concern for the welfare of the common man pushed him into joining the defunct People's Redemption Party. Unlike regular politicians, Chinua with his colleagues did not join politics for personal gain. He joined to help create a just society in his country. He had hoped that a political party running on the agenda to improve the lot of the down-trodden, would eventually revolutionize the society for the better.

Chinua's colleagues in Biafra's National Guidance Committee repeatedly said he was driven by a very deep and sincere concern for the common man. Obiechina said:

> You would say that a writer, who has to preserve his high degree of skepticism, would not be so concerned about the fate of little people. It is not so with Chinua. What brought me very close to him was his commitment to the interest of the Biafran masses.[5]

When Johnson Okudo repeatedly said of Chinua, "*Madu ka o bu; o bu ka madu, ezigbo madu ka o bu*," he was merely stressing the fundamental goodness of a person who embodies all that is good in a human being. Chinua's relatives and his employees said of him, over and over, "*O bu onye n'atupuru madu uche*- he is one mindful and considerate of others people's needs."

A couple of examples will suffice to demonstrate Chinua's consideration of other people's needs. Chinua and his wife paid for Mrs. Ugwoke and her daughter to travel from Nigeria to the U.S for the wedding of Chinelo Achebe at Bard College. After the wedding, Mrs. Ugwoke offered to stay and help out with housework at Bard. It was a reasonable offer because Mrs. Achebe could use such help, since she

---

[3] Dr. John U. Achebe, interview with Egejuru.
[4] Dr. Sam Okoli, interview with Egejuru.
[5] Prof. E. Obiechina, interview with Egejuru.

and her husband were all alone. However, when they learned from Mrs. Ugwoke that she had not made proper arrangements for the care of the children she left in Nigeria, the Achebes rejected her offer. They told her to go home and make the necessary arrangements for the care of her children. Mrs. Ugwoke returned to Nigeria but did not go back to Bard to stay with the Achebes. It was Mrs. Ethel Momah who talked of this incident. She cited it as an example of how Chinua and his wife put the needs of others ahead of their own. Mrs. Momah's story was corroborated by Ugwoke's children. Without any prompting, they talked of their mother's trip to America:

> Our mother wanted to stay back and help Mrs. Achebe with the care of her husband, but when she heard from our mother that there was nobody looking after the rest of us at home, she told her to return to Nigeria. She told her that she could come back after making arrangements for our care. So, our mother returned. Now we are all grown up.[6]

A similar incident had occurred earlier when Reuben offered to join the Achebes in the U.S. They were ready to accept Reuben's offer, but when they learned that his aging mother who depended very much on her son, was against Reuben's plans, the Achebes backed down. They felt that the old woman's needs outweighed their own. Indeed, not many Nigerians would give much thought to the old woman's need. They would instead, try to convince her of the greater monetary rewards she would be reaping from her son's move to America. But Chinua thought differently because he felt intimately the needs of another human being whose very life depended on the services of another human being.

For Esther Ogadi, the meaning of Chinua lies in his eagerness to recognize another person's humanity. She spoke of how Chinua practices what he preaches:

> Achebe doesn't know he is a great man. All he cares is that you are a human being. He and I worked in mutual trust. He was concerned about my well being, even in family matters. When I had a very serious family problem, he gave me time off to settle the problem and stabilize myself.[7]

Like several other interviewees, Esther said she could not find adequate words to describe her former boss:

---

[6] Ngozi Ugwoke and her siblings, interview with Egejuru.
[7] Esther Ogadi, interview with Egejuru.

Where do I begin? Is it in his non-discriminatory attitude towards all people? Is it his humility, his kindness, his goodness towards all? He is simply a rare human being. God washed his hands clean before he created Chinua.[8]

Reuben went even further in his examples of Chinua's humane treatment of his fellow human beings. He recalled the type of treatment he received from his boss:

> We worked well together for ten years. When he trusts you, he will not disturb you when he assigns a job to you. In the morning when I greet him, he shakes hands with me. When he notices that you are low in spirit, he asks you what the problem is. If it is money problem, he gives you money or he gives you invoice. If you come late to work, he will ask if anything happened in your home, and if you explain, he understands. When we travel to his hometown without his wife, he trusts me to clean his bedroom. He gives me money to buy things and cook our meals. When we travel far and stop at a restaurant, we sit at the same table to eat. Sometimes when we travel to his town, he will give me beer to wash down my food. If we go to a function or ceremony that involves eating, he will make sure that I eat. Instead of me not to eat, Prof. will starve to make sure that I eat and drink. He took very good care of me each time we traveled. Prof. cannot be compared to anybody. He is too special of a human being.[9]

Certainly, there are employers who treat their employees well. But it is very rare to find an African "big man" who would sit at the same table to eat with his driver. The usual practice is to give the driver some money to go and buy something to eat. Perhaps, shaking hands with one's driver or secretary may not be such a big deal. But in Nigeria, it is rare to find an employer who would cheerfully respond to the employee's greeting let alone shake hands with him and ask about his family.

When C. L. Innes worked with Chinua for *Okike* Magazine, she was struck with the kind of courtesy her boss had toward his workers. She echoed what Esther and Reuben said, "He always treated people with great consideration and respect." She added that Chinua's rapport with his employees was not common among employers, be they Americans or Africans.

Chinua's junior colleagues at Nsukka talked about his humane treatment of people. Udechukwu spoke for his colleagues:

---

[8] Esther Ogadi, same interview.
[9] Reuben Alumona, interview with Egejuru.

Madu ka o bu -he is human. There are not many men of his stature who would step down to the level of junior colleagues. He can come to your house. He's not like others who are too conscious of age and status, and would rather send for you. But Chinua will come to your house or office, no matter how old you are, or who you are. He can descend to the lowest level of human ladder to deal on a human level with all.[10]

---

[10] Obiora Udechukwu, interview with Egejuru.

18

A man of integrity

It is somehow foolhardy to attempt a rank ordering of so many good qualities jostling for space in one individual. It is safe to say that integrity is among the qualities at the top of the list of Chinua's good qualities.

There is no better or higher testimony to Chinua's integrity than his appointment as Goodwill Ambassador for the United Nations, in January 1999. It is because of his uprightness that the United Nations, whose gestures are constantly viewed with skepticism, chose Chinua to speak for them. Whatever the qualifications are, integrity and respectability must be there. As shown by the words of interviewees, Chinua has a certain *gravitas* about him. Many compare his ideas and opinions to those of wise men of earlier times. People crave for and respect his opinion. Simply put, Chinua inspires trust, and any messages coming through him would resonate with trustworthiness.

Even when people do not use the word integrity to describe Chinua, its meaning is often implied in their testimony or comment. For example, Augustine Achebe said of his brother, " Chinua is not one you can attract with money. Once something is right, he will continue to stick with it. You can't sway him with money. He is a man of the old."[1] Chinua's integrity compelled his townspeople to literally cry out to him for help. Their town needed a man of unquestioned uprightness, a man who commanded the respect of all Ogidi people, to step in and save them from socio-political anarchy.

In an ironic twist of fate, that same integrity that attracted Ogidi people to Chinua would also alienate him from the powerful Ndichie. Chinua and other progressive people in Ogidi saw the need to restore some of the traditional ways of doing certain things in their town. For instance, the old way of choosing the Igwe used to be fair and free of corruption, and the people wanted to restore that practice. They also called for the rotation of the Igweship, to eliminate monopoly of that powerful office by one family or kindred. Surprisingly, Chinua's

---

[1] Augustine Achebe, interview with Egejuru.

proposal to return to traditional 'clean' politics angered the Ndichie who had been selling their votes, then picking and choosing candidates without regard to traditional protocol. Of course, in Nigeria it is common practice for highly placed citizens to sell their opinion and vote for as little as a mesh of pottage. Therefore, Chinua's call for clean politics was a real economic threat to the corrupt Ndichie. By standing firm against corrupt and powerful officials, Chinua reminded those who are caught in the whirlpool of corruption the world over, that it is possible to stay clean in a thoroughly corrupt society.

One keeps going back to Chinua's role in Biafra's National Guidance Committee. This is because, that body he chaired provided a priceless opportunity for those who worked with him, to observe him at close quarters and comment on his character. It was Chinua's integrity that made him the obvious choice of leader for the group. Nzimiro testified to Chinua's integrity that earned him the respect of the high and the mighty. As a left winger, Nzimiro nearly lost his life for criticizing Biafran policies. Fortunately for him and others in his camp, "Chinua was the man giving us cover, defending us because Ojukwu respected him too much." S. J. Cookey alluded to Chinua's integrity in most of his observations about the man. For instance, he stated that members of the National Guidance Committee were of diverse ideological orientations. "However diverged the view, everyone respected Chinua and accepted his summary of the proceedings, because everyone believed him to be genuine. He is an individual you can conveniently associate with without any reservations."[2] Reinforcing Cookey's observation, Obiechina added, "Chinua's integrity was the driving force behind the National Guidance Committee." After he enumerated the various ways Chinua demonstrated his integrity, Obiechina concluded, "I could go anywhere with a man like that."[3]

Nepotism is a common practice across the world. It is even considered a virtue in many third world countries like Nigeria. But this is one "virtue" that Chinua refuses to embrace. Ironically, some of his relatives saw his refusal to use his position to advance their interests, as a point of weakness. One of them in a dejected voice confessed:

> We would like him to use his position to help us so we can come out like him. We thought that we his relatives would have things smoother and easier. But he wants each man to make himself. He

---

[2] S.J. Cookey, interview with Egejuru.
[3] E. Obiechina, interview with Egejuru.

treats his children the same way. This is the problem we have. We think he should serve our interest with his position.[4]

On the other hand, some of his nephews admired him for not practicing nepotism. One said, "He is not a typical Nigerian. I could not go to him and ask him to help me get into the University. Some people do compromise their position, but he will not."[5] Another said, "His sense of fairness prevents him from practicing nepotism, he is upright to a fault. In the African value system, this is a weakness."[6] Yet another said:

> Nobody goes to ask him for favours that spell nepotism. If you want a special favour which is against the rule, he will quickly tell you, 'we make the rules and we can't break them.' He is very kind and can go out of his way to help you if it is legitimate.[7]

Like all good teachers, Chinua upholds his professional integrity. For instance, it has become a habit in Nigeria for lecturers to literally sell passing grades to students who had not worked for the grades; female students are notorious for buying grades with sex. Through his own example, Chinua made students know that a few good professors can still be found in Nigeria. He did not compromise his grading standard to please any student. Some of the students admitted that he was too demanding and he expected a certain quality of work that most students were not interested in pursuing. Nonetheless, they applauded his integrity. His secretary, Esther Ogadi commented that his standard of grading was too high for today's youth. "Instead of him to compromise his integrity by lowering his standard, he accepted his children's advice and retired," said Ms. Ogadi. Indeed, Chinua retired much earlier than his colleagues expected. However, this is not to suggest that he retired because his academic demands are too high for today's youth. He had some other very important reasons; he wanted to devote more time to his writing and to securing the future of *Okike* magazine.

One of Chinua's classmates, G. Eneli strongly believes that high integrity is a common trait found in men who went through Umuahia/Ibadan route in their education. Eneli asserts:

---

[4] Tochukwu Okocha, interview with Egejuru.
[5] Dr. John U.D. Achebe, interview with Egejuru.
[6] Dr. Okey Ikpeze, interview with Egejuru.
[7] Prof. Nnaemeka Ikpeze, interview with Egejuru.

When you hear of fraudulent practices in Nigeria, you can't think of any of us Umuahia/ Ibadan products, involved in it. Our principal Mr. Simpson told us, 'you don't get something for nothing'. Chinua is not the type you associate with anything bad.[8]

Of course, one can dispute Eneli's claim, yet, he points out an important fact about Chinua: he follows good teaching from his parents and from his teachers, and one of the lessons he learned and lives by, is moral integrity.

---

[8] Chief Godfrey Eneli, interview with Egejuru.

19

An unwavering loyalty

Loyalty, a catchword for love and commitment is among the virtues extolled in Chinua. From members of his family to his friends and colleagues, testimonies poured in about his genuine love and commitment to persons, groups and causes.

True to the Igbo saying: "Beauty begins from the home," Chinua's loyalty starts with himself. Can one be loyal to oneself? Yes. If not, why then do we say that such and such a person refuses to accept who or what he is? Chinua has remained loyal to who he is despite his achievements and international fame. He expresses his loyalty to his nuclear family by tenaciously guarding their privacy. His abiding love for his immediate and extended family members is so total that he consciously avoids verbalizing or describing it. "There is something about our relationships which is difficult to put in words," he said of himself and his siblings. "I prefer not to turn this relationship into words because it is something of great value," he said of the love between him and his wife. With this type of inexpressible love for his family, Chinua's loyalty to his family cannot be questioned. By his own example of remaining simple and humble despite his fame, he has saved his family members, especially his children, from agonies and tragedies that befall those who live off the fame and fortune of their loved ones. Because he has taken his fame in stride, his children have learned to do the same. His daughter Chinelo said:

> We were never able to come out and say, 'my father is Chinua Achebe.' People expect you to come out and proclaim who you are, and when we don't, people tell us we are behaving abnormally. We have been lucky, people have tried to leave us alone.[1]

Chinua did not speak about relationship with any of his friends. He didn't have to; they all spoke on his behalf and did so glowingly. A

---

[1] Chinelo Achebe, interview with Egejuru.

An unwavering loyalty 155

number of them spoke of his respect and value for friendship. He once wrote to Sam Nwoye, "The greatest of friendships may move in mysterious ways." This was in allusion to their friendship over the years. Nwoye was the chairman at Chinua's wedding reception. Nwoye said: "He came back after twenty-five years to make me chairman of his silver wedding anniversary."[2] Obviously Chinua didn't want any other person to play a role reserved for Sam. It was a question of loyalty.

Frank Ellah said: "Our friendship went beyond classmates. It is not every friend you go to after forty years of being classmates."[3] Ellah made that remark because he went to Chinua when he needed some advice on a book he was writing.

V.C. Ike said he had always sought guidance and advice from Chinua from the time they were students at Government College Umuahia. Ike fears that this relationship is now threatened by distance.

> We had a kind of elder brother/younger brother relationship, for he was ahead of me at Umuahia and at Ibadan. I feel bad that a gap is developing between us because of distance; there's no phone to talk to him. But I have decided to write him once in a while even if I don't get any reply.[4]

Ben Uzochukwu another close friend from Umuahia days recalled:

> We met in 1944 as new entrants to Government College. Within the first week, there was something that brought us together. That thing was his headmaster, Mr. Ikegwuonu who was a close relative of mine. We have maintained correspondence over the years. When I got married to an expatriate lady in 1962, Chinua and Christie acted as parents of the bride. I still call him Albert. It gives me great pride to have him as my friend.[5]

C. C. Momah spoke passionately of his friendship with Chinua.

> We've been friends since 1944 from secondary school. I was the best man at his wedding and Vincent Ike was the best man at my wedding. What makes Chinua special as my friend is that he is a special human being. I can't locate any downs in our friendship. It's just time and distance that restrict our seeing each other often. I am very proud of our friendship. I wouldn't want to change any

---

[2] Sam Nwoye, interview with Egejuru
[3] Frank Ellah, interview with Egejuru.
[4] V.C. Ike, interview with Egejuru.
[5] Ben Uzochukwu, interview with Egejuru

aspect of it. We didn't indulge in letter writing but each time we meet, it's like we've never parted.[6]

Ulli Beier met Chinua at Ibadan in 1950. Chinua was among the students who took a course in Phonetics from him. Even then, Beier's impression of Chinua was that of an extremely thoughtful, serious and reliable fellow. Shortly after, Beier left the University for another job in his country. He kept in touch with Chinua and gradually their friendship developed. In 1966, the crises leading to the Nigerian civil war forced Beier out of the country. He still managed to keep informed about Chinua's whereabout and activities. At the end of the war, he made haste to visit Chinua at Nsukka. Speaking of his reunion with Chinua, Beier said:

> Our encounters over the last quarter of a century were always brief but rewarding. I felt that in spite of the long time that had passed, we could pick up our relationship exactly where we had left. And throughout the years, I always had that sense of trust and reliability. I knew that wherever and whenever I would meet Chinua, he would be the same. He wouldn't suddenly change, nor would our relationship.[7]

Loyal as ever, Chinua visited Beier a couple of times in his home in Germany. Beier said he felt guilty because he did not attend the celebration to mark Chinua's 60th birthday at Nsukka. He was unable to get leave from his University at that time. However, Beier marked the occasion in his own way. "To honour him I translated some of his poems into German and published a limited edition with illustrations by Obiora Udechukwu. I believe that Chinua's poems have not been appreciated sufficiently."[8]

Professor Ejike who is very fascinated by Chinua's personality, choked back tears as he talked about his friendship with the man. "He has been like a big brother to me for more than twenty-five years. Chinua is someone I would like to be with on a daily basis without missing an event."[9]

Some of Chinua's friends are sometimes so overcome by his commitment to their relationship that they try to keep some distance to avoid betraying or hurting it. For instance, C. L. Innes said:

---

[6] C.C. Momah, interview with Egejuru.
[7] Ulli Beier, interview with Egejuru.
[8] Ulli Beier, same interview.
[9] Prof. Ejike, interview with Egejuru.

"I am lucky to have known him. I have always had a double feeling about him and I had to remind myself that he is human. There is a fear of exploiting our friendship. So, I restrain from seeing or talking to him as much as I would like, for fear of betraying the relationship.[10]

Aigboje Higo met Chinua in 1964. They later became family friends. Higo thinks there's something in Chinua that makes him irresistible to people. He asserted, "I don't know of anyone who would meet Chinua and not fall in love with him. I mean it in the deep sense of appreciation." While some friends lamented that Chinua didn't write them as often as they would like him to, Higo alone claimed, "Chinua keeps up writing and replying to letters. He is committed to relationships, all his friends receive tons of letters from him."[11]

So much has been made of Chinua's Presidency of Ogidi Town Union because of the manner in which he secured that position. Under normal circumstances, a man without the *ozo* title cannot become President of that awesome body. Besides, very few Ogidi men would have the courage, not to speak of the patience to preside over that body. Chinua's acceptance of that office took more than courage, intellectual preparedness and patience. It took a genuine love and commitment to the well-being of Ogidi people.

Chinua shows loyalty to his people in different ways. The most outstanding demonstration of his loyalty to Ogidi is answering their call for help. As his friend Dr. Agulefo put it, "Disharmony and disintegration were facing Ogidi" and the people needed a man who commanded the respect of all Ogidi to step in and save the town." If Chinua did not love and respect his people, he would have turned down their offer. He not only restored the confidence of the people in their Town Union, he made ambitious plans for the development of Ogidi town. For the love of Ogidi, Chinua was unafraid to propose measures that were distasteful to the powerful Ndichie. With strong opposition coming from that powerful click, a man of lesser conviction and superficial commitment, would have given up the Presidency at the end of one term. But Chinua went in for a second term. His determination to restore the traditional ways of doing things the right way in Ogidi, almost cost him his life. As Dr. Agulefo logically reasoned, "It was in the process of driving across the country in the service of Ogidi Town Union, that he met the motor accident that almost took his life."[12]

---

[10] C. L. Innes, interview with Egejuru.
[11] Aigboje Higo, interview with Egejuru.
[12] Dr. N.T.C. Agulefo, correspondence with Egejuru

Another way that Chinua demonstrates his loyalty to Ogidi is by speaking their dialect. This might come as a surprise because we are expected to speak our mother tongue. However, for the western educated Igbo, speaking the mother tongue is no longer a given. Most western educated Igbo people are quick to abandon their language for English. Therefore, speaking Igbo language becomes a test of wills and a demonstration of loyalty to the group. It is in this context that several people made it a point, to mention that Chinua respects the culture and tradition of his people. He holds conversation with Ogidi village folks in Ogidi dialect. One seemingly minor incident made a group of Ogidi youth realize the depth of Chinua's knowledge of Ogidi dialect. It happened when Chinua was speaking to them. In the course of his speech, Chinua explained the double and true meanings of OSU (pronounced *awsu*), not to be confused with *osu* (*oh-soo*, outcast). Tochukwu who was in the group concluded: "That shows he knows our dialect very well. When he addresses an Ogidi crowd, he does not throw in English words. He is careful to avoid ands and buts."[13]

In *Things Fall Apart* and *Arrow of God*, Chinua talks about characters who killed or tried to kill the sacred python. But readers are unable to tell from his novels how the writer feels about the python in Ogidi tradition. However, a story by one of his nieces throws some light on the matter. There was an incident after the Biafran war when the Achebe clan was residing in their Headquarter, the compound of Isaiah and Janet Achebe. Chinua's niece, Janet Achebe talked about that incident:

> One day, a python came into the house and we were throwing things at it. Uncle Chinua came out; he was very angry. He shouted at us, reminding us that if we killed the python, we would be in trouble with Ogidi people. I don't know why he didn't want us to kill the python.[14]

Chinua didn't want them to kill the python not because he is necessarily an animal rights activist. It's because he appreciates and respects Ogidi tradition. Unlike his own father who did everything to protect Chinua and his siblings from Ogidi culture and traditions which he equated with pagan ways, Chinua has initiated his own sons into the cult of masquerades of Ogidi. Furthermore, when his daughters were engaged, Chinua made sure that the traditional background check was done on each groom and his family. He made sure the last and the most important ceremony in the marriage negotiation - *igba nkwu*, was

---

[13] Tochukwu Okocha, interview with Egejuru.
[14] Miss. Janet Achebe, interview with Egejuru.

performed. Though Chinua was in the U.S. the ceremony was performed at Ogidi because it is specifically for Umunna, the men of the kindred. His brother, John deputized for him and presided over the ceremony.

Loyalty to Ogidi is subsumed in his loyalty to the ethnic Igbo. "Chinua is Igbo to the core", was repeated by almost all the interviewees. Yet, several Igbo scholars, including Chinua, couldn't give a clear explanation of what it means to be Igbo to the core. What one can confidently say is that Chinua immerses himself completely in Igbo ways of life. His novels and essays on Igbo worldview and cosmology are the best witnesses of his love and commitment to the group. It is due to his dispassionate exploration of Igbo culture and tradition, that he earned the praise name, *Onu nekwuru Igbo*, the mouth that speaks for the Igbo, culturally that is.

Chinua was committed to the Biafran cause not because of his Igbo origin. He saw that the Igbos had been grossly wronged. Because of his fierce sense of justice, Chinua would fight for justice for any group whose human rights were trampled upon. He would have equally condemned his people if they had been wrong. So convinced was he of the legitimacy of their cause, that he risked his life and a blossoming literary career to support them. When the Biafran leader needed people to go round the world and plead the case of Biafra before foreign nations, Chinua was among the first people he summoned. Chinua did not hesitate to step forward despite the apprehension of his family members. Those who worked with him at that time, witnessed first hand, how hard Chinua worked, as he thought of solutions to the most mundane problems facing a beleaguered people.

A few interviewees like Ejike, Obiechina and Johnson Okudo called Chinua *Nwa afo Igbo* -a birth child of the Igbo, as opposed to an adopted child or a pretender to the Igbo parentage. The term is used for one who is thoroughly immersed in the culture and tradition of the land. Chinua is not only loyal to Igbo culture, he adheres very closely to Igbo code of conduct. This conduct hinges on four values: Humility, Evenhandedness, Rationality and Objectivity. Each of these words has a cluster of conducts around it, while the four act together as the pillars of Igbo morality and ethics known as *Odinani* and *Omenani*.[15]

"I believe the reason for choosing Chinua as the chair of Biafra's National Guidance Committee was his close contact with Igbo culture," claimed S. J. Cookey. And T.C. Nwosu asserted that Biafra's Ahiara Declaration with Chinua as its chief composer, was a synthesis of what it is to be Igbo. "When they lost the war," Nwosu said: "The Igbos lost

---

[15] Prof. Ejike, expounded on Igbo morality and ethics (*Odinani and Omenani*) during the interview.

the opportunity of demonstrating to the world, the Igbo ethos, Igbo sense of achievement, Igbo perfectionism, Igbo excellence and Igbo drive." These qualities are united in Chinua.

Furthermore, Chinua observes the traditions he describes in his novels. Ejike remarked that Chinua starts every event with *igo ofo* in which he invokes the spirit of the ancestors and pours libation to them; that he takes the tradition of breaking kola nut very seriously. In three hours of conversation, which Ejike recorded, "Chinua spoke to Igbo posterity. There was his usual posture of hope for our people. He believes the struggle for justice should be collective and families should remain points of focus."[16] Despite his undeniable loyalty to the group, Chinua is not blind to the negative qualities of the Igbo. He specifically despises their loudness and often times, empty posturing.

An aspect of Chinua's loyalty to the Igbo is his deep understanding of their strengths and weaknesses. Because of his knowledge of the Igbo, he was able to work with them at Nsukka to restore their morale after the war. Obiechina recalled: "There were people who, in the name of the federal government, felt they had to trample on Igbo people because we lost the war. Chinua called a meeting to deal with it. We didn't have to behave as if we were waiting to die."[17] It was to deal with aggravations and insults heaped on them that Chinua started publishing *Nsukkascope*, a periodical that became a morale booster for Igbo people during the years of reconstruction.

The majority of Igbo people appreciate Chinua. For instance, in 1996, Igbo U.S.A organized an appreciation diner party in honor of Chinua. In his short thank you speech, Chinua stated that although he had received countless awards and honors from innumerable institutions and organizations, the recognition and appreciation of him by his own people meant the most to him. With that admission, he demonstrated his understanding of the Igbo dictum, "Goodness/Beauty begins at home." As a true son of the Igbo, he knows that one who is only respected by outsiders and despised by his own people lives in shame and misery. By securing the recognition, the respect and appreciation of his people, Chinua considers his accolades complete.

The circle of Chinua's loyalty expands from the ethnic Igbo to the country as a whole. Even before there was a Biafra, Chinua's loyalty to Nigeria was unquestionable. Before the war broke out, there was a mass exodus of Igbos from different parts of the country. Chinua did not rush back to Igbo land. He remained at his job in Lagos even though he had learned that Hausa soldiers where looking for him. It was only when it became very obvious that the soldiers meant to harm

---

[16] Prof. Ejike, same interview.
[17] Prof. Obiechina, interview with Egejuru.

him, that he risked the journey back home. If he were not committed to his country, he would not have needed as much persuasion as he received from his co-workers before he finally left.

Immediately after the war, Chinua took his children on a short tour of the war torn Igbo land. It was his way of reassuring them that there was still hope for them in the country. His daughter Chinelo recalled the tour: "I remember him taking us around after the war, the broken up roads, the potholes; it was so dreary. He told us we have so much to look forward to. It was a very successful mission."[18]

And Higo who spent much time with Chinua after the war had this to say:

> When the war ended and there was this genuine feeling of no victors no vanquished, Chinua was prepared to say, 'let's see if these mistakes could be rectified.' He went beyond the civil war to see it as a manifestation of the ills of society. So he wrote *The Trouble with Nigeria*; that all Nigerians might look at themselves, the enormous resources and the waste.[19]

Chinua's scathing but candid criticism of Nigeria in *The Trouble with Nigeria*, ironically demonstrates his continued loyalty to his country. If he were not so concerned for the future, why would he spend his time pointing out the errors of the past? By pointing out why and how things went wrong politically for the country, the writer hoped the future politicians would do better. As if that were not enough, Chinua joined the People's Redemption Party. "He did it to raise the spirit of the people who wanted to create a party for the future," Ejike observed. His commitment to justice and fairness to the common man in Nigeria forced him into politics, an act that most of his close relatives and friends considered out of character. But all those who truly know the depth of his love for his country do not consider his joining a political party, out of character. Bola Ige noted that "Chinua is anxious to make every Nigerian remember his roots." Evidently, Chinua's loyalty to Nigeria has never wavered despite the trauma of the civil war. The seriousness with which he takes his Nigerian roots is seen in the moving words he spoke to the crowd that thronged to welcome him at the Lagos airport during his brief visit after nine years of absence. "I feel it is like a ritual of a sort," he said, " and I must make contact with the soil of Nigeria."[20]

---

[18] Chinelo Achebe, interview with Egejuru.
[19] Aigboje Higo, interview with Egejuru.
[20] Chinua, posted on the Internet by the Associated Press, lifted off the Lagos *Guardian* newspaper, August 25, 1999.

As further proof of his continued loyalty to his country, Chinua eagerly answered his country's call to duty when he joined the select group of scholars who revised the Nigerian constitution. In another national project, he was the leader of one of the groups assigned to compose a new national anthem. In yet another project, he wrote the words of the anthem commemorating the Black Festival of the Arts and Culture in 1976. In return, the Nigerian government showed its appreciation of Chinua's numerous services, by honoring him in 1979 with their highest civilian award, the National Merit Award, twenty-one years after he had brought honor to his country with the publication of *Things Fall Apart*. Nigeria's show of appreciation of Chinua was repeated in September 1999 when they gave the novelist their first National Creativity Award, twenty years after giving him the National Merit Award.

From his country, Chinua's loyalty reached out to embrace the black race. "Chinua's concern for the black man is his driving force. His gospel translates into '*Onye aghala nwa nne ya*' - let no one leave his kinsman behind."[21] Kinship to Chinua is not necessarily with his fellow townsmen or countrymen or black men, but kinship with all humans. In his lecture on Conrad's racism, Chinua pointed out white people's racist attitude in their refusal to recognize their kinship with black people. Thus, exposing the plight of black people in their relationship with the white world, became a motivating factor in Chinua's literary career. From the very beginning, his mission has been the restoration of dignity to the black race. In his public lectures he invariably addresses the iniquitous rider-and-horse relationship between the white man and the black man.

Chinua has a deep-seated commitment to the issues affecting black people. Speaking about the impact of Chinua's works on Blacks in the Diaspora, Thelwell said:

> The work of Chinua was as important for us as it was for Africans trying to define themselves as independent people outside the pejorative definitions of them by Europeans. Encountering Chinua's work was a revelation.[22]

During Chinua's stay at Amherst, his black colleagues noted the depth of his commitment to the black race. His lecture on Conrad convinced everyone that Chinua is never afraid to go against the grain, to confront the custodians of western literary canon. He is never afraid

---

[21] Prof. Ejike, same interview.
[22] Michael Thelwell, interview with Egejuru.

or embarrassed or inhibited from immersing himself in the cultural legacy of black people.

Despite Chinua's unrelenting criticism of the western world in their reluctance to share kinship with the black world, he is not bitter towards them. He does not run down their world. He continues to advise them to recognize the humanity and the presence of black people in the world. Chinua is very concerned about a possible nuclear threat to the entire world. He is equally concerned about the global consequence of ozone depletion. In the closing words of a lecture he gave at Loyola, New Orleans in 1992, he addressed the issues of coexistence and interdependence. He quoted a character in Hamidou Kane's *Ambiguous Adventure* who said to a French man, "We have not had the same past you and ourselves, but we shall have strictly the same future. The era of separate destinies has run its course." Then Chinua concluded, " If that is so, we had better learn to appreciate one another's presence and to accord to every people their due of human respect."[23]

Chinua's loyalty that started with himself and his nuclear family gradually soaked through the central fabric of humanity to its outer fringes.

---

[23] Chinua, *African Commentary*, Nov. 1989, p.54.

20

An empowering force for others

Over the years, Chinua has been putting his ideas to work not only for constituted bodies like the Nigerian Broadcasting Service, the Association of Nigerian Authors or Ogidi Town Union, but also for individuals. A number of his fellow writers who were interviewed claimed him as mentor. His classmate and well-known author, Mabel Segun acknowledged Chinua's role in her development as a writer. She said she had difficulty getting her first book, *My Father's Daughter* accepted for publication. She presented the manuscript to Heinemann and Heinemann asked her to lengthen the book as a condition for publishing it. When she refused to do as they directed, Heinemann rejected her manuscript. When Chinua became the editor of Heinemann's African Writers Series, Segun told him about her book. Chinua asked to see it and: "It was he who gave it to African University Press to publish. He was always helping and encouraging writers."[1]

In the same vein, V.C. Ike paid tribute to Chinua as his mentor:

> It's Chinua who gave me the confidence to emerge as a novelist. It was something that was impossible until I saw him do it. As a friend, he has always been willing to help me, and to see him make it, gave me the confidence that writing is not unattainable, and in fact, he gave you that feeling that the goal is not unattainable.[2]

Even when Chinua does not directly advise other writers on their works, he still unconsciously influences them. John Munonye was asked if Chinua influenced him in any way and he said, "People say my writing resembles his. He affected my writing in the sense that he was the first to write, so we wanted to do what he did."[3] What Munonye said is equally true for many writers who started writing many years after Chinua. For instance, when Phanuel Egejuru was writing her novel, *The Seed Yams Have Been Eaten*, she did not consult Chinua *per*

---

[1] Mabel Segun, interview with Egejuru.
[2] V.C. Ike, interview with Egejuru.
[3] John Munonye, interview with Egejuru.

se. However, whenever she wanted to render an Igbo thought into English, she asked herself: "How would Chinua phrase this?"

On a number occasions when Flora Nwapa spoke of her rise as the first woman novelist from west Africa, she never failed to mention that she sent the manuscript of her first novel, *Efuru* to Chinua for comment. After reading and commenting on the manuscript, Chinua recommended that she submit it to Heinemann for consideration. Nwapa did and Heinemann published her novel in 1966. Chinua also reached out to a fledging Nigerian poet, Mamman Vatsa. The case of Vatsa is particularly interesting because Vatsa was a Major General in the Nigerian army. In Nigeria there is the feeling that the military is anti-intellectual. Besides, soldiers are not normally encouraged to aspire to intellectual accomplishment. Therefore, a soldier from northern Nigeria writing poetry was quite unusual and exciting. Chinua's sense of fairness came to the fore and "when he saw Major General Mamman Vatsa's manuscript, he said that Vatsa should be encouraged," Arthur Nwankwo recalled. Chinua spoke to T.C. Nwosu about Vatsa's manuscript and recommended that Nwosu publish it. Nwosu published Vatsa's collection of poems, *Reach for the Skies, Poetry of Abuja*.[4]

Chinua's mentoring and inspiring of writers were not confined to young creative writers. Frank Ellah was Chinua's classmate at Ibadan. They have remained friends since then. After the Nigerian civil war, Ellah became a senator in the Rivers State. However, his tenure was brief because he soon resigned from the position. It was unprecedented for a Nigerian to resign from political office. Ellah decided to write a book to explain why he took such a drastic measure. However, before undertaking such a feat, " I found it necessary to consult good thinkers. I went to Chinua because he is the type who would inspire confidence. It's not everybody you go to talk to."[5] It was Chinua who wrote the forward to Ellah's book: *Nigerian Creation of States*.

Chinua is not known for throwing his weight around, but when there is a good cause, he would use his influence to achieve a positive end. Such was the case when he helped launch the writing career of young James Ngugi of Kenya. It all started when Chinua was attending the first conference of African writers held at Makerere University in Kampala Uganda in 1962. Young James Ngugi who was a student there, went to see Chinua and talked to him about his novel in the making. He gave the manuscript to Chinua who took the time to read it before the conference was over. Chinua was impressed with the manuscript so, he recommended some changes. He personally gave the

---

[4] Both Arthur Nwankwo and T.C. Nwosu talked about Chinua's patronage of Vatsa.
[5] Frank Ellah, interview with Egejuru.

manuscript to Van Milne, a representative of Heinemann at the conference. He recommended that they consider the manuscript for publication. In the end Heinemann published Ngugi's first novel, *Weep Not Child*, in 1964. From that positive and constructive encouragement, Ngugi's career as a writer took off.[6]

In 1980, the Noma award for publishing in Africa was awarded to the Senegalese writer, Mariama Ba, the author of *So Long a Letter*. At that ceremony, Ba met Chinua for the first time. Through an interpreter, she told Chinua that she started writing after reading *Things Fall Apart*.[7] Even when younger writers do not go directly to Chinua for advice, they still get inspiration from him. Several black writers, including African Americans like Toni Morrison, Maya Angelou, Yusef Komunyakaa, have acknowledged Chinua as a source of inspiration.[8] Now, African writers in different European languages experiment with their various adoptive languages because Chinua did it and succeeded. Thus, from his broadcasting days when he mentored many young Nigerians of various ethnic groups, Chinua has been busy mentoring and inspiring writers from all over the world.

---

[6] This is a known fact in African literature circles; Ohaeto refers to it in his book *Chinua Achebe*, Indiana University Press, 1997, pp. 91-92.
[7] Ibid. 216.
[8] Ibid. 283.

21

A generous soul

Generosity as applied to Chinua Achebe, is not only the willingness to share with others, but also a nobility of heart and a pronounced absence of meanness. It is not surprising that a man, who passionately despises obsessive accumulation of wealth, would be quick to share his "wealth" with others. Wealth here is not only material possession but also spiritual and intellectual endowments.

A number of people, who were asked to list Chinua's good qualities, said it was difficult to qualify the man in human terms. It came down to asking them point blank if Chinua possessed this or that quality. For instance, they were asked if he was generous. To this question, C. C. Momah replied, "There's no way he cannot be a generous man. He is generous with his time, his advice and his criticism. He is careful with money, but he is everything you would want in a host."[1]

Like most people, Chinua gives money to individuals in dire need of it. In addition to helping individuals, he spends money on worthy causes. A few examples will suffice to show that Chinua spends his money when it comes to supporting worthy causes. Theo Vincent shared some of his personal experiences spanning more than twenty-five years of friendship with Chinua. He talked about the problem that Nigerian members of PEN international always have with paying their annual dues. Because they cannot afford five hundred naira annual fee, many young Nigerian writers who are interested in PEN cannot join. As a last resort:

> We went to Chinua to complain that we couldn't pay our dues to PEN international. Chinua wrote a check for two hundred dollars to cover dues for twenty members. That's the kind of person I am talking about.[2]

Ngozi Ugwoke, a final year student at the University, told a moving story of how Professor Achebe and his wife adopted her family

---
[1] C.C. Momah, interview with Egejuru.
[2] Theo Vincent, interview with Egejuru.

literally. It started in 1980 when Ngozi's mother, did Mrs. Christie Achebe's hair in her small hair "saloon". Mrs. Achebe was so impressed with the hairdresser's patience and quiet disposition that she became friends with her. Ngozi then narrated what that friendship led to:

> Since then, Mrs. Achebe and her husband have been helping our family. They even paid fees for our dad who was then a student at the University of Calabar. They paid for medical expenses for an operation to correct the deformed legs of our youngest sister. They are paying school fees for her now. They have given us this accommodation in their premises free of charge. They continue to help us even after Professor Achebe's accident. For example, our mother and our youngest sister went to America for the wedding of Achebe's daughter Chinelo, and Mrs. Achebe and her husband paid all the expenses.[3]

It was in their home in Achebe's boy's quarter, that Ngozi and her four younger siblings were interviewed. Their mother was out on errands in the village. It was in view of Chinua's generosity that Ngozi gave him the praise name, *aka n'emelu ora* - the hand that ministers to the people. Her younger brother called Chinua, A MAN OF THE PEOPLE.

Dr. J.U. Achebe had not seen his uncle Chinua since he worked with the team that gave the first emergency treatment to him at Enugu in 1990. He was asked if his uncle had written him since the accident. He said that Chinua's wife wrote him from Paddocks hospital but "She talked mainly about the child they were sponsoring at the hospital, about the financial aspect of the child's operation." In this way, Dr. Achebe inadvertently corroborated Ngozi's story. So, here is a wife whose husband's life was hanging in the balance, talking about their financial responsibility for an operation on a child who is not even their own child! It is obvious that Mrs. Achebe and her husband discussed the health care of this young child even as her husband lay in a hospital bed, struggling for his own life.

Reuben, his driver talked about the kindness and generosity of the Achebes without being asked. "Prof is concerned about his employees' welfare. If you lost a relative, he gives you money even if he could not come to your house at that very time." Reuben gave an instance when his brother, whom the Achebes knew very well, died while Chinua was in Europe and his wife was in Lagos. The day his brother died, Reuben was scheduled to pick Mrs. Achebe from the airport; he kept the appointment. As soon as Mrs. Achebe got into the car, she asked him

---

[3] Ngozi Ugwoke, interview with Egejuru.

why he looked so haggard and forlorn. He told her what had happened. "Madam wept. She gave me some money to start buying kola nuts. She said that she and her husband would pay their condolence visit when her husband returned from his travel. That's the kind of people they are." Reuben also mentioned Chinua's other acts of generosity toward him:

> When it comes to gifts, he gives me clothes twice a year. And when he gives you used clothing, only you, the receiver will notice that that piece of clothing has been used. Another person will think you just bought the clothes. He gives me a complete set of safari suit. He gives shoes too. He gives you something with a clean heart. He doesn't dash you something anyhow.[4]

Chinua's friends and relatives talked of his generosity as a matter of fact. His friend and mentor Johnson Okudo said, "Chinua's gifts to me are countless, money, clothes and drinks." His cousin Ernest Achebe explained how much he owed Chinua for his career and livelihood. He credited Chinua with helping him get the training he needed to function in society. Chinua wrote letters on his behalf. After he graduated he got a job in the broadcasting establishment. Ernest said: "My relationship to him helped me in my career. He is a man with a large heart."[5]

Chinua paid school fees and gave pocket money to his young nephews and nieces. He bought books for some of them. He continues to give money and other gifts to his sisters. To Africans, especially to the very old, it is just part of the culture to help one's relatives, especially if one is more financially secure. Therefore, there is nothing unusual about Chinua paying school fees for his nephews and nieces. He owes it to them by virtue of being their uncle! Yet, every African knows that most rich people in Africa today do not help their poorer relatives. Most of them prefer to patronize non-members of their family because those people flatter them and sing their praises. They donate huge sums of money at fund raising events to show off their wealth. They live in mansions while their relatives squat in shanty towns. Besides, the more Africans get westernized, the less they consider themselves obligated to help members of their extended family. Yet, Chinua remains loyal to his culture; he sticks to the old ways of doing things. But most important of all, his giving spirit would not let him turn his back on his needy relatives. His relatives on the other hand, understand that things have changed; relatives are less obligated to take

---

[4] Reuben Alumona, interview with Egejuru.
[5] Ernest Achebe, interview with Egejuru.

care of one another these days. They recognize that Chinua's help to them is not in response to some traditional obligation. They know that he reaches out to them because it is in his nature to be generous.

Chinua's generosity was also evident in the way he responded to students when he visited Loyola University in New Orleans in 1992. Dr. Julian Wasserman described what he called an "amazing moment." This happened shortly after Chinua had finished talking to a group of students. There was some difficulty getting him back into the van. As the driver was about to move, a group of students who had travelled from a distance to see Achebe, came running to the van. Chinua spoke to the driver and the mechanism was lowered again. Dr. Wasserman said: "He did not give them two minutes, he took time talking to them. His type of generosity embodies giving without creating a debt or the feeling of owing on the part of the receiver."[6]

There are not many people willing to share their ideas or the secret of their success in a certain venture. These days, those who do share their ideas usually do so at a fee. They may write a book on "How to get published" or they get paid to give a public lecture on the subject. Chinua is among the few successful writers who are willing to share their ideas, and he does so at no fee. Several African writers, some of whom were interviewed, told stories of how Chinua helped them become successful writers. He invited them to send him their manuscripts, which he read and made suggestions for improvement. Sometimes he suggested specific publishers who were most likely to publish their works. It was not only in writing that he encouraged people. He mentored several young Nigerians in broadcasting. Obiora Udechukwu and Osmond Enekwe were among the younger colleagues he took under his wings, groomed and handed over responsibility to them. Udechukwu said, "Chinua behaves this way because he knows what we call *okutu azu* -begetting of successors." Out of the goodness of his heart, Chinua worked hard to establish solid foundations for various projects which he handed over to others to manage.

It is because of Chinua's generosity of spirit that he recognizes the potential in others to accomplish things on their own and he gives them the opportunity to do so. Because of his generous spirit, Chinua gracefully hands over the baton to his disciples just like the moon in the Igbo proverb, "*Onwa tie, o chalu ibe ya-* the moon shines and steps aside for its fellow moons to shine." Even though Chinua is no longer the editor of O*kike* magazine, he continues to solicit funds from foreign donors, to help his successors carry on with its publication. And one must not forget that he started *Okike magazine* with part of the money that Ulli Beier sent to help him out after the Biafran war. Most other

---

[6] Prof. Julian Wasserman, interview with Egejuru.

people would have kept all the money to themselves. After all, they were under no obligation to invest it in the magazine. Therefore, one can say that Chinua's generous spirit made him put out the money for the magazine. The same largeness of heart made him tell his colleagues that Ulli Beier was the one who provided the money to start with. Chinua would not take the credit.

"Time is money," is a popular slogan. Today, TIME is priceless! There are people who would give you money and other gifts instead of a fraction of their time. Therefore, when Momah said that Chinua is generous with his time, he hit on an important fact. Many scholars who have interviewed Chinua can testify to his generosity with time. For example, Egejuru is among those who have benefited from the gifts of his time, and of accommodation in his home. He even offers transportation to take the interviewing guest to the airport or to the bus depot. Egejuru travelled to Achebe's home at Bard a couple of times for interviews. But when Chinua realized that her questions were inexhaustible, he suggested that they continue the interview over the telephone to cut down on her travels. Throughout the years that she worked on Achebe's biography, Egejuru continued to interview him over the phone. And he always patiently and graciously answered all her questions.

Members of African Literature Association would agree that no other African writer of Achebe's stature, has participated in the Association's annual conferences as many times as Achebe. Not even his limited mobility would stop him from travelling long distances to honour invitations from organizations and educational institutions to make speeches and give lectures. Why does he continue to spend his time in this manner? From what one knows of Chinua's aversion for material wealth, one can say that monetary compensation has little if anything to do with his honouring invitations. He is simply generous with his time as he is with his money, his ideas, his advice and his criticism. Chinua is one who willingly shares his wealth because he strongly believes that wealth, in any shape or form is meaningless, unless it is used in the service of others.

In possession of his soul

Observations and comments by friends and relatives show that Chinua has an utter disdain and disregard for material possessions. In fact, the automobile accident that almost killed him has been blamed in part, to Chinua's indifference to material wealth. Several people shared the opinion that the accident could have been avoided if Chinua had used his own private car or even a University vehicle (he was entitled to one). Instead, he rented a car that was apparently not road-worthy. Among those who expressed a mild anger, was Achebe's friend, Aigboje Higo who commented:

> There are basic necessities that one must have, but Chinua doesn't think there are necessities that one must have. There is no reason Chinua shouldn't have his own car waiting at all times. But he couldn't be bothered with paraphernalia. Even his wife has had to adjust to his total disregard for worldly things.[1]

Chinua's accident sent his nephew, Emeka Okocha on a guilt trip. He was working for the company, "Land Flight", from which his uncle rented the car. Emeka felt very bitter because:

> I knew the inadequacies of the company, but I didn't know my uncle was one of our patrons. This only goes to show you the type of person uncle Chinua is. He is not the type to invest in flashy cars, that's our regret. Many people felt he could have used something better.[2]

During the Biafran war, many people like Chinua, who had the opportunity to visit foreign countries, engaged in profitable trading; they stashed money away in foreign banks. Others who were in charge of distributing supplies donated by charitable organizations,

---

[1] Aigboje Higo, interview with Egejuru.
[2] Emeka Okocha, interview with Egejuru.

misappropriated commodities meant for the people. Chinua was a Biafran ambassador-at-large. He roamed the world seeking for recognition and aid for Biafra. He had access to items donated to the masses. But he never saw the Biafran situation as one that provided opportunity for private accumulation of wealth. His sister Zinobia recalled, "Throughout his travels, my brother never came home with any type of merchandise, not even a match stick."[3]

Chinua's attitude to material wealth is very unNigerian. For instance, most Nigerians like to show off their wealth by building elaborate mansions, making large donations of cash at functions, or throwing lavish parties to celebrate one minor occasion or the other. But these gestures do not seem to appeal to Chinua. For many Nigerians, and indeed, to some of his relatives, Chinua's indifference to material possession, is a point of weakness. For these people, it is a given that a man of his calibre should engage in outward show of importance. His nephew, Dr. Okey Ikpeze commented, "Here in Nigeria, one would expect him to live in a palace, instead of a modest two story building he has in the village." What is more, Chinua will no longer be living in this modest two-story building. Because, in order to accommodate his present wheel chair bound life, a two-bedroom bungalow has been built next to the first house. This bungalow was nearing completion by early 1996. There is nothing fanciful about this bungalow. The rooms are very spacious and have wide doors for easy access and movement. Dr. Ikpeze continued, " With his books, he should be a millionaire, but he is not. People wouldn't even pay him for books they bought from him."[4] At one point, his sister Grace asked Chinua's wife why her husband wouldn't collect money from those who bought books from him. Chinua's wife said to her sister-in-law, "This brother of yours, does he look like someone who can collect debt from his debtors?"[5] His nephew hit on an important avenue to wealth these days -books. Writers and even ordinary intellectuals now have agents to promote their works or ideas, for commercial purposes. Agents would push a book to be adapted to a movie or a play or a musical, or be adopted for school or college courses. Yet, a celebrity like Chinua has no official agent to promote his works or arrange and negotiate payments for lectures and speeches. In fact, one admirer of Chinua's genius, Dr. Michael Mbabuike found it insupportable that a famous writer like Chinua had no agent. Mbabuike was appalled by the way people often took undue advantage of Chinua's generosity. People offered him very little or no money at all for making speeches or giving

---

[3] Zinobia Ikpeze, interview with Egejuru.
[4] Dr. Okey Ikpeze, interview with Egejuru.
[5] Grace Okocha talked of her conversation with Chinua's wife.

public lectures. Consequently, Mbabuike appointed himself Chinua's unofficial agent. He was particularly interested in making sure that Chinua received adequate monetary compensations for his public appearances. This was easier said than done. Because, many academic acquaintances of Chinua's who could not afford to pay the type of fee befitting Chinua, would bypass Mbabuike and go directly to Chinua and invite him to come and speak on their campus for a fraction of what writers of his stature would earn, and he would go.

Many Nigerians of Chinua's standing would be quick to use their influence to get whatever they desired from the country. But Chinua does not ask the government for anything, though he renders useful services to the country. Chinua's long time friend, Ben Uzochukwu believes that Chinua seems to lack the acquisitive instinct of many Nigerians. Uzochukwu, recalled how much it took him to persuade Chinua to purchase one of the flats that the government had for sale in Lagos. Few, if any Nigerian, would hesitate to buy a flat or several flats from the government, because they might end up not paying for those flats. They would instead, bribe government officials in charge of the program.

Another example of Chinua taking just what he needs, is provided by Arthur Nwankwo. When Chinua was planning to buy a piece of land at Enugu, he went to the bank to borrow some money. He wanted to put up some building on the land. Nwankwo, who accompanied him to the bank, recalled: " When we went to see Chief Celestine Oli, managing director of African Continental Bank, I thought Chinua would ask for a huge amount of money like one million naira but he asked for sixty-five thousand naira only."[6] Chinua eventually abandoned the project when an avaricious business tycoon, sent his thugs to demolish the foundation. Rather than serve the interest of corrupt officials who would certainly be bribed by the offending party, Chinua withdrew the case. Furthermore, Chinua quickly returned the money to the bank with interest. For an average Nigerian, that was a heaven-sent fortune that should never have been returned to the bank. Later, Chinua was asked about the incident and he confirmed Nwankwo's story. In the conversation that followed, he indirectly gave another important reason why he did not continue to pursue the case in court. He quoted what Mr. C. Fine often says, " *Esemokwu aburo nni-dispute is not food.*"[7] Obviously, Chinua would rather feed on real food to nourish his body and soul. He would avoid altercations that would only cause restlessness to his soul. For him then, living a clean and

---

[6] Arthur Nwankwo, interview with Egejuru.
[7] Chinua, telephone interview with Egejuru.

peaceful life is much better than owning all the wealth in the world and the headaches that come with it.

It must be noted that Chinua's distaste for inordinate material wealth started much earlier before he became world famous. For instance, when he gave up Medicine for a general degree in Arts, he was well aware of the monetary gain and prestige associated with the medical profession. He was equally aware of the uncertainties that surround a profession in the Arts. Yet, he settled for an uncertain future that became more so at the end of his final year at the University. "After graduation, I left the University not having any definite idea of what to do."[8] He did not at that time regret his choice because he felt deeply that the wealth and prestige of a medical doctor were not his priority. That he remained steadfast in his conviction is seen in the conversation he had with his very young daughter Chinelo. The child had asked him why he left Medicine when he could have been a rich doctor. He had told her, that being a doctor was good, but one should not be a doctor because of the money a doctor makes. When he was questioned on the same issue of leaving Medicine for Arts, he said he would have been a second rate doctor and he would have been unhappy too. From his youthful days when most young people are too eager to join the race for material wealth, Chinua's mind was already made up against that race. One might be tempted to attribute his attitude to his Christian upbringing. Perhaps he had taken to heart, the teachings of Jesus against excessive accumulation of wealth: "It is easier for a camel to pass through the eye of a needle than for a rich man to enter the kingdom of heaven" and "What will it profit a man to gain the whole world and lose his soul?"[9]

---

[8] Chinua, face to face interview with Egejuru.
[9] Words of Jesus found in Luke, 18:25 and Matthew 16:26 respectively.

23

A beautiful leisureliness

Chinua inherited his calmness and legendary quiet disposition from his parents. According to Chinua himself, quietness is a trait that runs on both sides of his family. He couldn't think of anyone in his lineage who wasn't quietly disposed. In fact, some members of his family see this trait as a point of weakness in Chinua. Ukamaka Ikpeze remarked:

> Sometimes when there is the need to speak out at once, he would not. He withdraws to watch events. It is a general fault with them all. My mother does it too. Before they talk, things have gone wrong.[1]

Chinua displays a beautiful leisureliness in his approach to many things that other people would normally fuss about. All his friends agree that he is never a hurried man. At the secondary school, he was known to be deliberate and slow. His classmates called him a slack because he was too slow in getting started on things. Talking about Chinua's laid back attitude, Ben Uzochukwu said: "He was not a slacker in a bad sense. He bides his time, you could never hurry him."

At the University, Chinua's classmates also noted his quietness and self-control. Bola Ige saw himself as a foil to Chinua:

> I was more of a trouble-maker than he, but in his own quiet way, he was firm. I was notorious for bugging people but Chinua was more into fashioning definitions for the *Bug*. He was not as vocal or boisterous as C. C. Momah or I. He was calm and disciplined.[2]

As a new recruit of the Nigerian Broadcasting Service, Chinua did not rush around to impress his senior colleagues. He maintained his quiet disposition. Two of his colleagues remembered that " he was very

---

[1] Ukamaka Ikpeze, interview with Egejuru.
[2] Bola Ige, interview with Egejuru.

self effacing when he came in. He didn't push himself. He would talk at meetings only when he was invited to."[3]

Chinua's ability to remain calm when everyone around him seemed to be going insane was cited by all those who have observed him at close quarters. Higo stated that Chinua's ability to relax is not given to many. Higo then gave an example. It happened on the day that Ibadan University awarded an honorary doctorate degree to Chinua. For that occasion, the Igbo community at the University arranged a beautiful ceremony of masquerades. Five minutes to the time, Chinua was still not ready to go. Higo and the others who were to accompany Chinua were ready and sweating profusely. They kept urging Chinua to hurry up. But he didn't see any reason for their fuss. "We have five minutes," he told them.[4]

It is difficult to imagine anyone who could maintain his "cool" in the midst of war. Yet, Chinua seemed to have done so during the Biafran war. A couple of those who worked closely with him at that time testified to his incredible composure in moments of extreme crisis. With all the problems that members of the National Guidance Committee had to deal with, "Chinua never lost his cool. Even under stressful situations he still remained calm and determined."[5]

> Chinua is calm and sedate; he is highly principled and detached from mundane things. Their father brought them up in that way. They have a way of seeing things; things that worry you don't worry them.[6]

What most people remember about Chinua at their initial meeting with him is his quiet nature. Soyinka recalled the first time he encountered Chinua. At that time he was a budding writer and he used to send short stories to Chinua at NBS. Soyinka said:

> I used to pop in there to do these short stories. I remember this quiet person, no real direct communication as such. I saw more of him in Lagos. We crossed one another along corridors, greeting hello, no real intimacy; not much conversation to make you say you know somebody in depth.[7]

---

[3] Both Michael Olumide and Sam Nwaneri made the comment in separate interviews.
[4] Higo told the story to illustrate Chinua's unhurried nature.
[5] E. Obiechina, interview with Egejuru.
[6] Ikenna Nzimiro, interview with Egejuru.
[7] Wole Soyinka, interview with Egejuru.

It was after the Mbari club had taken off that real interaction started. Even then, Chinua only attended the cultural events from time to time. This was mainly because he lived in Lagos while other members of the club lived at Ibadan where they held their meetings. However, considering that Chinua literally gave the club its name, one would have expected him to be more than "a sleeping partner," as Soyinka described his attendance and participation in the club. Again, his laid-back attitude prevented him from asserting himself.

Chinua's first visit to Amherst was a social disaster due in part to his self- effacement and composure. Added to this was the mistake of not introducing him formally to the group he was supposed to address. It was a social event for African American graduate students. Before the organizer had a chance to introduce Chinua, the students got into a political argument. Chinua just sat there quietly while they completely ignored him. Finally, he had to leave without addressing them because someone had come to take him to another place he was scheduled to appear. Chinua did not storm out fuming. Instead, "He withdrew graciously."[8]

The second time he returned to Amherst to teach, his reserved and quiet nature gave his colleagues a wrong impression of him. Because he had just come out from a civil war in his country, his hosts assumed that he possessed the sensibility of an insecure refugee. They were careful to limit their demands on him. But then, when a constant stream of journalists and scholars started coming to speak to him, they realized he had another profession and political life going on. They realized they were not just giving him a place of refuge. So, they stopped feeling sorry for him but made real effort not to demand that he be involved in the pedestrian mundane life of the University. It didn't take long before they all realized that the man was naturally quiet and unpretentious.

Some people view Chinua's calmness as a form of detachment or withdrawal. Unable to define Chinua's habit of withdrawing to a corner to watch people and events, Aniebo called it "a watching detachment." He went on to describe it: " You could feel the detachment, yet he is aware of things going on around. Even though he appeared detached, I could still tell him things and I did." Aniebo contrasted Chinua with Cyprian Ekwensi to further stress Achebe's type of quietness: "When Ekwensi is there, everything moves around him but with Chinua, you couldn't see anything."[9]

---

[8] Michael Thelwell, interview with Egejuru
[9] Ifeanyi Aniebo, interview with Egejuru.

Uzochukwu also talked of Chinua's withdrawal. "Chinua can cut himself off if he feels he does not like what is going on. He can withdraw to his shell and he does it often as a protective measure."[10]
On the other hand, C. C. Momah doesn't think his friend is detached. "He has always seemed a little more serious than others, but the seriousness doesn't translate into detachment. He enjoys people's company."[11]

Obiechina holds another view of Chinua's quietness. He remarked:

> He is private domestically; he is not a surface creature. As for detachment, he is not detached when it comes to issues that require attention and plain speaking. Chinua withdraws when there is a lot of histrionics and demonstration. I would not regard that as detachment but as good sense.[12]

Chinua demonstrates this good sense by distancing himself from the less attractive qualities of the Igbo. For example, the Igbo people are loud, theatrical and demonstrative. Chinua strongly disapproves of these qualities, so he pulls away when his people engage in them.

One of the groups Chinua put together during the Biafran war was the Manuscript Committee. Their job was to keep track of whatever bits of writing people were doing at that time. T.C. Nwosu who was in the group admired Chinua's relaxed way of going about things. Nwosu said: "He didn't like being fussy. He wouldn't intrude upon anything. He would let the noisy ones make their noise and he would do the intellectual thing."[13]

---

[10] Ben Uzochukwu, interview with Egejuru.
[11] C.C. Momah, interview with Egejuru.
[12] E. Obiechina, interview with Egejuru.
[13] T.C. Nwosu, interview with Egejuru.

24

A delicate sense of humour

If there is one thing that stands out in Chinua's works, it is the humour with which he coats serious issues. Much of this humour goes unnoticed by non-Nigerian readers because they do not share the author's social and cultural references. Most Nigerian readers find Achebe's novels very entertaining because they are packed with humour. Achebe's daughter Nwando expressed the sentiment of many Nigerian readers when she said, "Whenever I am reading *A Man of the People*, I fall down laughing."

It is not only in his novels that he indulges in humorous descriptions of characters and situations. Chinua has the ability to joke with the most painful of national issues and personal lives. In *The Trouble with Nigeria* he seriously denounces the blatant miscarriage of leadership in his country. Yet, every sentence in that book sounds like a joke.

He is even more humorous in real life. Members of his family said he always sent them rolling in laughter at family gatherings, especially when he mimicked people. Both his brother John and his sister Zinobia said that Chinua inherited his sense of humour from their parents, especially from their father.

Chief Aigboje Higo described Chinua's gift for making people laugh in these words: "Conversing with Chinua is like having a meal of jokes, especially when he is relaxed with you."

And C.C.Momah observed:

> He's not just funny; you enjoy listening to him talk. He is the best conversationalist I know. If you see how he slips in words, he will send you rolling with laughter, but in the end he makes very profound statements.[1]

Despite these testimonies, very few interviewees could provide samples of Chinua's jokes. This was because they couldn't remember

---

[1] C.C. Momah, interview with Egejuru.

them. Why was it difficult to remember Chinua's jokes? Soyinka provided a plausible explanation:

> Chinua is one of the most quietly witty persons I know. He has a way of inserting little jokes in the midst of conversations. As with all good witty material, it is always related to an event. The jokes that one remembers are those unstructured or tailored to the occasion. Chinua is not a storyteller such as would say, 'oh, have you heard this one?' and he will tell you a hilarious one. One remembers jokes like that. His are momentary, they are difficult to remember.[2]

Mabel Segun had a different description of Chinua's humour and jokes. She said: "He has an English sense of humour, subtle, sarcastic sometimes. He doesn't crack African jokes. African jokes are too broad, his are subtle."[3]

Chinua is known to hold back laughter when he throws his bombs of jokes. Bola Ige gave an instance: " We are in Aigboje's house, Chinua walks about and throws one bomb of a joke, and you look at his face, it's dead calm. He is a taut person. Either he programs himself to be self controlled or it is part of him."[4]

Ifeanyi Aniebo watched Chinua sitting in a corner at a birthday party. Chinua seemed to be mentally recording what was going on. Then, Aniebo noticed that:

> Once in a while he will throw out a little thing and people will crack up and the man will not be affected at all. His jokes are quietly said, so you don't attach importance to them. Surprisingly, the appropriateness of these jokes makes you forget them.[5]

Michael Thelwell recalled a joke of Chinua's that seemed tailored to the moment. It happened during a faculty meeting at Amherst. A faculty member made vicious charges against James Baldwin, accusing him of anti-Semitism. As they were embroiled in their discussion of those charges, Chinua walked in and listened for a while. He then said to them, " The Igbos have a proverb that says, 'when a tsetse fly lands on your penis, you approach it carefully.'"[6] That proverb stopped them all in their tracks. Although this proverb sounds vulgar and funny, it

---

[2] Soyinka, interview with Egejuru.
[3] Mabel Segun, interview with Egejuru.
[4] Bola Ige, interview with Egejuru.
[5] Ifeanyi Aniebo, interview with Egejuru.
[6] Michael Thelwell told of the incident.

makes a profound statement to the effect that delicate situations call for cautious approaches.

One of Chinua's friends invited a woman to his house while his wife was away. Unfortunately for the man, his wife returned suddenly. Luckily for him, Chinua drove in almost at the same time of the wife's return. The man rushed to Chinua and whispered to him; he asked him to help him get the lady out through the back door. Chinua kindly obliged and spirited the lady away. Later on, Chinua called his friend and said to him, "I am not he who takest away the sins of the world."[7] He had rescued his friend, but he had to let him know in a humorous manner, that he didn't go about being an accomplice in shady deeds.

As a young bachelor working at NBS, Chinua invited one of his female colleagues to dinner at his house. While he was driving her back to her place, a police officer stopped them and asked Chinua, "whosai you pick am -where did you pick her from?" Chinua responded, "From my house."[8] This incident was fictionalized in *No Longer at Ease* when Obi and Clara were sitting in Obi's car at the beach and a police man came and asked Obi the same question Chinua was asked.

V.C. Ike recalled a joke that Chinua made when Ike wrote him about his degree exam result. Both of them studied the same subjects at the University. Ike came out in the second division as Chinua did earlier. In his letter, Ike jokingly bragged that he and Chinua were then equal because they obtained the same result. Ike said: "He wrote me back a short letter saying: 'was it not St. Paul who said that there are many stars in the firmament but some shine brighter than others?' So, he wasn't ready to accept the idea that we were at par."[9] Although this was a joke between friends, Chinua used the opportunity to comment subtly on individual characteristics. Indeed, stars are shaped the same, but they vary in the degree of their brightness.

C.C. Momah remembered a number of jokes in Chinua's letters to him. One was about the incident with Ike. In a slightly altered version, Chinua wrote to Momah, "St. Paul said that one star differs from another in glory. St. Paul would have illustrated his point with a master's degree if he had it at the time." In another letter to Momah, Chinua said: "I really believe there's something wrong with my writing style, even when I write with studied negligence as in my last letter to you, I am accused of elegance. It's just too bad you know. It's like being a member of the Royal family, nothing you do escapes comment." In the same letter, Chinua told his friend of "two rather obscene jokes I heard recently. One of the jokes was about a Mr. Smith

---

[7] V.C. Ike told the story to illustrate Chinua's subtle joke.
[8] V.C Ike recalled the story as Chinua told it to him.
[9] Ike recalled Chinua's joke in a letter Chinua wrote to him.

who asked his four-year old son what he wanted for his birthday. The boy said he wanted a baby brother. His father told him the time was too short, for his birthday was only two weeks away. The boy told his father to put more men on the job. At the end of the jokes, Chinua warned his friend, "After reading these jokes, please destroy these sheets. I don't want such awkward manuscripts to be produced when I shall have become a great man."[10] It appears those sheets were not burnt or if they were, his friend remembered the jokes and told them to researchers asking for samples of jokes from the great man.

Chinua even takes his jokes to the meeting of Ogidi Town Union. On one occasion he wanted to make a point about the mistake people often make when they agree with you on something without thinking it over. He illustrated: "When we salute in Ogidi, we say '*kwenu!*' and we respond '*yaah!*' But you will be *kweying* without knowing why you are *kweying*."[11] Who else but Chinua would think of making a verb out of a salutation? Yet, he used the joke to caution people to consider the consequences of their actions before taking them.

In the most mundane of situations, Chinua can find a joke to fit. At a lunch in the house of Professor Ejike, the house-boy did not put the knives and forks in their proper positions. Ejike got angry with the boy and started scolding him. Chinua said to Ejike, "Leave the boy alone, don't you see that the things of the white man are confusing to him?"[12] This was an innocent funny remark, yet it addressed the confusion that western ways have wreaked on the African mind.

Sometime in late 1987, Egejuru drove from Rhode Island to Wellesley College in Massachusetts to listen to Chinua's public lecture. She ran into Chinua on his way to the Hall. He was very surprised to see her there. So, he asked what she was doing there. She told him that she had just come from Nigeria and was looking for a job. He laughed and asked her, "Do you mean that a high powered person like you couldn't find a job in Nigeria?"[13] The idea of Egejuru being high powered was very funny indeed, but the funnier and ironic truth was that many high-powered Nigerians could not find jobs in their country. Thus, in that seemingly innocent question, Nigeria's waste and abuse of its human resource were ridiculed.

As saddened as Chinua was by the Nigerian civil war, he could on occasion, crack jokes or laugh at jokes about the war. He told a little anecdote to Ulli Beier. On several occasions he and his family had to evacuate before the advancing Nigerian soldiers. They moved to

---

[10] C.C. Momah made reference to these jokes in Chinua's letters to him.
[11] Ben Ogbogu, during an interview with Egejuru, recalled the joke by Chinua.
[12] Prof. Ejike cited it as an example of Chinua's wisdom permeating his jokes.
[13] Chinua ran into Egejuru unexpectedly in Massachusetts and made that comment.

different towns and lived in different houses. Towards the end of the war, they had to move one more time. This time, one of his children said to him, "Daddy you must be very rich, you have so many houses."[14] No doubt the child's innocent but false impression of his father's wealth, contrasted sharply with the reality of the moment.

It is very remarkable that Chinua's humour is deeply entrenched in his wisdom. He does not crack jokes just for the sake of jokes. Like his normal utterances, his jokes are well crafted and to the point. As in his sentences, nothing is wasted in his jokes. In addition to making profound statements in his jokes, Chinua can sometimes insult you in a very decent but subtle manner with his jokes.

---

[14] Ulli Beier recalled the joke in a correspondence to Egejuru.

Chinua and the Nobel Prize

As far as Chinua could remember, he has been nominated five times for the Nobel Prize. The nominations started as far back as the nineteen seventies. Many of his admirers are disappointed and some are outraged that he hasn't won the coveted Prize. Why he hasn't won the Prize remains a matter of conjecture.

Without any prompting, most of the interviewees made comments on the topic and gave their own reasons why Chinua hasn't won the Prize. Some of their remarks deserve to be included in a biography of Chinua Achebe:

> "Probably why he has not won the Nobel laureate is that he has not played the political game it entails." [1]
> " Part of his inner complexity could be seen in his nonchalant attitude toward the campaign to get the Nobel Prize in literature."[2]
> " Chinua is not a controversial figure. He is not a lavish man, may be that worked against him in the Nobel Prize." [3]

For a couple of Chinua's admirers, no honorific awards or symbolic prizes like the Nobel Prize could do justice to his literary achievements. For example, someone asked T.C. Nwosu what he thought about Achebe as a candidate for the Nobel Prize. He responded:

> Achebe is the quintessential African black man, Igbo to the core. His works are yet to be understood. He is too deep and too profound. His profundity transcends all these prizes and awards. How do you price the priceless? How do you quantify the unquantifiable? His role in literature is yet to be appreciated. Achebe does not speak the language of Nobel Prize judges.[4]

---

[1] Victor Nwankwo, interview with Egejuru.
[2] Arthur Nwankwo, interview with Egejuru.
[3] Godfrey Eneli, interview with Egejuru.
[4] Dr. T.C. Nwosu, interview with Egejuru.

Soyinka brought up the Nobel Prize issue when he wanted to address the question of weak points in Chinua:

> The so-called bad blood which seems to be between us was created by his acolytes. One of them wrote me awful letters accusing Skip Gates of pushing me for the Nobel Prize. This fellow wrote me a Festschrift whose sub-text was, 'How dare anybody speak of Wole when Chinua is there?' I don't believe Chinua was aware of the extent that fellow went. Chinua must accept a little of the blame (for the escalation of the verbal warfare between their adulators).[5]

Soyinka believed that Chinua's lack of response when a situation called for his intervention was a point of weakness in the latter's character. He felt that Chinua should have intervened to stop his adulators' attack on him but he didn't. According to Soyinka, Chinua's silence led to unnecessary counter attacks and insults on him by Soyinka's supporters.

Michael Thelwell lamented what he called the destabilizing influence of western honorifics and prizes on African literature. He went on to say:

> Truly great writers never had to go out of their way to create rituals that emphasize their importance and accessibility. Achebe is very important and accessible without self-promotion or self-aggrandizement. He doesn't need to do that. In some places, the eagle that flies too low is mistaken for a crow. Achebe never had to fly too low.[6]

In other words, for Thelwell as well as for Nwosu, Achebe's worth cannot be measured in prizes. More importantly for Thelwell, Achebe, the eagle will not fly too low to pander to western recognition and rewards. What explains Europeans' reluctance to give their prize to Achebe, he believes, is the latter's defiance of European intellectual arrogance, coupled with his total commitment to the cultural legacy of black people.

Thelwell then proceeded to tell a joke that was purportedly circulating among western scholars of African literature:

> Two western academicians are talking about Nigerian literature. One asks the other, ' Who is Nigeria's greatest writer?' He answers, ' Soyinka of course.' He asks again, ' And what is his greatest book?' He answers, '*Things Fall Apart*'.[7]

---
[5] Wole Soyinka, interview with Egejuru.
[6] Michael Thelwell, interview with Egejuru.
[7] Thelwell, same interview.

Points of weakness

"There is no one without BUT" is an Igbo saying that underscores the fallible nature of humans. Therefore, one expects Chinua's relatives and friends to know and talk about his faults or weaknesses. Consequently, every interviewee was asked the question: "What are Chinua's weaknesses?"

Surprisingly, it was difficult to get anyone to mention any faults or points of weakness in Chinua's character. Most of his friends correctly stated that it was difficult to find fault in a person you admire and respect so much. None of his siblings could think of any points of weakness. Among his children, only Chinelo answered the question with, " That's a difficult question. You have to put your mind to it to find one." It was when she was talking about how her father always carried out any resolutions that she hit on something that appeared like weakness in her father: "He smoked when he was young but when he decided against it, he just stopped."[1]

One of Chinua's nephews said that weakness is a matter of perception. What some people might consider weakness might be considered strength by other people. For instance, one nephew considered a point of weakness the fact that Chinua never uses his position and influence to advance the interest of his relatives. By African system of values, one is expected and encouraged to practice nepotism. By refusing to abuse his position for the benefit of his relatives, Chinua is considered unAfrican. However, another nephew sees it as strength. "His sense of fairness prevents him from practicing nepotism," he claimed. In the same vein, a fellow writer felt that Chinua could have used his influence to help some of them get teaching positions or go on speaking tours to the U.S. and to other parts of the world. And since he had not purportedly done this, he is deemed self-centred and that's a point of weakness.

Chinua found it amusing that some people actually thought he had no fault. He readily admitted to one specific fault which he shares with

---

[1] Chinelo Achebe, interview with Egejuru.

his siblings. They are all too quiet and too cautious. Things could and do go wrong while they are literally dragging their tongues. Chinua explained:

> We don't try to force things or make things happen. This is one aspect of our nature which could be good or bad. Therefore, if you let things be too much, they could get out of hand.[2]

S.J. Cookey argued that it could be better sometimes not to respond to a call for action. He said, "When someone is crying out for you to do something and you don't, it's not necessarily a point of weakness. It could be a sign of strength."[3]

Soyinka saw the negative aspect of doing nothing when you are required to do something. He gave two examples in which Chinua's silence or intervention led to some ugly situations. In the first instance, Chinua's acolytes/disciples worked on *Okike* with Chinua; because of these sub-editors, the magazine "became tribalistic to an obscene level," claimed Soyinka. He felt that Chinua should have done something to prevent that development, but "he chose not to do anything." Soyinka continued: "Our adulators are there, we didn't create them, but it becomes the responsibility of the writer to ensure a kind of distance between him and them." Apparently, Chinua did not create that distance. Another occasion was when Chinua objected to a national funeral for Awolowo and in addition referred to the man as an ordinary tribal chief. In response, Awolowo's followers including Soyinka's acolytes, attacked Chinua in the newspapers. Chinua fired back at them. Soyinka was disappointed that Chinua allowed himself to be drawn into the ugly Awolowo debate. He saw Chinua's counter attack as an example of his black pull at work.

Arthur Nwankwo cited Chinua's excessive trust in people as a point of weakness. "This leads to misjudgement of character and disappointment," Nwankwo claimed. He gave an instance of how having too much trust in people hurt Chinua. It happened when an admirer of Chinua's asked to borrow fifteen thousand pounds sterling from Chinua. He needed the money to renovate his house and sell it. He promised to return the money after selling his house. Chinua referred the man to Nwankwo who saw through the man and refused to lend him the money. The man went back to Chinua who then lent him the money. "Chinua trusted the man and so he gave him the money," Nwankwo said. Five years later, Chinua wrote Nwankwo to help him track down the man and recover his money. Nwankwo could not find

---
[2] Chinua, interview with Egejuru.
[3] S.J. Cookey, interview with Egejuru.

the man and he doubted that the man would ever return that money to Chinua.[4] On the other hand, Dr. Ejike cited Chinua's over trusting nature as a sign of an excellent mind. "Such a person gives you the benefit of the doubt before he finds a reason to distrust you," Ejike claimed.

Chinua is impatient with "fools", not fools in the sense of St. Paul. According to Obiechina, this "foolishness" has to do with an attitude of complacent self-glorification and self righteousness. It has to do with a form of wickedness, where somebody is out to sow seeds of disruption and to inflict pain on others." Chinua does not disguise his disdain for such people and he puts them down in public in the manner of Okonkwo of *Things Fall Apart*. This attitude could be considered a point of strength, Obiechina concedes. Among the Igbo however, one has to be more tactful in dealing with such aggravating people.

Ulli Beier confirmed Obiechina's observation in a story he told about Chinua. He did not consider it a fault in Chinua to be impatient with fools. If anything, it's a sign of courage and good sense. He narrated an incident that happened in Berlin in 1979 at the Horizonte Festival. During a luncheon, some senior German officials made derogatory remarks about East Berlin and how unfree writers were beyond the wall. Chinua who responded on behalf of the writers answered with quiet dignity. He told the conferees that he came from a country that had just survived a civil war, but he hadn't come to Germany to wash his dirty linen in public. He went on to say that he and other African writers had come to meet and exchange ideas with their fellow writers. They had not come to Berlin to be involved in the cold war. Beier mentioned this incident because it threw light on Chinua's character. Beier said: "He does not suffer fools gladly, and at public gatherings he could put them in their place firmly and clearly but without being aggressive."[5]

In Nigerian parlance, Chinua damns or disgraces publicly, people who like to prove they are important when they are worthless and empty. Chinua can subtly throw somebody's stupidity at his face or firmly put him in his place. For instance, after his speech at Loyola in 1992, the audience was invited to ask questions. One man expressed his disappointment that Chinua had phrased a sentence in a certain manner. He wondered if Chinua would mind rephrasing his sentence and choosing his word more cautiously. Chinua laughed and said he stood by his sentence. He then advised the man to phrase his own sentences in whatever manner he pleased when and if he wrote his own book; the audience exploded in laughter and applause. On another occasion at

---

[4] Arthur Nwankwo, interview with Egejuru.
[5] Ulli Beier, correspondence to Egejuru.

Austin Texas in 1998, someone in the audience wanted to know what Chinua thought about the socio-political situation in Nigeria. "Is the situation really out of control as people claim?" asked the man. Chinua responded with an Igbo counter question: "When you hear that a man's house has fallen, do you ask if the ceiling came down with the roof?"[6] Chinua's counter question simply made the audience realize that the man's question was a confounding demonstration of stupidity. Instead of telling the man point blank how stupid his question was, Chinua pushed the responsibility to an Igbo saying, and still got his point across. While some people might consider Chinua's blunt way of silencing fools a mark of strength, some others, especially Igbo people might consider the approach tactless if not brutal.

At Ogidi, Chinua attended a function where he met some of his childhood playmates. They joked about some of the things they did in those good old days. Some got a good laugh by making up stories. Well, one of the playmates started bragging that he used to throw Chinua down in wrestling (though he never wrestled with Chinua). He caused some laughter. Then Chinua asked him: "And how far did your wrestling prowess get you?" In the end Chinua drew a thunderous laughter with his subtle but damning retort.[7]

During her interview with Chinua, Egejuru started by explaining that she wanted to focus specifically on the human as opposed to the literary side of the writer. Before he took any of her questions, Chinua took some time to explain to her that a person cannot be easily compartmentalized. He used Egejuru as his example of showing how an individual can be so many different things. After his long illustration he concluded:

> I don't draw a line between the human story and the literary story, because to me it is one story, though I understand that one at a distance can separate them. I don't think in those categories particularly. I am not saying that these categories don't exist or are not valid, they are. For me it is one story. There is no way you can say this is it or that is it. This is how I perceive of the world in life. We are many different things. To me the best is to be able to hold all these together without the various components fighting against one another.[8]

---

[6] Chinua's speech at the African Literature Association Conference at Austin Texas, March 1998.
[7] Tochukwu Okocha cited the incident as an example of Chinua's ability to put fools in their place.
[8] Chinua, interview with Egejuru.

Instead of telling Egejuru straight away that her idea was debatable if not valid, he did it in a subtle manner. Where another person might keep quiet to avoid embarrassing the questioner, Chinua would not. Besides, he would use the opportunity to deliver a valuable lesson.

For Victor Nwankwo, Chinua has one weak point and that is: "You never can tell when he is unhappy with you no matter how discerning you are. You can only guess what he would do or say under certain circumstances." Again, this is in keeping with his extreme self-control.

One is finally left with a vague notion of what actually translates into weakness as it relates to Chinua. Some of his friends and colleagues said they could not associate him with anything bad. Higo seemed to speak for all admirers of Chinua when he said: "Chinua cannot help himself if people see him as faultless."[9]

---

[9] Aigboje Higo, interview with Egejuru.

27

Praise names for Chinua

Naming among the Igbo people is a quasi-sacred undertaking, because a name is often considered a spirit that inhabits it bearer. A person's name is believed to play itself out in the life of the named. Therefore, it is crucial to choose a good and fitting name. In most cases, the circumstances surrounding a baby's birth determines its name. This is why it is rare to name a baby before it is born.

Like birth names, praise names must fit the bearer. A praise name is like a badge of honour and recognition for a person. As the term implies, a praise name is a form of flattery that is meant to recognize positive achievement or good behaviour. It can also reflect a person's character. A praise name is not to be confused with a nickname because the latter does not often praise or flatter but can in fact, denigrate a person.

Praise names flatter the receiver's ego and make him feel good. Among the Igbo for instance, to greet a titled man properly, you must first call him by his praise name. By doing that you show him that you recognize his social status and respect it. Furthermore, you put him in a good mood and establish a good rapport before you start a serious conversation with him. Because of the role praise name plays in daily greetings among the Igbo, it is also known as salutation or greeting name.

A person can choose his or her own praise name because that person knows himself/herself better than other people do. A person can also receive praise names from other people who know him or her very well.

UGONABO -two eagles- is the praise name that Chinua chose for himself. There wasn't any elaborate ceremony to mark the occasion because the name was not accompanied by an *ozo* title. But Chinua called together a few elderly men in his village to let them know that he had taken a praise name. With that gesture, he sort of "registered" his salutation name with his people.

Though Chinua is not known to flatter the ex-colonial masters, he makes no apologies for his colonial inheritance (western education).

Chinua is not unique in this inheritance; every colonized African is heir to it. However, Chinua is among the very few westernized Africans who feel comfortable straddling African and European cultures. The best demonstration of his adaptation to these two worlds is his use of language. Whether he is expressing an idea in English or Igbo, he always finds the exact word or words in each language. Where he cannot find the exact English equivalent of an Igbo word, he creates an English expression that perfectly articulates his Igbo ideas. His mastery of both Igbo and English enables him to create specific idioms to verbalize Igbo thoughts and ideas in English.

Ugonabo is Chinua's way of saying that he is a child of two worlds and that he feels equally comfortable in both. He has been able to internalize his Christian upbringing and still remain rooted in Igbo tradition. Ulli Beier believes that:

> The strongest point in Chinua's character is his integrated personality. It is this integrated personality that gives him his sense of security, his reliability, his sober and well-considered judgment.[1]

Because Chinua is confident in himself, he is able to accommodate many different influences effortlessly. With his unfailing good judgment, Chinua hit upon a praise name that captures the essence of a well-balanced individual. Indeed, the significance of *Ugonabo* can only be fully appreciated by those who understand the symbolic nature of the eagle in Igbo culture. The eagle makes rare appearances and to spot two eagles sitting back to back is a rare occurrence. Chinua casts the figure of two eagles sitting comfortably back to back, a truly singular phenomenon.

EAGLE-ON-IROKO, the theme of the symposium marking the 60th birthday of Chinua, is the praise name bestowed on him by humanists and academicians, especially those in the field of African literature. *Eagle-on-Iroko* rivals *Ugonabo* in weight and significance. It combines the two most powerful symbols in Igbo land. The *iroko* is the king of trees just as the eagle is the king of birds. When an eagle lands on the dome of an *iroko*, it adds its beauty and strength to the *iroko*'s and thus draws more attention to the tree and the bird. A combination of these two monarchs yields an ultimate symbol.

Speaking of the appropriateness of this symbol, Theo Vincent said:

> Chinua's elusive humanity needed to be captured in words. When I saw the *Eagle-on-Iroko*, I couldn't think of anything better. To use

---

[1] Ulli Beier, correspondence to Egejuru.

these two powerful symbols to capture the essence of one man, one isn't able to invent anything comparable.[2]

Chinua is the eagle of African literature poised at the helm of the continent. He beautifies Africa with his writings and draws more attention to it. At the same time, this world he perches on, amplifies his figure and draws attention to him. In this *Eagle-on-Iroko*, one perceives strength, beauty, duality and balance, and one perceives greatness.

UGO MMUTA -Eagle of Knowledge is the praise name that his friend and fellow novelist, John Munonye came up with. He called Chinua a philosopher and the quintessential learned man. For him, Chinua is a genius who effortlessly makes one fall in love with his ideas and words.

IKEJIMBA -Strength that upholds the nation is a titular praise name and the highest ranking official in the king's cabinet at Ogidi. Igwe Amobi of Ogidi gave that title to Chinua on behalf of Ogidi people. *Ikejimba* is a term loaded with meaning. A comparable analogy is the central pillar of a house.

In his position as the President General of Ogidi Town Union, Chinua performed duties that earned him the title of *Ikejimba*. He stepped in to hold his people together when they were literally falling apart. He drew up an agenda to rid Ogidi politics of corruption. He came up with progressive ideas that would launch Ogidi into the 21st century.

IFE EJI MALU OGIDI -That for which Ogidi is known, is a sonorous praise name coined by Chinua's mentor, Johnson Okudo. In this name, the old man proclaimed Chinua the identity of Ogidi. This is important because Chinua was not the first Ogidi man to make the name of his town known beyond their immediate Idemili region. Before Chinua's time, there was Mr. Atuanya, an uncle of Mrs. Agnes Achebe. He was so huge that Ogidi people gave him the praise name, *OKASI OGIDI* (the biggest one of Ogidi). Probably because of his size, he became a policeman. When Mr. Atuanya went to work in Owerri province, the people of Owerri were captivated by his gigantic and imposing personality. He soon became known in Owerri as OGIDI POLICE- Ogidi, the police. He had such a hold on Owerri people that they regularly included his statue in their Mbari exhibitions. Eventually, he passed into Owerri legend as a super giant, because of his size, Mr. Atuanya made the name of Ogidi known in other parts of Igbo land. However, the fame he brought to his town was still local; it came from another region of the country. On the other hand, Chinua

---

[2] Theo Vincent, interview with Egejuru.

brought worldwide recognition and fame to Ogidi with his publications and lectures across the globe.

ONYENKUZI- Teacher- is the praise name that Obiechina gave to Chinua. In an elaborate article titled, "In Praise of the Teacher: A Tribute to Chinua Achebe," Obiechina explored the pedagogic role of Chinua the artist and novelist. This tribute was a confirmation of Chinua's indirect claim to that title many years earlier. In his essay, "The Novelist as a Teacher," published in his collection, *Morning Yet on Creation Day* (1965), Chinua explained and equated the role of the novelist to that of a teacher. Chinua's primary motive for writing was to straighten the crooked image of Africa fashioned by Europe. His secondary aim was to help Africans and black people in general to regain their lost dignity and self -confidence. Chinua saw this process of self- reclamation as a matter of "education in the best sense of the word." And he is the one doing this work of educating his people.

The dictionary definition of teacher falls short of the weighty connotation of its Igbo equivalent, *Onyenkuzi*. The word is a metaphor drawn out of smithery. A smith puts a piece of crooked metal on an anvil and straightens it with hammer blows. *Onyenkuzi* literally straightens crooked ideas and information. He gives desirable shape to a mass of knowledge. In a more refined application, the role of *Onyenkuzi* becomes multi-layered. Obiechina compared teachers to great founders of world religions; they were also teachers as well as moral and social philosophers. Like a philosopher, a teacher brings knowledge and enlightens people. *Onyenkuzi* is a custodian of moral and ethical values, he makes sure that the moral and ethical paths of his community are straight.

The teaching profession has lost its prestige and respect in recent times. But that does not diminish the stature of truly great teachers who effect changes in their worlds. Feeling that readers might misunderstand the word teacher, Obiechina explained why his application of it to Chinua is appropriate:

> When I speak of Achebe as a teacher, I am casting my mind back to happier times for the teaching profession; to its golden age, when it was not defined in material terms but by a certain spiritual plenitude; a sense of real achievement in pursuit of the high goals of a civilization's ideal values. I am talking of that time when the teacher bore a special burden for spreading of enlightenment; when the teacher played a special role in bringing knowledge and clarity to dispel mental and moral confusion.[3]

---

[3] E. Obiechina, "In Praise of the Teacher: A Tribute to Chinua Achebe," paper presented at the *Eagle-On-Iroko: Chinua Achebe at 60* symposium, Feb. 1990

Chinua is a teacher in the original and best connotation of the word. He has a passion for spreading the truth and dispelling ignorance. When we look at the entire body of his works, we see a textbook of the quintessential teacher and novelist instructing and enriching the lives of his readers. He has positively changed the way Africa is perceived in the world today. And one would agree with Obiechina that, "in Chinua, more than in most modern writers, the reader is taken to school and elaborately instructed without being aware of it, and therefore, without resenting the experience of the teacher."

ONYE NCHIKOTA – one who gathers and organizes things in an orderly manner. The imagery implies bringing together things scattered or strewn about. It was his sister Grace that gave him this praise name. Chinua has the gift of bringing together things scattered about. This gift is seen in his role as a leader of different organizations or his role as editor of journals and other collections of works. It is seen in his launching of organizations like the Association of Nigerian Authors. It was Chinua who brought the Achebe clan together for a historic visit to their motherland. He is very successful in holding his nuclear family together.

ONYE OKA OKWU is a verbal crafts-person. This is Egejuru's praise name for Chinua. This name reflects his creative use of language, especially his expertise in creating English expressions to capture Igbo ideas. Chinua's verbal craftsmanship stands above the rest of his artistic talents. Through his works, readers have come to know the Igbos as " people of the word." Reading a novel by Chinua is like listening to an Igbo *Onye Oka Okwu*, the excellent manipulator of words. As *Onye Oka Okwu*, he combines in proper context, several elements of traditional discourse. Thus, he strews his speeches and writings with proverbs, idioms, anecdotes, maxims and other derivatives of verbal manoeuvring. Chinua combines the qualities of two great speakers in his works -Ezeulu in *Arrow of God* and Egonwanne in *Things Fall Apart*. Ezeulu is the sophisticated *onye oka okwu* who combines refinement of speech and verbal creativeness. Egonwanne's "sweet tongue can change fire into cold ash. When he speaks, he moves men to impotence."[4] Olumide's observation about Chinua's gift with words is relevant here: "Chinua has developed the certainty of the power that can be wielded by the pen and the word. He's a very successful speaker. Whatever he did, that gave him the edge."[5] Chinua's power with words has already earned him a place among the few who, by the stroke of the pen, have caused changes to occur in the world.

---

[4] Chinua Achebe, *Things Fall Apart*, Heinemann, 1958, p.141.
[5] Michael Olumide, interview with Egejuru.

PATHFINDER: This praise name appropriately captures Chinua's accomplishments as a frontiersman in diverse endeavours. He definitely showed many writers of African descent, the way to write novels. Many of the valuable projects he initiated attest to his role of path finding. He put his gift of path finding to practical use when he chaired the Biafran National Guidance Committee. All those who worked with him in that Committee claimed that most of the brilliant ideas associated with that body came from Chinua. After that war, he found the way to harness the artistic potentials of the survivors by founding *Okike* magazine. He paved the way for self-regeneration and morale boosting of the Igbo by founding the journal, *Nsukkascope*. It is interesting to note that Mrs. Agnes Achebe, who called her brother-in-law "My Pathfinder," did not know that Chinua played the same role for so many other people and for so many durable projects.

GOD-BLESSED: Chinua's friends and relatives view him as a favoured child of God because he received countless good gifts from God. When Michael Thelwell called Chinua "God-Blessed" as a praise name, he meant it in the Jamaican sense. In Jamaica, A God-Blessed person is a special emissary of the gods. This person is invested with special qualities of spirit; anybody who comes in contact with him or her is also blessed and inspired. A God-Blessed man has a certain aura of being elected for higher service. He is high-minded. He has hardly any enemies and he is positioned to be an example for many. Chinua fits the picture of a Jamaican God-blessed man.

NWA CHUKWU KEZIRI –'A child well created by God' implies that God put everything he knew about crafting or creating a human being into producing this particular child. As a praise name for Chinua, it means he is a masterpiece of God's creation. Esther Ogadi who coined this name said that God took extra care to wash his hands very clean before he created Chinua.

SHAKESPEARE OF AFRICA as a praise name seems to push the analogy too far if one considers the nature and volume of Shakespeare's writing. However, this praise name draws attention to the significance of both writers' works for their historical epochs. Both writers chronicled the events of their worlds and times in two different genres. Shakespeare became a household name in Elizabethan drama; Chinua has become a household name in African novel.

ODOGWU NWOKE: The word *Odogwu* is not easy to define but its implication is easy to grasp by the Igbo. An *Odogwu* combines in his or her character and achievements, the best, the admirable and the praise worthy. *Odogwu* also connotes heroism.

OKA IBE -He that is far superior to his peers. Professor Ejike who coined this praise name was thinking of Chinua's achievements as a novelist and his ability to successfully merge his Christian upbringing and his African experience. This successful marrying of two different cultures is not an easy task for many westernized Africans.

OKPE UDO -Peace maker or peace negotiator refers to Chinua's role in restoring harmony to the conflict-ridden Ogidi Town Union. It also fits well to the role he played as the Chair of Biafra's National Guidance Committee. Those who served under him gave him much credit for preventing acts of violence against those who questioned the policies of the Biafran government.

AFA EJI AGA NA MBA -A name that accompanies one on a journey to other lands, is the equivalent of a passport. Chinua's relatives and friends said his name opens doors. Wherever they go and mention Chinua's name, people attend to them much faster; people are also friendlier to them.

ONYE EJI EME ONU is one you brag about. You are too eager to boast of this person and claim him as a relative or friend. All of Chinua's relatives and friends agreed that it's a blessing to be related or associated with him.

AKA N'EMELU ORA -The hand that ministers to the people is a praise name that reflects Chinua's generosity and his readiness to serve his fellow human beings.

A MAN OF THE PEOPLE genuinely loves the people and is concerned for their welfare. He in turn is loved and supported by the people.

EKWU EME: One who speaks and acts upon his words.

STOREHOUSE OF HONOURS is Soyinka's praise name for Chinua. It reflects the countless honorific awards and citations that Chinua has amassed over the years.

Man of the century: a truly great man

Undoubtedly, Chinua has achieved greatness through his literary career. However, to some of his admirers, he was born great. An example is his brother John's account of the circumstances surrounding Chinua's birth. This account has supernatural, if not superstitious overtones. Chinua's father was told in a dream that his yet-to-be-conceived son would be a great man. He proceeded to look for a name that would suit a man of great stature. A friend suggested an appropriate one- Albertus Magnus. Though Magnus was dropped for Chinualumogu, the innate greatness remained to be played out. Or as Chinua's sister Grace put it: "*Afa onye nachojie*- a man's name seeks him out." The greatness implied in Chinua's name would eventually seek him out.

In 1979 when Chinua won the first Nigerian National Merit Award, a group of artists gathered to celebrate with him at Nsukka. A minstrel from Aguleri Awka captured Chinua's impact and greatness in this praise song: "*Ogidi mutalu gi ife dili fa nma*- Ogidi gave birth to you and their fortune changed for the better." But Ogidi wasn't the only one that gained from the birth of Chinua. The entire Igbo people gained from his creative works and scholarly essays. Through his works, other groups in the world came to know about the Igbo world. Because of the recognition he brought to Igbo culture, a number of Igbo scholars refer to Chinua as a "Great Happening to the Igbo."

Because Chinua brought international fame to Igbo culture, he has been compared to Oluadah Equiano, the ex-slave and the first Igbo man to write about the Igbo in his autobiography, *The Interesting Narrative of the Life of Olaudah Equiano* or *Gustavus Vassa, the African*. Chinua admires Equiano and makes references to him in his writings and speeches. Speaking of Achebe and Equiano, Obiechina said:

> Chinua and Equiano are the quintessential great Igbo people. They are a credit to the race because of their international recognition.

Equiano is so high that even though he just passed through Virginia, African Americans claim him and place him first on their list of great black people. Achebe is the same, not just a great man but a great symbolic figure.[1]

Some of Chinua's relatives are so overwhelmed by his role and place among the Igbo that they could not resist a sacrilegious comparison. His sister-in-law, Agnes Achebe found a fitting analogy in Simeon's *Nunc Dimitis*, when Simeon recognized the infant Jesus as the Christ, a light to lighten the gentiles.[2] Agnes said:

> I ask for God's forgiveness if I liken Chinua to Jesus Christ. Just as God created Christ and made a woman to give birth to him to save his people, so did God put Chinua in our midst as a light to lighten the world about the Igbo. What he has done for us is not easy to tell.[3]

Another sister-in-law, Lucy Achebe referred to the same bible passage in her evaluation of Chinua's greatness. "Chinua is the light that lightened the world about the black race and the glory has come back to Igbo people. Is this sacrilegious?" she asked.[4]

Knowing the Christian background of these women, one would not be surprised at their choice of analogy. Yet, they are not the only people who couldn't resist the temptation of placing Chinua in a biblical context. For instance, the retired executive chairman of Heinemann Educational Books (Nigerian branch), Chief Aigboje Higo went even further when he said:

> I don't have adequate words to express my perception of Chinua. I feel humbled when I see him. I thank God that there are such mighty creations to indicate to us the greatness of God. There is that thing that sets Chinua apart from all of us.[5]

His best friend, C. C. Momah was asked to characterize Chinua in a few words. He said:

> It is difficult to qualify the man in human terms. From our childhood, nobody had any idea that Chinua would become larger than life. As a classmate, I couldn't imagine his *akala aka*, the imprint of greatness in the lines on his palms. The scope of his

---

[1] E. Obiechina, interview with Egejuru.
[2] Reference to Luke 2:25-32, the baby Jesus is received by Simeon in the Temple.
[3] Agnes Achebe, interview with Egejuru.
[4] Lucy Achebe, interview with Egejuru, she referred to the same passage in Luke.
[5] Aigboje Higo, interview with Egejuru.

achievement is abnormally out of proportion. There must be some other hand at work.[6]

Greatness is difficult to measure. However, one can point to a few tangible indicators of Chinua's greatness. On September 22, 1991, the *Times* of London published its list of 1000 "Makers of the 20th Century." Chinua Achebe was on the list! It is true that Chinua has received more than a score of honorary doctorate degrees. Yet, one cannot compare a University's search for candidates for honorary degrees to a media search across the globe, for 1000 Makers of the Century. Therefore, one can only imagine the astronomical number of candidates that had to be scrutinized before the final list was drawn. Making that list definitely put Chinua in a rare bracket.

It is hardly an exaggeration to say that Chinua helped to reshape western thinking on Africa by the stroke of his pen. As he has explained in numerous lectures and in his essays, Chinua wrote his first novel to balance the distorted picture that Europe had painted of Africa for centuries. However, he went much further in his subsequent works to tell the story of the continent's encounter with the West from Africa's perspective. In the end, Chinua's seemingly simple novels affected the consciousness of a whole generation of white and black readers. It not only altered western thinking on Africa, it also altered the way black people all over the world think of themselves and the African continent.

For more examples of tangible indicators of Chinua's greatness, one can compare his global impact with other great figures of literature. For instance, a few writers like Shakespeare imposed their will and definition upon a historical epoch. One can claim that Chinua did exactly the same thing for his epoch; he imposed his will and his definition of Africa on the world of his time. It's no wonder that Ikenna Nzimiro called Chinua, "the Shakespeare of Africa." Ultimately what Achebe would leave for future generations is a body of work that constitutes a historical and cultural record.

Considering the enormous task of being Africa's number one storyteller and cultural griot, one can claim that Chinua has done more than other African novelists to "tell" the story of his continent. After all, it is rare in most cultures, especially developing cultures, for a writer to emerge and be appropriate and equal to the fundamental issues and conflicts of his time. In literary, historical, political and cultural senses, Chinua has proved himself appropriate and more than equal to

---

[6] C.C. Momah, interview with Egejuru.

the major issues and conflicts of his generation and this indeed, attests to his greatness.

In his essay "African Literature as Celebration", Chinua recalled how the Irish *Times* carried a prominent story in which a very kind columnist referred to him as "the man who invented African Literature." When it was Chinua's turn to make a presentation, he "took the opportunity of the forum given me at the symposium to dissociate myself from that well-meant but blasphemous characterization."[7] Blasphemous or not, the columnist expressed the sentiments of millions of readers, for whom Chinua Achebe has become synonymous with African literature. For an author to have such a grip on the consciousness of a generation of readers, he must be unique.

Furthermore, Achebe went beyond the world of literature, beyond the black world to other worlds, to broader human concerns. We know that when western scholars speak of universality (a word that Chinua wants to be banned from the English language) of a work, they usually mean how closely that work resembles a western work. Chinua's work does not fit into western concept of the universal. His work is uniquely anchored in African culture and experience. Yet, he gets so deep into the reactions of the individual to his culture and his environment, that these reactions become uniquely human. In other words, Chinua goes into African culture to reach what is universally human. He does this deliberately in his art and purpose; very few writers do that successfully. Once more, the circle of positive contributions expands from Ogidi to the Igbo, to Africa and the black race, to the human community. Again, it was Chinua's former houseboy Dickson who captured the global range of Chinua's impact in this crude statement: "Although he was born here at Ogidi and has been given titles at Ogidi, Chinua is now universal property."[8] Dickson's declaration ties in with Ulli Beier's tree imagery of Chinua's gradual rise to fame.

> The greatness of Chinua lies in the fact that he grew seamlessly from very firm local roots towards his broader worldwide concern. He simply grew like a tree that becomes larger and adds a new ring to its stem every year.[9]

Things Fall Apart, the most widely read African novel has eclipsed all other works of Achebe. It has effectively become the identity of its author. It is impossible to speak of Achebe's greatness without dragging in the book that paved his way to greatness. The global

---

[7] Chinua Achebe, *African Commentary*, Nov. 1989, p.51.
[8] Dickson Odukwe, interview with Egejuru.
[9] Ulli Beier, correspondence to Egejuru.

influence of *Things Fall Apart* has been explored in numerous critical works and essays. Many writers of African descent have testified to the inspirational role of that novel on their own writings. Scholars and critics of African literature would agree that no other African novel has attained the level of popularity of this one novel. This novel is not only popular, it has attained the stature of a great book by anybody's standard. An acclaimed medievalist, Dr. Julian Wasserman of Loyola University, New Orleans evaluated Achebe and his novel in the light of "Great Soul" theory of literature. This theory correctly claims that we do not meet many great souls in real life. However, it asserts that to spend an hour reading a book by a great soul like Shakespeare or Milton, is to spend an hour in the presence of greatness. Thus, Wasserman asserts that to spend an hour reading *Things Fall Apart* is to spend an hour in the presence of greatness. He further regretted that more than nine out of every ten people who read Achebe would not meet him in person, because if they had the opportunity to meet him in person as he did, they would certainly feel his greatness.[10]

In 1992, Achebe gave a rough estimate of sales and translations of the novel. At that time, it had sold eight million copies in English translation alone. It had been translated into some fifty languages, including Kiswahili. In the fall of 1992, *Things Fall Apart* was one of 46 World Literary Classics issued in Everyman's Library.

In 1995, the New York Public Library celebrated its Centenary. Part of the celebration was an exhibition of one hundred " Books of the Century", written between 1895 and 1995. *Things Fall Apart* was on the exhibit and in the volume, *BOOKS OF THE CENTURY*, published by Barnes and Noble. Since an artist is reflected in his or her work, and if the work is considered unique, it attests to the uniqueness of its creator. If Achebe's definitive work is listed as the book of the century, it does rub off on the fact that the writer is the man of the century. After all, there is an organic relationship between the artist and his work.

To say that *Things Fall Apart* is a great book is now an understatement, because the word great has become so clichéd that it has lost its significance. The fact remains that the novel and its author have attained the stature of greatness. There is a joke that purportedly started circulating among western academicians after Soyinka won the Nobel Prize in literature. These academicians hailed Soyinka as the greatest Nigerian writer. But then, they innocently but erroneously, called him the author of *Things Fall Apart*! In the twisted logic of these academicians, a Nigerian winner of the Nobel Prize in literature, must be the author of that country's greatest novel. Though this might be a joke, it echoes a profound truth of the powerful position of Achebe's

---

[10] Julian Wasserman, interview with Egejuru.

novel on the world literary scene. It also intimates that the author deserves the Nobel Prize in literature.

Indeed, Achebe's literary career cleared the path for his journey towards international fame and rewards. But he has gone beyond his writings to become a uniquely respected and powerful personality in his own right. Dr. Botstein, President of Bard College was unrestrained when he expressed his views of Achebe as one of the few great men he has encountered:

> There is an aura about him that sets him apart. He has a universal and unqualified respect and affection of people all over the world. I couldn't say that about anyone else. For me, his meaning lies in the fact that in his presence, I never forget what separates but does not alienate us from one another. He manages to assert and maintain distinction and still holds the common ground. He does not approach issues of life with predictable formula. He is intuitive, articulate and specific. Upon all that, he is warm and honest. He has a wonderful relationship with his wife and children. He is a man of unfailing graciousness. I am profoundly impressed by his spirituality.[11]

Many of those interviewed spoke passionately of Chinua as one who is complete. People are drawn to his writing and auditoriums are jammed when he makes public speeches. Commenting on the magnetic nature of Chinua's personality, John Munonye said: "Apart from Nelson Mandela, no other African pulls as much crowd as he does."[12] Chinua effectively pulled in the whole world when the United Nations appointed him their Good Will Ambassador in matters of health. There is no better testimony of the respect he commands in the world. There is no higher recognition of his genuine concern for the welfare of humanity. This gesture by the United Nations seems to say, "Wait, he's not yet complete till the world as one body has honoured him."

Chinua's sister Grace called him *onye nchikota* -one who gathers and organizes people or puts things together. This could be seen in various projects and organizations he set up and managed successfully over the years. He groomed younger colleagues and handed projects over to them. Most importantly, he inspired and mentored writers and younger colleagues across the globe. Indeed, Chinua's greatest achievement might turn out to be his mentoring and inspiring others to follow in his footsteps. For, in his march towards greatness, Chinua took many people along with him. In this way, he embodies an Igbo

---

[11] Dr. Leon Botstein, telephone interview with Egejuru.
[12] John Munonye, interview with Egejuru.

saying: " A great man is not just great for himself, he is an empowering force for others."

Considering all of Chinua's achievements, the respect he commands all over the world, and particularly of his innumerable near-perfect human qualities, one could easily join Michael Thelwell in saying, "It's almost an honour and a benefaction to be a contemporary of Chinua Achebe."[13]

---

[13] Michael Thelwell, interview with Egejuru.

Appendix

Honorary doctorate degrees awarded to Chinua Achebe: 1972-1999

1972	Datmouth College, Hanover, New Hampshire, USA
1974	University of Southampton, UK
1975	University of Stirling, Scotland, UK
1976	University of Prince Edward Island, Canada
1977	University of Massachusetts at Amherst, USA
1978	University Ife, Nigeria
1981	University of Nigeria, Nsukka
1982	University of Kent, Canterbury, UK
1984	Mount Allison University, New Brunswick, Canada
1984	University of Guelph Ontario, Canada
1985	Franklin Pierce College, New Hampshire, USA
1989	Westfield State College Massachusetts, USA
1989	Open University of London, UK

1989   University of Ibadan, Nigeria

1990   Georgetown University, Washington D.C., USA

1991   University of Port Harcourt, Nigeria

1991   Skidmore College of Saratoga Springs, New York, USA

1991   School for Social Research, New York, USA

1991   Hobart and William Smith Colleges, Geneva, New York, USA

1991   Mary Mount Manhattan College, New York, USA

1992   City University of New York, USA

1993   Colgate University, Hamilton, New York, USA

1994   Fitchburg State College, Massachusetts, USA

1996   Bates College, Lewiston, Maine, USA

1996   Harvard University, Cambridge, Massachusetts, USA

1998   Brown University, Providence, Rhode Island, USA

1998   Syracuse University, New York, USA

1999   Ohio Wesleyan University, Delaware, Ohio, USA

1999   Trinity College, Hartford, Connecticut, USA

Index

Achebe,
- Agnes, 4, 25, 30, 115, 194, 197, 200
- Albert Chinualumogu, 8, 199
- Augustine, 2, 5, 12, 28, 65, 150
- Chidi, 83, 89, 94, 101, 102, 103, 104, 106, 108, 109, 110, 112, 116
- Chinelo, 29, 30, 72, 75, 78, 81, 83, 100, 101, 104, 105, 109, 110, 146, 154, 161, 168, 175, 187
- Christie, 89, 98, 99, 112, 109, 108, 103, 104, 100, 102, 116, 142, 168
- Ernest, 115, 132, 169
- Frank, 4, 12, 129, 113
- Grace, 127, 128, 134, 139, 173, 199, 204
- Ihechukwu, 76, 77, 83, 91, 103, 104, 105, 109, 110, 111, 116
- Isaiah Okafo, 1, 2, 3, 4, 5, 6, 8, 111
- J. U. Dr., 77, 168
- Jane, 85, 113, 114
- Janet, 3, 4, 6
- John, 8, 9, 18, 19, 20, 21, 25, 28, 180, 199, 77, 113, 114, 126, 134, 159
- Julius, 8
- Lucy, 10, 115, 116, 128, 131, 200
- Nwando, 102, 104, 106, 107, 109, 111, 112, 137, 180
- Oyibo, 5, 113, 125, 132
- Zinobia Ikpeze, 5, 8, 12, 13, 14, 18, 26, 46, 99, 134, 173, 180

Achebe, Chinua
- a complex simplicity, 127, 131, 132
- a generous soul, 167, 168, 169, 170, 171, 173
- a great humanist, 145, 146, 147, 148
- a man of integrity, 150, 151, 152, 153
- a man of the people, 66, 136, 168
- a man of truth and justice, 140, 141, 142, 143
- a model student and son, 25
- a student in the faculty of Arts, 31
- academic brilliance, 16, 19, 20, 21, 22
- admission to university college Ibadan, 26
- afraid of school, 14, 15
- age grade, 6
- an empowering force for others, 164
- an unwavering loyalty, 154, 155, 156, 157, 158, 159, 160, 162, 163, 169
- and the nobel prize, 185
- approachable & accessible to all, 131, 132, 133
- aptitude for story telling, 9
- as a big *alusi*, 118, 119
- as a family man, 98
- as a man of ideas, 120
- as a man of wisdom, 118, 119, 120
- as a philosopher, 123
- as a prefect, 22
- as a sage, 119, 120

-as a teacher, 195, 196
-as ambasador of biafra, 173
-as goodwill ambassador for UN, 150, 204
-as man of the century, 199
-as president of Ogidi town union, 69, 70, 71, 133, 141, 157, 164, 183, 194, 198
-as president of PEN, 73
-as pro-chancellor of ASUTECH, 69
-as pro-emeritus, 68
-as senior research fellow, Nsukka, 45
-as the Shakespeare of Africa, 201, 202, 203, 204, 205
-as visiting professor, 71, 72, 74
-at Bard College, 87
-automobile accident, 76, 172
-awards, 95
-beautiful leisureliness, 176, 177, 178
-birth, 8
-bond with father, 12
-both birthday, 74
-childhood years, 13
-commitment to Biafran cause, 159
-delicate sense of humour, 180, 181, 182, 183, 184
-extra curricular activity, 25
-from Nekede Central School to Government College Umuahia, 19
-gentle as a lamb, fierce as a lion, 134, 138, 137, 136, 135
-gift of reading people, 119
-his Christian faith, 115, 116, 117
-his dress sense, 127, 128, 129
-his inner voice, 7, 29
-his simplicity, 128, 129, 130, 131
-home, 90
-in NBS/NBC, 38-41

-in possession of his soul, 172, 173, 174, 175
-inner voice, 98,99
-intellectual courage, 138
-intellectual performance, 118
-lecture on Conrad's Heart of Darkness, 57, 162
-meaning of, 147,145
-meeting with same Baldwin, 61, 71
-miraculous recovery, 79
-nickname, 19
-on to Arts, 98
-opposition to the proposition for a National funeral for Awolowo, 136
-parentage, 1
-participation in school activities, 32
-picking up the pieces, 53
-point of weakness, 173, 186, 187, 188, 189, 190, 191
-praise names 192, 193, 194, 195, 196, 197, 198
-primary and secondary education, 16
-qualities, 41, 51, 127, 135
-relationship with children, 104, 105, 106, 107, 108, 109, 110, 111
-relationship with people, 128
-relationship with wife, 101, 102, 103
-retirement years, 64
-return to Nsukka, 59
-road, 95
-running back home, 43, 44
-scholarship, 21, 26, 30
-school mates, 27
-senior research fellow, 56
-sixtieth birthday, 155
-switch from science to art, 27, 28, 29, 30, 175
-the accident, 76
-tittle, 27

-triumphal return, 91
-truthfulness, 140, 141, 143
-turning point, 74
-use of Igbo proverbs, 119, 120
-visit to Abuja, 95
-weak points, 24
-wedding, 100, 155
-wisdom, 13
-work experience, 36
-working for Biafra, 46, 47
Adi, 83
African Commentary: A Journal for People of African Descent, 73, 123
African Continental Bank, 174
African Literature Association, 171
-conference, 61, 132
African Writers Series, 121, 122, 164
Aggrey Memorial Grammar School, 20
Agulefo, 28, 70, 118, 157
Ahiara declaration, 47, 48, 49, 50, 122, 159
Ajayi, J. F. Ade, 32
Akpan, 67
Alumona, Reuben, 78, 118, 119, 130, 147, 148, 168
Ambiguous Adventure, 163
Amobi, *Rev.*, 8
An Image of Africa: Racism in Conrad's" Heart of Darkness, 137, 138
Anambra State University of Technology, 77, 78
Anene, A. C., 32
Angelou, Maya, 166
Aniagolu, Justice, 47
Aniebo, Ifeanyi, 85, 132, 135, 181
Another Africa, 90
Anthills of the Savanna, 68, 72, 80
Anyiwo, 16, 17, 26
Arrow of God, 2, 23, 75, 158, 196
Ashby lecture, 36
Association of Nigerian Authors, 62, 63, 68, 75, 125, 164, 196
Atuanya, 194

Awka College for Teachers, 2, 3
Awolowo debate, 188
Awolowo, Obafemi, 71, 136
Azikiwe, Nnamdi, 136

Ba, Mariama, 166
Babaginda, Ibrahim, 69
Badejo, Victor, 43, 44
Badsen, G. T., 4
Baldwin, 71, 181
Bard College, 87, 88, 89, 146
Barnes and Noble, 203
Beattie, Angela, 39
Beier, Ulli, 55, 56, 64, 123, 124, 156, 170, 171, 183, 189, 193, 202
Beyond Pardon, 25
Biafra's think tank, 47
Biafran cultural council, 55
Biafran war, 52, 122, 123, 132, 138, 172
-National Guidance Committee (NGC), 143,146,151,159, 177
Biobaku, S. O. 24, 137
Black festival of arts and culture, 162
Books of the century, 203
Botstein, Leo, 88, 89, 204
British Broadcasting Corporation (BBC), 42
-staff school, London, 40
British Council, 78
Brook, Gwendolyn, 80
Buchan, John, 25

Cambridge University, 25, 36
Cary, Joyce, 25
Cawson, Frank, 44
Chapel of Resurrection, 110, 111
Chijioke, 27
Christians, 4
Citadel Publishing House, 121
Clark, J. P., 54, 69, 123
Clay, M. Berhta, 25
Cookey S. J., 50, 122, 138, 145,

151, 159, 188
Crow, Jim, 62

Daily Times, 26
Darmouth College, 74, 75
David Okoye, 3
Denis Memorial Grammar School, 6, 20, 25
Dennis mix, 94
Dennis, Archbishop., 93
Diamond, Stanley, 88, 89
Dickson, 134, 139, 202
Dictionary, 19
Directorate of Culture, 51

Eagle-on-Iroko, 74, 75, 76, 85, 128
Education, 5, 6
Effiong, 54
Efuru, 165
Ejeguru, 164, 171, 183, 190, 191, 196
Ejike, Prof., 78, 82, 110, 135, 140, 141, 145, 156, 159, 160, 161, 183, 189, 198
Eke, Ifegwu, 48
Ekwensi, Cyprian, 52, 178
Ekwueme, Alex Chukwuma, 64, 93, 102
Elizabethan drama, 197
Ellah, Frank, 33, 155, 165, 119
Elphik, 39
Emodi, Okechukwu, 54
Enekwe, Osmond, 60, 69, 170
Eneli G., 152, 153
Enugu coal mine massacre, 35
Equaino, Gustavus, 83, 199
Ete, Inyang, 54
European fiction, 25
Ezekwesili,
Ezeoke, Ume, 44
Ezilo, James, 27, 36, 37, 38, 59, 144

Festival of arts and culture, 131

Fine, C., 174
Fisher, 23
Ford Foundation, 64
Fourth Dimension Publishing Co., 121
Frankel, H. L., 78

Gates, Skip, 186
Government College Umuahia, 11, 20, 21, 23, 25
Graham Douglas, Amachree Christiana, 33
Greene, Graham, 25
Gustavus Vassa, The African, 199

Haggard, Rider, 25
Harriman, Leslie, 27
Hazley, 80
Headquaters, 4, 132, 158
Heinemann Publishers, 40, 121, 164, 166, 200
Higo, Aigboge, 84, 120, 157, 161, 172, 177, 180, 191, 200
Hill, Alan, 40
Horizonte festival, Berlin, 189

Igbo USA, 125, 160
Ige, Bola, 27, 32, 33, 35, 66, 119, 161, 176, 181
Igwe Amobi VI of Ogidi, 70, 194
Ihekweazu, Edith, 74
Ike, V. C., 33, 34, 82, 99, 127, 155, 164, 182
Ikenga family union, 92
Ikoku, 67
Ikpeze, Nnaemeka, 114, 115, 142
Ikpeze, Okey, 173, 140
Ikpeze, Ukamaka, 132, 176
Imodu, Michael, 66
Innes, C. L., 23, 57, 58, 148, 156
International Conference of Writers & Artists, Budapest, 88, 89
Inyang, 26
Irish Times, 72, 202

Jaodu, Yemi, 123

Kane, Hamidou, 163
Kanu, Aminu, 65, 66, 67, 68
King's College Lagos, 23
Kodilinye, 54, 59, 143
Komunyakaa, Yusef, 166
Ku klux klan, 62

Lagos State University, 72
Land flight, 76, 172
Layola University New Orleans, 170
Literature as Celebration", 74
London Television's South Bank Show, 74
London University, 35, 36

Mahfouz, Naguib, 90
Makerere University, Kampala, 165
Mana Assumpta Cathedral, Owerri, 92
Mandela, Nelson, 204
Mary Mount Girl's Secondary School, 142
Mbabuike, Micheal, 173, 174
Mbari Institution, 72, 74, 121, 124, 125, 178
Melanby, Kenneth, 34
Menakaya, 22
Merchant of Light, 36, 37
Mgbemena, *Canon*, 36
Milne, Van, 166
Milton, 203
Mohammed, Murtala, 59
Momah, Christian, 21, 22, 31, 34, 82, 100, 103, 125, 155, 187, 171, 176, 179, 180, 182, 200
Momah, Ethel, 99, 108, 116, 147
Monday class, 14
Morning Yet on Creation Day, 195
Morrison, Toni, 166
Moyers television series, 72
Moyers, Bill, 72

Mphahele, Eskia, 123
Mr. Johnson, 25
Munonye, John, 123, 164, 194, 204
My Father's Daughter, 164

National creativity award, 95, 162
National merit award, 95, 162, 199
Ndem, *Prof.*, 47
Ndi'chie, 70, 76, 83, 150, 151
Nekede Central School, 18, 19
New York public library, 203
Ngugi, James, 165
Ngwoke, Ngozi, 167,168
Niger House, 22
Nigeria Creation of States, 165
Nigerian Broadcasting Corporation, 41, 42, 100
Nigerian Broadcasting Service, 38, 39, 40, 41, 98, 142, 164, 176, 177, 182
-talks production department, 39, 131
-department of external service, 41
Nigerian civil war, 43, 46
Nigerian federal inspector of police, 91
Nile House, 23
Nnolim, *Prof.*, 135
No Longer at Ease, 2, 19, 182
Nobel prize in literature, 137, 203, 204
Nsukkascope, 53, 54, 55, 144, 160, 197
Nunc Dimitis, 200
Nwaneri, Sam, 41
Nwankwo, Arthur, 64, 65, 121, 146, 165, 174, 188
Nwankwo, Victor, 121, 135, 191
Nwapa, Flora, 165
Nwoga, 60
Nwoko, Dema, 123
Nwonodi, Glory, 52
Nwosu, T. C., 52, 54, 68, 159, 165, 179, 185, 186
Nwoye, Sam, 100, 131, 155

Nyerere's Arusha declaration, 47
Nzekwu, Onuora, 52
Nzimiro, Ikenna, 47, 48, 49, 50, 54, 122, 143, 144, 151, 201

Obasanjo, Olusegun, 59, 95, 131
Obgonna, Ephraim, 19
Obiechina, Emmanuel, 47, 50, 51, 52, 60, 66, 67, 81, 122, 140, 144, 146, 159, 160, 179, 189, 195, 199
Obinna, Anthony, 92
Odenigbo lecture, 92, 93, 94
Odukwe, Dickson, 37, 38
Ogadi, Esther, 68, 138, 146, 152
Ogbogu, Ben, 37, 70, 129
Ogidi
-masquerade cult, 111
-missionaries in, 2, 5
Ogidi town union, 70, 71, 75, 76, 85, 95, 133
Ojukwu, Chukwuemeka, 46, 48, 49, 122, 143, 151
Okara, Gabriel, 52
Okeke, Mrs., 13
Okeke, Uche, 123
Okigbo, Christopher, 45, 121,123
Okike, 55, 58, 60, 63, 64, 65, 69, 123, 148, 152, 170, 188, 197
Okocha, Emeka, 86, 114, 139, 172
Okocha, Grace, 10, 11, 14, 18, 25
Okocha, Tochukwu, 70, 85, 108, 113, 115, 132, 158
Okoli, Chinwe Christie, 98
Okoli, Sam, 116, 146
Okongwu, 17, 21
Okoro, 27
Okudo, Johnson, 1, 4, 6, 76, 141, 146, 159, 169, 194
Okwundu, 139
Oli, Celestine, 174
Olumide, Micheal, 40, 41, 42, 71, 120, 132, 196
Olumiyiwa, 27
One (1000) "Makers of the 20th Century", 201
Onyemelukwe, C. J., 92

Opara, Ralph, 123

Paddocks hospital England, 78,79
Parrinder, Geoffrey, 31
PEN International, 167
Peoples Redemption Party, 65, 66, 146, 161
Phelps, Gilbert, 40
Praise names for Chinua,
-a man of the people, 198
-afa eji aga na mba, 198
-aka n'emelu ora, 198
-eagle on iroko, 193
-ekwueme, 198
-God-bless, 197
-ife eji malu Ogidi, 194
-ikejimba, 194
-nwa chukwu keziri, 197
-odogwu nwoke
-oka ibe, 198
-okpe udo, 198
-onye eji eme onu, 198
-onye nchikota, 196, 204
-onye oka okwu, 196
-onyenkuzi, 195
-pathfinder, 197
-shakespeare of Africa, 197
-storehouse of honours, 198
-ugo mmuta, 194
-ugonabo, 192, 193
Prester John, 25

Reach of the Skies, Poetry of Abuja, 165
Republic of Biafra, 45
-national guidance committee, 48, 49
Rockefeller Foundation, 42

Sarduana, 136
Segun, Mabel, 32, 33, 34, 164, 181
Shagari, Shehu, 136
Shagari's government, 66

Shakespeare, William, 197, 201, 203
She, 25
Simpson, William, 21, 23, 153
Slater, Adrian, 23, 24
So Long a Letter, 166
Soyinka, 54, 66, 67, 69, 75, 84, 85, 123, 124, 131, 137, 177, 178, 181, 186, 188, 198, 203
St, Monica's School, 3, 6
St. Luke's Anglican Mission, Ogidi, 14
St. Micheal's, Aba, 21
St. Pauls's Anglican Church, Ogidi, 3
St. Peter Anglican Church Ogidi, 92
St. Phillip's Central School Ogidi, 16
St. Phillip's Church Ogidi, 3
St. Simon's Anglican Church, 8
Stanford University, California, 75
Stevenson, P. Charles, 89
Swados, Havey, 56

The Bug, 33, 35, 176
The Heart of the Matter, 25
The Herald, 33, 34
The Interesting Narrative of the Life of Olaudah Equiano, 199
The Last Laugh & Other Stories, 72
The Return of She, 25
The Rise and Fall of the Roman Empire, 27
The Seed Yams Have Been Eating, 164
The Sorrows of Satan, 25
The Sword, 34
The Trouble with Nigeria, 67, 136, 161, 180
Thelwell, Michael, 57, 58, 82, 83, 85, 138, 162, 181, 186, 197, 205
Things Fall Apart, 1, 2, 3, 4, 24, 25, 40, 62, 94, 114, 116, 121, 142, 158, 162, 166, 189, 196, 202, 203

Times of London, 201
Tripple eminence award, 75

Udechukwu, Ada, 59, 60, 61
Udechukwu, Obiora, 56, 60, 64, 69, 129, 130, 131, 141, 148, 156, 170
Udo, Kenneth, 1, 2, 37
Ugwoke, Grace, 139, 146, 147
Union Igbo, 93, 94
University College Ibadan, 26, 177
University of Connecticut, 58
University of Kent, 23, 24
University of Massachusetts, Amherst, 56, 62, 71, 72, 137
University of Nigeria, Nsukka (UNN), 53, 74, 75, 85, 89, 125, 143, 144
University Teaching Hospital, Enugu, 77
Uzochukwu, Ben, 22, 24, 34, 65, 82, 155, 174, 176, 179

Vasta, Mamman, 68, 165
Vincent, Theo, 73, 82, 135, 167, 193
Voice of Nigeria, 41, 43

Warner, Miss, 3
Wasserman, Julian, 170, 203
Weep Not Child, 166
Welch, *Prof.*, 36, 39
Wellesley College, Massachusetts, 183
Winter, Ella, 55
Wiwa, Saro, 63
world literary classics, 203
World War II, 23
Writers week, Adelaide, 61

Yakubu, Gowon, 59
Yusuf, Hassan, 67